Poems

IN THE MAKING

After writing a poem, one should correct it all over.

— POPE

WALKER GIBSON
NEW YORK UNIVERSITY

HOUGHTON MIFFLIN COMPANY · BOSTON

CONTENTS

CHAPTER THREE

COLERIDGE · *An Explanation by Literary Origins*

CHAPTER FOUR

POE · *A Dubious Explanation by the Maker Himself*

CHAPTER FIVE

POPE · *Disorder in the Making and Order in the Poem*

CHAPTER SIX

RICHARDS · *Poetic Process and Literary Analysis*

PREAMBLE

What a useful study it might be for a poet, to compare in those parts what was written first, with the successive alterations; to learn his turns and arts in versification; and to consider the reasons why such and such an alteration was made.

— Spence

I have often thought how interesting a magazine paper might be written by an author who would — that is to say who could — detail, step by step, the processes by which one of his compositions attained its ultimate point of completion.

— Poe

One poet's example is only his adaptation of his personality to the demands of poetry, but if it is clearly stated it may help us to understand other poets, and even something of poetry.

— Spender

If, then, we can reconstruct for the moment when Coleridge fell asleep over *Purchas His Pilgrimage*, the elements, even in part, of that subliminal chaos, we shall have taken a long step toward the clarification of our problem.

— Lowes

To help us in the fascinating business of looking over the craftsman's shoulder while he is actually at work, we have a greater wealth of material than for any other poem of Keats . . . .

— Ridley

Often the inspection of such material does give us new insight into the author both as a personality and as a craftsman. However, we must remember that: Even if we had a record of every such single step involved in the actual writing of a poem, of the exact order in which revisions were made, of the author's dreams and personal quandaries during the writing, of his borrowings from other authors or from situations in life itself . . . even if we had a mountain of such data, we should have but a fraction of the information needed to chart fully the work's genesis.

— BURKE

For myself, I can only say that a knowledge of the springs which released a poem is not necessarily a help toward understanding the poem.

— ELIOT

Poetry is so much more than a source for low-down on the lives of the poets.

— RICHARDS

At any rate, as long as there is poetry there will be curiosity about its genesis.

— SHAPIRO

POEMS IN THE MAKING

A High-Class Kind of Gossip

This book places before the student several different ways of talking about the making of poems — or what is called the creative process. The student of poetry may choose among a variety of accounts of these processes, based on different kinds of evidence and different points of attack. He is also confronted with a more fundamental question: what is the relevance of any or all of these accounts to his own richer appreciation of poetry. As the quotations in our Preamble suggest, this is not a question with a single answer.

Chapter One offers an explanation of genesis by manuscript versions — the familiar examination of various drafts and worksheets used by the poet. Keats' difficulties in certain sections of "The Eve of St. Agnes" are elaborately and sometimes amusingly reconstructed by the English scholar M. R. Ridley, with a view to reconstructing something of the actual experience that Keats presumably went through over a few days in early 1819.

Chapter Two demonstrates the same kind of manuscript analysis, with the difference that one of the accounts is a post-mortem explanation by the poet himself, Stephen Spender. Using manuscripts available at the huge collection of such materials at the University of Buffalo, Karl Shapiro examines some versions of two of Spender's poems. Then Spender himself, in a much-admired article called "The Making of a Poem," discusses some of his operations in composing a third poem. All three poems are reprinted here in their final forms.

Chapter Three turns to another way of discussing what happened to the poet — an explanation by literary origins. Here we review John Livingston Lowes' famous piece of detective work into Coleridge's reading just prior to his writing of "Kubla Khan." This is followed by a well-mannered but devastating attack on such scholarly goings-on by T. S. Eliot. The question here raised directly — and relevant as well to our first two chapters — concerns the relation between *explanation* and *understanding*. The student is invited to ask himself whether, as Eliot argues, understanding a poem has nothing to do with its origins. Is literary detective work outside "the frontiers of criticism" or isn't it? And what does one's answer imply about what one thinks "criticism" is or ought to be?

Chapter Four offers another sort of problem — testimony about the making of a poem from the poet himself, but testimony that most people have considered suspect. Here the student, with or without further research on Poe, may decide for himself whether the poet's account of the composition of "The Raven" is or is not plausible. Kenneth Burke's recent comment on Poe's essay may suggest a way in which Poe may be taken seriously after all.

Chapter Five probably raises the most complex problems of all, partly because the poem in question, the First Epistle to Pope's "Essay on Man," is itself so wonderfully rich and subtle. Again we return to an abiding question: how does the evidence we have about Pope's creative processes relate to our experience of reading the poem, or to our evaluation of it? In Spence's entertaining *Anecdotes* we hear what purports to be the voice of Pope himself speaking about his own aims and problems, both in the "Essay on Man" and in general. George Sherburn then shows us that Pope's methods of planning and working may account for the logical organization — or disorganization — of his poem. Thus Pope's habit of working on several poems at once may have resulted in what Sherburn calls the "fragmentary" quality of the "Essay." Sherburn suggests that Pope would have been wiser — truer to his creative process perhaps? — if he "had been content to leave his verse units as fragmentary reflections" rather than trying to make a coherent system out of them. But R. A. Brower goes at the question entirely differently. Acknowledging some logical shortcomings, he looks to another kind of organization, that of style and tone and allusion. Ignoring Pope's "disorderly" creative process, Brower sees a literary order in the poem nevertheless. The student needs to face this debate in terms of his own experience of the poem: how has his knowledge of Pope's working practices assisted his understanding of "An Essay on Man"?

Finally, in a witty address to a group of sophisticated linguists (Chapter Six), I. A. Richards closes our collection on another warning note. Arguing for a critical language that is "fundamentally linguistic," he doubts that his own creative experience has a great deal to do with helping a reader read his poem. The writers in this book certainly represent various persuasions, but they would probably all agree with one of Richards' concluding remarks: "Poetry is so much more than a source for low-down on the lives of the poets."

The creative process has traditionally been divided into three parts, in a chronological order. First there is the original inspiration, and this everybody agrees is the most difficult to discover and define. Anyone can experience the difficulty simply by asking himself, about any reasonably original or useful idea he has created, "Just how did *that* come to me?" The second stage is the initial rendering of the original "thought" in words on paper — the writing down of the first draft, the first notes, or whatever, with inevitably mysterious consequences about the agreement or disagreement of these notes with the original "idea." Third and last, there is the development from the first "rough" words into the final and finished product.

Strictly speaking, it is only with this third stage that this book is concerned — and very inadequately at that. The mysteries of the first two stages — how the original idea occurred to the poet, and how that idea became transformed into its first verbal expression — are truly insurmountable. As Jung has told us, in what Karl Shapiro calls "one of the most discouraging statements concerning the creative activity ever written," "Any reaction to stimulus may be explained; but the creative act, which is the absolute antithesis of mere reaction, will for ever elude the human understanding." Kenneth Burke's remarks, quoted in the Preamble, are worth repeating here: "Even if we had a record of every such single step involved in the actual writing of a poem, of the exact order in which revisions were made, of the author's dreams and personal quandaries during the writing, of his borrowings from other authors or from situations in life itself . . . even if we had a mountain of such data, we should have but a fraction of the information needed to chart fully the work's genesis."

But Burke goes on to concede that, "though studies of this sort can't possibly go deep enough, they do provide us with a high-class kind of gossip that is often worth the effort." We will have to take our comfort in that. This book offers the interested reader "a high-class kind of gossip"; it pretends to do no more. Let us hope it will be worth the effort.

CHAPTER ONE

An Explanation by Manuscript Versions

JOHN KEATS

The Eve of St. Agnes

The Eve of St. Agnes

JOHN KEATS

(There was a belief in medieval times that on St. Agnes' Eve, January 20th, a girl, with proper preparation, might dream of her future husband, who would appear to her as in a vision and kiss her and feast with her.)

1

St. Agnes' Eve — Ah, bitter chill it was!
The owl, for all his feathers, was a-cold;
The hare limped trembling through the frozen grass,
And silent was the flock in woolly fold:
Numb were the Beadsman's fingers while he told
His rosary, and while his frosted breath,
Like pious incense from a censer old,
Seemed taking flight for heaven, without a death,
Past the sweet Virgin's picture, while his prayer he saith.

2

His prayer he saith, this patient, holy man; 10
Then takes his lamp, and riseth from his knees,
And back returneth, meager, barefoot, wan,
Along the chapel aisle by slow degrees:
The sculptured dead, on each side, seem to freeze,
Imprisoned in black, purgatorial rails:

3

Knights, ladies, praying in dumb orat'ries,
He passeth by, and his weak spirit fails
To think how they may ache in icy hoods and mails.

3

Northward he turneth through a little door,
And scarce three steps, ere Music's golden tongue 20
Flattered to tears this aged man and poor;
But no — already had his death-bell rung:
The joys of all his life were said and sung;
His was harsh penance on St. Agnes' Eve:
Another way he went, and soon among
Rough ashes sat he for his soul's reprieve,
And all night kept awake, for sinners' sake to grieve.

4

That ancient Beadsman heard the prelude soft;
And so it chanced, for many a door was wide,
From hurry to and fro. Soon, up aloft, 30
The silver, snarling trumpets 'gan to chide:
The level chambers, ready with their pride,
Were glowing to receive a thousand guests:
The carved angels, ever eager-eyed,
Stared, where upon their heads the cornice rests,
With hair blown back and wings put crosswise on their breasts.

5

At length burst in the argent revelry,
With plume, tiara, and all rich array,
Numerous as shadows haunting faerily
The brain new-stuffed, in youth, with triumphs gay 40
Of old romance. These let us wish away,
And turn, sole-thoughted, to one Lady there,
Whose heart had brooded, all that winter day,
On love, and winged St. Agnes' saintly care,
As she had heard old dames full many times declare.

6

They told her how, upon St. Agnes' Eve,
Young virgins might have visions of delight,
And soft adorings from their loves receive
Upon the honeyed middle of the night,
If ceremonies due they did aright; 50
As, supperless to bed they must retire,
And couch supine their beauties, lily white;
Nor look behind, nor sideways, but require
Of Heaven with upward eyes for all that they desire.

7

Full of this whim was thoughtful Madeline:
The music, yearning like a God in pain,
She scarcely heard: her maiden eyes divine,
Fixed on the floor, saw many a sweeping train
Pass by — she heeded not at all: in vain
Came many a tiptoe, amorous cavalier, 60
And back retired; not cooled by high disdain,
But she saw not: her heart was otherwhere;
She sighed for Agnes' dreams, the sweetest of the year.

8

She danced along with vague, regardless eyes,
Anxious her lips, her breathing quick and short:
The hallowed hour was near at hand: she sighs
Amid the timbrels, and the thronged resort
Of whisperers in anger or in sport;
'Mid looks of love, defiance, hate, and scorn,
Hoodwinked with faery fancy; all amort, 70
Save to St. Agnes and her lambs unshorn,
And all the bliss to be before to-morrow morn.

9

So, purposing each moment to retire,
She lingered still. Meantime, across the moors,

Had come young Porphyro, with heart on fire
For Madeline. Beside the portal doors,
Buttressed from moonlight, stands he, and implores
All saints to give him sight of Madeline,
But for one moment in the tedious hours,
That he might gaze and worship all unseen; 80
Perchance speak, kneel, touch, kiss — in sooth such things have been.

10

He ventures in: let no buzzed whisper tell:
All eyes be muffled, or a hundred swords
Will storm his heart, Love's fev'rous citadel:
For him, those chambers held barbarian hordes,
Hyena foemen, and hot-blooded lords,
Whose very dogs would execrations howl
Against his lineage: not one breast affords
Him any mercy, in that mansion foul,
Save one old beldame, weak in body and in soul. 90

11

Ah, happy chance! the aged creature came,
Shuffling along with ivory-headed wand,
To where he stood, hid from the torch's flame,
Behind a broad hall-pillar, far beyond
The sound of merriment and chorus bland:
He startled her; but soon she knew his face,
And grasped his fingers in her palsied hand,
Saying, "Mercy, Porphyro! hie thee from this place;
They are all here to-night, the whole bloodthirsty race!

12

"Get hence! get hence! here's dwarfish Hildebrand: 100
He had a fever late, and in the fit
He cursed thee and thine, both house and land:
Then there's that old Lord Maurice, not a whit

More tame for his gray hairs — Alas me! flit!
Flit like a ghost away." — "Ah, Gossip dear,
We're safe enough; here in this arm-chair sit,
And tell me how —" "Good saints! not here, not here!
Follow me, child, or else these stones will be thy bier."

13

He followed through a lowly arched way,
Brushing the cobwebs with his lofty plume; 110
And as she muttered "Well-a — well-a-day!"
He found him in a little moonlight room,
Pale, latticed, chill, and silent as a tomb.
"Now tell me where is Madeline," said he,
"O tell me, Angela, by the holy loom
Which none but secret sisterhood may see,
When they St. Agnes' wool are weaving piously."

14

"St. Agnes! Ah! it is St. Agnes' Eve —
Yet men will murder upon holy days.
Thou must hold water in a witch's sieve, 120
And be liege-lord of all the Elves and Fays
To venture so: it fills me with amaze
To see thee, Porphyro! — St. Agnes' Eve!
God's help! my lady fair the conjurer plays
This very night: good angels her deceive!
But let me laugh awhile, — I've mickle time to grieve."

15

Feebly she laugheth in the languid moon,
While Porphyro upon her face doth look,
Like puzzled urchin on an aged crone
Who keepeth closed a wondrous riddle-book, 130
As spectacled she sits in chimney nook.
But soon his eyes grew brilliant, when she told
His lady's purpose; and he scarce could brook
Tears, at the thought of those enchantments cold,
And Madeline asleep in lap of legends old.

16

Sudden a thought came like a full-blown rose,
Flushing his brow, and in his pained heart
Made purple riot: then doth he propose
A strategem, that makes the beldame start:
"A cruel man and impious thou art: 140
Sweet lady, let her pray, and sleep, and dream
Alone with her good angels, far apart
From wicked men like thee. Go, go! I deem
Thou canst not surely be the same that thou didst seem."

17

"I will not harm her, by all saints I swear,"
Quoth Porphyro: "O may I ne'er find grace
When my weak voice shall whisper its last prayer,
If one of her soft ringlets I displace,
Or look with ruffian passion in her face:
Good Angela, believe me by these tears; 150
Or I will, even in a moment's space,
Awake, with horrid shout, my foemen's ears,
And beard them, though they be more fanged than wolves and bears."

18

"Ah! why wilt thou affright a feeble soul?
A poor, weak, palsy-stricken, churchyard thing,
Whose passing-bell may ere the midnight toll;
Whose prayers for thee, each morn and evening,
Were never missed." Thus plaining, doth she bring
A gentler speech from burning Porphyro;
So woeful, and of such deep sorrowing, 160
That Angela gives promise she will do
Whatever he shall wish, betide her weal or woe.

19

Which was, to lead him, in close secrecy,
Even to Madeline's chamber, and there hide

Him in a closet, of such privacy
That he might see her beauty unespied,
And win perhaps that night a peerless bride,
While legioned fairies paced the coverlet,
And pale enchantment held her sleepy-eyed.
Never on such a night have lovers met, 170
Since Merlin paid his Demon all the monstrous debt.

20

"It shall be as thou wishest," said the Dame:
"All cates and dainties shall be stored there
Quickly on this feast-night: by the tambour frame
Her own lute thou wilt see: no time to spare,
For I am slow and feeble, and scarce dare
On such a catering trust my dizzy head.
Wait here, my child, with patience; kneel in prayer
The while. Ah! thou must needs the lady wed,
Or may I never leave my grave among the dead." 180

21

So saying she hobbled off with busy fear.
The lover's endless minutes slowly passed;
The dame returned, and whispered in his ear
To follow her; with aged eyes aghast
From fright of dim espial. Safe at last
Through many a dusky gallery, they gain
The maiden's chamber, silken, hushed and chaste;
Where Porphyro took covert, pleased amain.
His poor guide hurried back with agues in her brain.

22

Her faltering hand upon the balustrade, 190
Old Angela was feeling for the stair,
When Madeline, St. Agnes' charmed maid,
Rose, like a missioned spirit, unaware:
With silver taper's light, and pious care,

She turned, and down the aged gossip led
To a safe level matting. Now prepare,
Young Porphyro, for gazing on the bed;
She comes, she comes again, like ring-dove frayed and fled.

23

Out went the taper as she hurried in;
Its little smoke, in pallid moonshine, died: 200
She closed the door, she panted, all akin
To spirits of the air, and visions wide:
No uttered syllable, or, woe betide!
But to her heart, her heart was voluble,
Paining with eloquence her balmy side;
As though a tongueless nightingale should swell
Her throat in vain, and die, heart-stifled, in her dell.

24

A casement high and triple-arched there was,
All garlanded with carven imageries,
Of fruits, and flowers, and bunches of knot-grass, 210
And diamonded with panes of quaint device,
Innumerable of stains and splendid dyes,
As are the tiger-moth's deep-damasked wings;
And in the midst, 'mong thousand heraldries,
And twilight saints, and dim emblazonings,
A shielded scutcheon blushed with blood of queens and kings.

25

Full on this casement shone the wintry moon,
And threw warm gules on Madeline's fair breast,
As down she knelt for Heaven's grace and boon;
Rose-bloom fell on her hands, together prest, 220
And on her silver cross soft amethyst,
And on her hair a glory, like a saint:
She seemed a splendid angel, newly drest,
Save wings, for heaven: — Porphyro grew faint:
She knelt, so pure a thing, so free from mortal taint.

26

Anon his heart revives: her vespers done,
Of all its wreathed pearls her hair she frees;
Unclasps her warmed jewels one by one;
Loosens her fragrant bodice; by degrees
Her rich attire creeps rustling to her knees: 230
Half-hidden, like a mermaid in sea-weed,
Pensive awhile she dreams awake, and sees,
In fancy, fair St. Agnes in her bed,
But dares not look behind, or all the charm is fled.

27

Soon, trembling in her soft and chilly nest,
In sort of wakeful swoon, perplexed she lay,
Until the poppied warmth of sleep oppressed
Her soothed limbs, and soul fatigued away;
Flown, like a thought, until the morrow-day;
Blissfully havened both from joy and pain; 240
Clasped like a missal where swart Paynims pray;
Blinded alike from sunshine and from rain,
As though a rose would shut, and be a bud again.

28

Stolen to this paradise, and so entranced,
Porphyro gazed upon her empty dress,
And listened to her breathing, if it chanced
To wake into a slumberous tenderness;
Which when he heard, that minute did he bless,
And breathed himself: then from the closet crept,
Noiseless as fear in a wide wilderness, 250
And over the hushed carpet, silent, stept,
And 'tween the curtains peeped, where, lo! — how fast she slept.

29

Then by the bed-side, where the faded moon
Made a dim, silver twilight, soft he set

A table, and, half anguished, threw thereon
A cloth of woven crimson, gold, and jet —
O for some drowsy Morphean amulet!
The boisterous, midnight, festive clarion,
The kettle-drum, and far-heard clarinet,
Affray his ears, though but in dying tone: — 260
The hall-door shuts again, and all the noise is gone.

30

And still she slept an azure-lidded sleep,
In blanched linen, smooth, and lavendered.
While he from forth the closet brought a heap
Of candied apple, quince, and plum, and gourd;
With jellies soother than the creamy curd,
And lucent syrops, tinct with cinnamon;
Manna and dates, in argosy transferred
From Fez; and spiced dainties, every one,
From silken Samarcand to cedared Lebanon. 270

31

These delicates he heaped with glowing hand
On golden dishes and in baskets bright
Of wreathed silver: sumptuous they stand
In the retired quiet of the night,
Filling the chilly room with perfume light. —
"And now, my love, my seraph fair, awake!
Thou art my heaven, and I thine eremite:
Open thine eyes, for meek St. Agnes' sake,
Or I shall drowse beside thee, so my soul doth ache."

32

Thus whispering, his warm, unnerved arm 280
Sank in her pillow. Shaded was her dream
By the dusk curtains: — 'twas a midnight charm
Impossible to melt as iced stream:
The lustrous salvers in the moonlight gleam;
Broad golden fringe upon the carpet lies:

It seemed he never, never could redeem
From such a stedfast spell his lady's eyes;
So mused awhile, entoiled in woofed phantasies.

33

Awakening up, he took her hollow lute, —
Tumultuous, — and, in chords that tenderest be, 290
He played an ancient ditty, long since mute,
In Provence called, "La belle dame sans mercy:"
Close to her ear touching the melody; —
Wherewith disturbed, she uttered a soft moan:
He ceased — she panted quick — and suddenly
Her blue affrayed eyes wide open shone:
Upon his knees he sank, pale as smooth-sculptured stone.

34

Her eyes were open, but she still beheld,
Now wide awake, the vision of her sleep:
There was a painful change, that nigh expelled 300
The blisses of her dream so pure and deep
At which fair Madeline began to weep,
And moan forth witless words with many a sigh,
While still her gaze on Porphyro would keep;
Who knelt, with joined hands and piteous eye,
Fearing to move or speak, she looked so dreamingly.

35

"Ah, Porphyro!" said she, "but even now
Thy voice was at sweet tremble in mine ear,
Made tuneable with every sweetest vow;
And those sad eyes were spiritual and clear: 310
How changed thou art! how pallid, chill, and drear!
Give me that voice again, my Porphyro,
Those looks immortal, those complainings dear!
Oh, leave me not in this eternal woe,
For if thou diest, my Love, I knew not where to go."

36

Beyond a mortal man impassioned far
At these voluptuous accents, he arose,
Ethereal, flushed, and like a throbbing star
Seen 'mid the sapphire heaven's deep repose;
Into her dream he melted, as the rose 320
Blendeth its odor with the violet, —
Solution sweet: meantime the frost-wind blows
Like Love's alarum, pattering the sharp sleet
Against the window-panes; St. Agnes' moon hath set.

37

'Tis dark: quick pattereth the flaw-blown sleet.
"This is no dream, my bride, my Madeline!"
'Tis dark: the iced gusts still rave and beat:
"No dream, alas! alas! and woe is mine!
Porphyro will leave me here to fade and pine.
Cruel! what traitor could thee hither bring? 330
I curse not, for my heart is lost in thine,
Though thou forsakest a deceived thing; —
A dove forlorn and lost with sick unpruned wing."

38

"My Madeline! sweet dreamer! lovely bride!
Say, may I be for aye thy vassal blest?
Thy beauty's shield, heart-shaped and vermeil-dyed?
Ah, silver shrine, here will I take my rest
After so many hours of toil and quest,
A famished pilgrim, — saved by miracle.
Though I have found, I will not rob thy nest, 340
Saving of thy sweet self; if thou think'st well
To trust, fair Madeline, to no rude infidel.

39

"Hark! 'tis an elfin-storm from faery land,
Of haggard seeming, but a boon indeed:
Arise — arise! the morning is at hand; —
The bloated wassailers will never heed; —

Let us away, my love, with happy speed;
There are no ears to hear, or eyes to see,—
Drowned all in Rhenish and the sleepy mead:
Awake! arise! my love, and fearless be, 350
For o'er the southern moors I have a home for thee."

40

She hurried at his words, beset with fears,
For there were sleeping dragons all around,
At glaring watch, perhaps, with ready spears —
Down the wide stairs a darkling way they found;
In all the house was heard no human sound.
A chain-drooped lamp was flickering by each door;
The arras, rich with horseman, hawk, and hound,
Fluttered in the besieging wind's uproar;
And the long carpets rose along the gusty floor. 360

41

They glide, like phantoms, into the wide hall;
Like phantoms, to the iron porch they glide,
Where lay the Porter, in uneasy sprawl,
With a huge empty flagon by his side:
The wakeful bloodhound rose, and shook his hide,
But his sagacious eye an inmate owns:
By one, and one, the bolts full easy slide: —
The chains lie silent on the footworn stones;
The key turns, and the door upon its hinges groans.

42

And they are gone: aye, ages long ago 370
These lovers fled away into the storm.
That night the Baron dreamt of many a woe,
And all his warrior-guests with shade and form
Of witch, and demon, and large coffin-worm,
Were long be-nightmared. Angela the old
Died palsy-twitched, with meager face deform;
The Beadsman, after thousand aves told,
For aye unsought-for slept among his ashes cold.

The Eve of St. Agnes

M. R. RIDLEY

About the 18th of January 1819 Keats went down to Chichester, to stay for a few days with "old Mr. Dilke," and on the 23rd he and Brown walked over to Bedhampton to stay with Mr. John Snook. There he was ill, and "did not go out of the Garden Gate but twice or thrice during the fortnight I was there." His comment on the trip, apart from the mention of two dowager card parties in Chichester, is that "nothing worth speaking of happened at either place." Well, opinions differ as to what is worth speaking of; but we find it hard to agree with Keats' estimate when we read his next sentence. "I took down some thin paper and wrote on it a little poem call'd St. Agnes' Eve." That was at least something which the readers of English poetry have thought worth speaking of ever since. It is true that, rightly or wrongly, Keats never did rate *The Eve of St. Agnes* so high as his friends then, and critics since, have rated it, and when we come to examine *Lamia* we shall I think discover the reason, and possibly agree with him. There is a wide difference, not so much in execution as in temper, between the two poems. And it is true also that Keats, fresh from his labours, which were disappointing him, on the far harder and greater *Hyperion*, must have felt, and was justified in feeling, that *The Eve of St. Agnes* was a slighter thing. But in its kind, even though that kind be slight, it is not far short of perfection. It has not the power of *Hyperion*, nor the

---

Reprinted, by permission, from *Keats Craftsmanship*, by M. R. Ridley (Oxford: The Clarendon Press, 1933).

"sort of fire" of *Lamia;* nor has it the superb and serene mastery of the greatest of his Odes. But Keats has at last entered triumphantly into his kingdom. There is none of the fumbling and the sense of insecurity which marred the beauties of *Isabella.* The control of the metre is complete; the narrative moves straight forward with neither halt nor hurry; the pictures have strength and clarity of line; and the outstanding page 96 / beauties, of which there are many, are not irrelevant adornments but parts of a harmonious whole. Whatever else *The Eve of St. Agnes* may be, it is the deliberate work of a trained craftsman; and as such it richly repays examination.

And for such an examination, to help us in the fascinating business of looking over the craftsman's shoulder while he is actually at work, we have a greater wealth of material than for any other poem of Keats, or for more than a very few other famous English poems. We have in the first place, all but seven stanzas of what is almost certainly the first draft of the poem, and we can watch the whole of its development. In the second place we can watch, as I hope to show, Keats' imagination working on his material, selecting from here, there, and everywhere in his reading, taking hints from Shakespeare and Mrs. Radcliffe, Boccaccio and Mother Bunch, and fusing them into his design.

There are extant, besides the printed version of the 1820 volume, four written copies of the poem, and the relations between these are of importance for our study.

1. A copy in Keats' own writing (wanting the first seven stanzas), now in the Widener library at Harvard University.
2. A transcript by Woodhouse, in the possession of the Marquess of Crewe.
3. Another transcript of Woodhouse, also in the possession of the Marquess of Crewe.
4. A transcript by George Keats, now in the British Museum.

Of these the first, the holograph, is almost certainly the first draft. It is so heavily corrected that it is hard to believe that there was any earlier state; and furthermore it is quite clear that in many of the stanzas the poet is writing as he composes; there are frequent false starts, half-lines scratched out before the whole new line is written, and other indications that this is not the work of page 97 / a man who is merely making final corrections in a more or less complete manuscript. Finally, the physical characteristics of this draft correspond with Keats' own description. The paper is so thin that in examining it one feels somewhat dangerously like Keats himself with his line of Shakespeare which he felt might be blown away. **page 98 /**

. . . .

The second aspect of Keats' craftsmanship which a study of this poem illumines is what is commonly called his "use of his sources." That is a dangerous phrase, and it is too often interpreted in a way which evokes a ridiculous picture of a creative artist sitting at his table surrounded by half a dozen books and flitting hurriedly from one to another in search of an idea or a phrase, feverishly turning the interminable pages of *The Mysteries of Udolpho* to find an oaken gallery, and then seeking in Shakespeare for an epithet for trumpets; picking a quince from *Romeo and Juliet,* a gourd from *The Arabian Nights,* and a complete dessert from *Paradise Lost;* and unable to draw a picture of a lover in his lady's chamber without going to Boccaccio to find it. No original artist works like that, but only a pedestrian compiler, "if such one there be," of inharmonious mosaic. But however original a literary artist is, part, and probably a large part, of the material on which his selecting and shaping imagination works is the reminiscences of his reading. And, so long as we do not jump too hurriedly to conclusions, the pleasure of watching the artist at work is greatly enhanced when we can watch him **page 101 /** shape and select. But the greater part of this material is in a kind of superior rag-bag of the artist's mind, in which the scraps are not docketed with their provenance, as though they were in a card-catalogue; so that he cannot tell to what kind of garment, owned by whom, this bit of flannel, or that piece of gingham, or that other attractive bit of silk originally belonged. It must be the commonest experience to any one who reads at all and who ever uses a pen, if for no more than writing letters, that he finds himself using phrases of which he does not know whether they are quotations, or half-quotations, or his own. So too, one may reasonably presume, with the artist. Occasionally, of course, one can see the artist at work on a specific and even acknowledged "source," as was Shakespeare in many of his plays, or Keats himself in *Isabella.* But, for the most part, "sources" are of the vaguer and less conscious kind, and the exploration of them is as seductive as it is perilous. The trouble is that the search after sources is too much like the collection of stamps or other objects of the collector's passion; and the discovery of a possible rarity, which the other collector has missed, is apt, in the first flush of enthusiasm, to make the collector unduly reluctant to examine the perforation and watermark. It will be as well, then, to consider for a moment what kind of evidence one can look for in estimating the probabilities that a suggested source was in fact a source. In the first place, the author may state in so many words, or indicate by other unmistakable signs, that he has read the author, book, poem, or passage in question. In the second place he may, by records however disjointed, so blaze the trails of his discursive reading and thinking, that the trained woodsman, if skilful enough and patient enough, can with some certainty follow him, as Professor Lowes followed Coleridge in the most brilliant piece of detective criticism that this century has produced. Again, still in the realm of external evidence, we may have the records of the author's friends as to his reading, whether in general, or specifically in regard to a particular piece of **page 102 /** work. When we move to internal evidence we are on much more treacherous ground. In the work of any writer we find innumerable parallels to the work of others. In some instances the parallel is so close, or involves such a striking word or collocation of words, that we feel that mere coincidence will not suffice to account for it, and that we are justified in saying, "This is a reminiscence, conscious or unconscious, of that." From such instances we move in a descending scale through the parallels which are introduced in notes by "This is probably a reminiscence of . . ." to those which have to be contented with "This may remind one of. . . ." This internal evidence never amounts to proof; and isolated pieces of it are of little more than casual interest. Its value is almost entirely cumulative; if we have reason to suspect that a given work is a source, every additional verbal parallel, or parallel in situation, greatly increases the probability that our conjecture is a sound one. And when both external evidence and a sufficient bulk of internal evidence appear to lead us in the same direction we may feel reasonably sure that we are on the author's trail.

I am going to suggest for examination, as the four main sources of *The Eve of St. Agnes,* apart from the folk-lore element, Shakespeare, especially *Romeo and Juliet;* Mrs. Radcliffe; *The*

Arabian Nights; and a French translation of Boccaccio's *Il Filocolo.*

Keats' familiarity with Shakespeare needs no proof. He regarded Shakespeare as his "Presider"; throughout the letters he is perpetually quoting him, and shows too that sure proof of familiarity which consists in quoting without the use of quotation marks; and two of his copies of Shakespeare, the folio now at Hampstead, and the edition in America, bear evidence of his careful reading of certain **page 103 /** plays in the shape of frequent underlinings and occasional annotations.

That Keats was at least acquainted with Mrs. Radcliffe's work appears from his own letters. Writing to Reynolds in March 1818 he says: "I am going among Scenery whence I intend to tip you the Damosel Radcliffe — I'll cavern you, and grotto you, and waterfall you, and wood you, and water you, and immense-rock you, and tremendous sound you, and solitude you." And writing to George and Georgiana Keats in February 1819, in allusion to the titles of his last written poems (*The Pot of Basil, St. Agnes' Eve,* and *The Eve of St. Mark*), he says: "You see what fine Mother Radcliffe names I have." Neither of these passages implies more than a nodding acquaintance. But when in *The Romance of the Forest* we find, as the refrain of one of the pieces of verse with which Mrs. Radcliffe tries, with imperfect success, to enliven the more tedious passages of her narrative, the line

> Love wave his purple pinions o'er my head

and then turn to Keats' early poem *To Hope*, and find as the last line of three verses

> And wave thy silver pinions o'er my head,

then we rub our eyes and begin to wonder. And when we read in the *Sicilian Romance* that "The sun, involved in clouds of *splendid* and *innumerable* hues, was setting," and remember that Keats wrote "*Innumerable* of stains and *splendid* dyes," and, further, that in the next line he first deletes his *damasked* for no very apparent reason to substitute *sunset*, then we wonder more, and begin to think that some further investigation along these lines might be illuminating. The idea that Keats, in *The Eve of St. Agnes,* was indebted to Mrs. Radcliffe was first **page 104 /**

propounded by Professor M. H. Shackford in a most interesting paper at which Miss Lowell aimed a boomerang which was much more destructive on its inward than its outward journey. But Professor Shackford confined her attention to *The Mysteries of Udolpho*, and, so limiting her own range, she missed, as I think and hope to show, discovering the range of Keats.

As to *Il Filocolo*, another American scholar, Professor H. Noble MacCracken, advanced the idea that Keats was indebted to this tale of Boccaccio. But he made the mistake of confining his attention to the original version, and the difficulties of supposing that Keats read *Il Filocolo* in the original are almost insuperable. Eight months later than the composition of *The Eve of St. Agnes* he could only manage Ariosto at the rate of "six or eight stanzas at a time," and that Keats could have ploughed through the infinite tediousness of *Il Filocolo* at a rate of progress so dragging as that to which his unfamiliarity with the language would have condemned him is a supposition which we would only entertain under the compulsion of the strongest evidence. Of such evidence, of evidence strong enough to outweigh the intrinsic improbability of his thesis, Professor MacCracken produced none at all. What he did show, and it was worth showing, was that there is a close parallel between the situation in *The Eve of St. Agnes* and the situation in one section of *Il Filocolo*, and one or two parallels in detail. But he adduced no verbal parallels which could persuade one to reject the probabilities. After all, the situation in *The Eve of St. Agnes* is not so peculiar that an imaginative artist could not invent it for himself, without recourse to a model; and if we were faced with the alternatives that Keats either read the romance in Italian or did not read it at all, there can be no doubt which of the two is the more page 105 / credible. On the other hand, the resemblances in situation are so close that, apart from the question of language, Professor MacCracken's thesis does not merit the cavalier dismissal which is all the attention Miss Lowell sees fit to accord it. We should feel happier if there were some way in which Keats could have read the *Filocolo*. And so there was. It is true that there appears to have been at that date no English translation of it. But there was a French translation. And from what Keats says himself, quite apart from the evidence of the Ronsard sonnets, and the probability, pointed out by Sir Sidney Colvin, that he had read Gombauld's *L'Endimion*, it appears that he had at least adequate facility in French. He begins his remarks about Ariosto with the comment, "In the course of a few months I shall be as good an Italian scholar as I am a french one." There is then no intrinsic improbability in the conjecture that Keats read Boccaccio's tale in French, and if he had read Mirabeau's translation of the *Decameron* he might well have looked round for other French translations of Boccaccio.

The internal evidence as to the sources will be more readily examined in detail in connexion with the different sections of the poem for which the particular sources seem to have been used.

I propose that we should examine the poem in some detail, trying to watch as it were both the mind and the hand of the craftsman, to see Keats' imagination working on his material, stimulated by some parts of it, modifying others, and rejecting others, and to see also his technical skill labouring to secure the finished result that he wants. In any such survey it is ridiculous to be dogmatic; the only person who can know how an artist's mind works is the artist himself, and even he is probably none too clear about it. On the other hand, perpetual qualification becomes tedious. I hope therefore that any reader page 106 / who is interested enough to follow this examination will realize that, outside deductions which can be safely made from an examination of the actual script of the holograph, where some degree of certainty is attainable, any blunt statement of what Keats did or did not do should be read with a tacit qualification of "probably" or "one may conjecture" which in the interest of brevity and clarity is suppressed.

The germ of the poem was a piece of folk-lore. And for all the wealth of beauty that sprang from it, Keats did not himself lose sight of what the seed had been, since in August of 1819, four months after the poem was structurally complete, he writes to Bailey of a poem "call'd St. Agnes' Eve on a popular superstition." What then was this popular superstition, and whence did Keats derive his knowledge of it? The commentators are content to refer us to Brand's *Popular Antiquities* and to Burton's *Anatomy of Melancholy*. Brand quotes Ben Jonson (or misquotes him):

> And on sweet St. Agnes' night
> Please you with the promised sight
> Some of husbands, some of lovers,
> Which an empty dream discovers

Burton is a very little more explicit:

> 'Tis their only desire if it may be done by Art, to see their husbands picture in a glass, they'll give anything to know when they shall be married, how many husbands they shall have, by *Crommyomantia*, a kind of divination with Onions laid on the Altar on St. Agnes' Eve or Night, to know who shall be their first husband. (III. ii. 3.1.)

I can see no reason to suppose that the subject "was page 107 / more probably suggested to Keats" by Burton than by Brand, or by Jonson direct: nor very much reason to suppose that it was suggested to him by either, since the two of them put together give us no more of the method of divination than a fasting dream. There seems no very cogent reason for pursuing a printed source at all. On the authority of Woodhouse the "subject was suggested by Mrs. Jones." It is perhaps enough title to fame for this mysterious lady that she is responsible for the inception of *The Eve of St. Agnes*, but at any rate that is all the title she has, since we know nothing else of her except that she borrowed a book from Keats. But it is reasonable enough to suppose that she was some one he met at Chichester, and tempting to suppose that it was actually on the 20th of January, when Keats was there, that she suggested the subject. If so, the least she could do was to tell Keats, if he did not know it already, the folklore about St. Agnes' Eve. At any rate Keats either invented, or learned from Mrs. Jones or from elsewhere, the details of the prescribed observances which are so signally lacking from Brand and Burton. In Keats we have the following points: the maiden must retire fasting; she must not look behind; she must not speak; she must lie on her back; if she follows the ceremonial she will see her adoring lover. The way in which the "ceremonies due" are catalogued does not read as though Keats were inventing them; and if we are determined to prefer a printed source to Mrs. Jones we shall find it in the shape of a chap-book entitled *Mother Bunches Closet newly broke open.* The relevant passages in this are as follows:

> Why then I will tell you in the first place, you must observe page 108 / St. Agnes's day which is the 21st of January, and on that day let no man salute thee; and at night before thou goest to bed put on the best shift thou hast, and when thou liest down, lay

thy right hand under thy head, and say these words, now the *God of love send me my desires;* then go to sleep as soon as possible, and you shall be sure to dream of him who will be your husband, and see him stand before you, and you may take notice of him and his complexion, and if he offer to salute thee, do not deny him, but shew him as much favour as thou canst.

That does not get us very far, but it is worth quoting for some interesting parallels which we shall notice later. Five pages later, however, we get more detail, and even though it is to do this time with St. Thomas, that need not seriously disturb us:

Take a St. Thomas's onion [what, one wonders in passing, is this mysterious vegetable?] pare it, and lay it on a clean handkerchief under your pillow; and put on a clean smock and as you lie down, lay your arms abroad, and say these words

Good St. Thomas do me right;
And bring my love to me this night,
That I may view him in the face,
And in my arms may him embrace

Then *lying on thy back* with thy arms abroad go to sleep as soon as you can, and in your first sleep you shall dream of him who is to be your husband and he will come and offer to kiss you; do not hinder him, but catch him in thy arms, and strive to hold him, for that is he.

This indeed gives us an unnecessary onion; but it gives us the lying on the back; it also gives us a clean smock, which Keats perhaps used, and the point that in the dream there will be an embrace, which is not indeed mentioned by Keats as part of the ceremonies due, except by implication in a finally rejected stanza of the second draft, but which does become the climax of the narrative.

A few pages later we revert to St. Agnes, with fuller detail:

But for all there be so many bad days in this month I can tell you of one day which is lucky, and many young men and maids **page 109 /** have a deal of heart's ease on that day, or the day after shall let you understand; it is the 21st. called St. Agnes' day. This St. Agnes has a favour for young men and maids and will bring to their bedsides their sweethearts if they follow my rules, on this day you must be sure to *keep fast,* and neither eat nor drink all that day, nor night, neither let man woman or child kiss thee on that day; and thou must be sure when thou goest to bed to put on a *clean shift* and the best thou has, and clean clothes on thy head; for St. Agnes loves to see all clean when she comes. When thou liest down lie as *straight as thou canst*, lay thy hands under thy head and say

> Now St. Agnes play thy part,
> And send to me my own sweetheart;
> And show me such a *happy bliss*,
> This night of him to have a kiss.

And be sure to fall asleep as soon as you can and before you awake out of your first sleep you shall see him come before you.

We still have not found directions for silence, but these also come later: "speak not a word" and "then go to bed without speaking a word."

Here then is a detailed statement of the ceremonies and their outcome, with the single exception of the prohibition against looking behind. There were probably other chap-books with much the same record of the details of the popular superstition, from which Keats could derive his knowledge, if he did not get it orally from Mrs. Jones. And we can leave Mrs. Jones and Mother Bunch, and possibly others, to share the distinction of being the old dames of stanza 5. If we incline to Mother Bunch there are at least two verbal parallels which may strengthen our inclination.

There then is the bare material of the superstition. It is time to turn to the poem and see what Keats made of it, and how he used the obviously wide latitude which it offers to the artist for expansion and embroidery and the interweaving of other themes.

In this examination of the poem I have made almost no attempt at general criticism, that type of criticism which page 110 / introduces the critic in the role of showman, with pointing finger indicating the beauties of the work. Such criticism will be found, if it is desired, in Leigh Hunt's *London Journal* for January 1835, where he printed the whole poem with a running commentary between the stanzas; and a revised version of this will be found in *Imagination and Fancy*. It shows Leigh Hunt at his best, and whatever we may think of Hunt as an original poet, his critical best was of a very high order. Other critics in turn have tried their hands at it; and perhaps one of the highest tributes we can pay to the poem is to say that it has emerged from this handling untarnished. But I think that critics would do well to take warning from a footnote in Sir Sidney Colvin's *Life of Keats.* There stands there, as he first wrote it, a long passage on two or three stanzas of *Isabella* which is as perfect a piece of expository criticism, in its restraint and taste and insight, as one can hope to find, a model of what such criticism should be. And yet, looking back on it after thirty years, its author notes that it now seems to him "somewhat officious and over-explanatory." If he felt so, I think that the rest of us had better keep our clumsy hands away from the exquisite and fragile beauties of such a poem as *The Eve of St. Agnes.* They are patent enough, not of that elusive kind that we need go looking for them behind a cicerone with a flash-lamp. And indeed *The Eve of St. Agnes* is one of those works which deserve, as I believe, the most patient and exact study that we can give them, and will most richly reward the patient reader by disclosing to him their beauties, as though Keats' shut rosebud should slowly expand before his eyes, but which resent, and punish, any attempt to force them to display those beauties. I have tried therefore in the remainder of this chapter to help the study, and leave the bud to expand as it chooses.

First, before he will introduce his main actors, Keats, with his dramatist's instinct, is going to set his stage, and **page 111 /** make the cold bite into the marrow.

1

St. Agnes' Eve — Ah bitter cold it was;
The owl for all his feathers was a-cold,
The hare limp'd trembling through the frozen grass,
And silent were the flock in sheltered fold —
Numb were the Beadsman's fingers while he told
His rosary, and while his frosted breath,
Like pious incense in a censer old,
Seem'd taking flight for heaven without a death,
Past the sweet virgin's picture while his prayers he saith.

There is the most astonishing cumulative effect of cold about this stanza as we feel in turn with the bird; the wild beast; the domesticated beast, partly sheltered; the man, indoors but still cold and numb; and the effect rises to its climax in the freezing picture of the frosted breath. And before the stanza is finished Keats is, I think, standing not in the chapel of his Radcliffean castle, but in one of the coldest places in all literature, where also it was "bitter cold," and where also it was silent, with not a mouse stirring, the platform before the castle at Elsinore.

In the second draft Keats altered *cold* to *chill*, primarily no doubt, as he explained in a letter to Taylor when protesting against this particular error in the proofs, to avoid the echo with *cold* on the next line; perhaps partly also to avoid the exact Shakespearean quotation. He corrected the fourth line to read *And silent was the flock in woolly fold;* the incense came more vividly *from* a censer, and there are two minor alterations in the last line. page 112 /

. . . .

24

For showing Keats the pure craftsman delighting in his mastery of his craft these next two stanzas* are unequalled in the poem. There is no emotional stress to distract, no excitement of action to hurry him. He is quietly setting his stage for the climax, and he can take his time over making it as richly perfect as it can be made. He remembers the arched windows and the stained glass from Mrs. Radcliffe and possibly the *deux escharboncles* from Blanchefleur's chamber; and he starts with a kind of fluent rough sketch.

A Casement ach'd

But let us make it bigger (? for more light and a better display of glass) and also more defined in outline; so

A Casement tripple archd and diamonded

(we notice that instinct for line, always strong in Keats, which gives first the outline of the window and then fills it with interesting tracery of the leading)

With many coloured glass fronted the Moon
In midst ~~of which~~ wereof a shilded scutcheon shed
High blushing gules, upon

* See illustration between pages 36 and 37 for Keats's changes in stanzas 24 and 25.

But, before the gules is shed on her, Madeline, who was left at the door, must be brought forward; so *upon* is deleted and a colon goes in after *gules;* and pictures from Mrs. Radcliffe come back to him; in one of which he remembers somewhere a silver cross which will catch the light:

> High blushing gules: she kneeled saintly down
> And inly prayed for grace and heavenly boon;
> The blood red gules fell on her silver cross
> And her white hands devout

(with, I think, an experimental change of *her white* into *whitest*).
page 149 /
Well, there at least is some of the material in the rough; but it will not do as it stands, if only for the purely technical reason that *down* will only rhyme with *moon* and *boon* if one is Burns. And apart from that there is a fumbling of touch in the repetition of *gules*. But most of the material is much too good to let go. So Keats takes it all to pieces, like a man making the stained-glass window of which he is talking, and begins to put the fragments together in a different design. And first he decides that Madeline had better be postponed till the next stanza. He will indulge himself with the luxury of a piece of pure description and give himself ample room for the development of the window and the moonlight. He starts by elaborating the window:

> A Casement tipple archd and high

presumably going to end *there was* but he concludes that this had better come at the beginning, and we get

> There was
> A Casement tipple archd and high
> All garlanded with carven imageries
> Of fruits & trailing flowers and sunny corn

which is excellent except that it does not rhyme; so *trailing* goes out and the line is completed with *ears parchd* ready to rhyme with the first line when the latter was transposed. But the transposition is not made, because there suddenly recurs to him a word ("knot-grass") from a passage which he had marked in *A*

Midsummer Night's Dream that will rhyme with the first line as he first had it in mind. So he starts all over again.

> A Casement high and tripple archd there was
> All gardneded [*he is in a hurry now*] with carven imageries
> Of fruits and flowers and bunches of knot grass;
> And diamonded with panes of quaint device
> Innumerable of stains and splendid dies
> As is the wing of evening tiger moths;
> And in the midst 'mong ~~man~~ thousand heraldries
> And dim twilight

page 150 /

At this point he sees how to give emphasis to both *dim* and *twilight* by separating them, and so cancels them to write

> And twilight saints and dim emblasonings
> A shielded scutcheon blushd with Blood of Queens and Kings

But now the sixth line is left hanging unrhymed. He makes a minor alteration in the seventh line, so that it starts *In midst whereoft;* then he feels that the line about the stains and dies, even though he is half-conscious that it is a reminiscence, is a fine line in itself, and that the line which follows, even apart from the easily secured rhyme, will not at present take the weight of its predecessor. So for the final touch for his stanza he begins the operation which makes of the tiger moths and their wings one of the richest of even his opulent lines. He first deletes it altogether and starts

> As is the tiger moths rich

no, let us have both a more significant word and an alliteration

> deep damasked wings

and then the force of association is too much for him; the splendid and innumerable dies when he first met them were the hues of sunset, and he acknowledges his debts by writing *sunset* for *damasked*, and so for the moment left the stanza, for once, we may hope, well satisfied. In the second draft he diminished the over-emphatic *s*'s of the third line by writing *fruit*, went back to the simpler *And in the midst*, and, surely rightly, reinstated *damasked*.

25

Keats is now ready to work into his design the other pieces that are left over, and, as he is no longer trying to compress into one stanza the material of two, he has space to develop the second part of his picture, the moonlight and Madeline. The impression of cold can be maintained page 151 / by the moon being *wintry*, and the picture of Madeline complete instead of a sketch.

Full on this Casement shone the wintry moon
And threw red gules on Madelines fair face

Red is redundant and becomes first *warm* and then *rich* (carried over from the deletion in the last stanza); *face* suffers from all possible disabilities; it suggests no feasible rhyme except *grace* which cannot be deferred till the fourth line; it is feebly Leigh Huntian; and in any case we do not want the heroine red in the face, even though by the operation of lunar cosmetics; so alter it to *breast*, and we have:

Full on this Casement shone the wintry moon
  And threw rich gules on Madelines fair breast
As down she kneel'd for heavens grace and boon
  Tinging her pious hands together prest
And silver cross

But the fourth line is not satisfactory, and also it occurs to him that the window of innumerable stains seems incapable of transmitting anything but gules, which is both illogical and dull; so he gets to work on the fourth line, and after a deal of experimentation, of which the stages are obscure, we arrive, with a dubious rhyme, at the end of the fifth line

Rose bloom fell on her hands together prest[1]
And on her silver cross soft Amethyst

[1] What exactly happened with this line is hard to determine. What we find in the draft, as nearly as print can represent it, is the following:

~~And~~ rose ~~with red~~ bloom fell on her hands together
~~Tinging her pious~~ hands ~~together~~ prest

The results of the first alteration were meant I think to be

Tinging with red her hands together prest

the second

And rose bloom on her hands together prest

the third

Rose bloom fell on her hands together prest

but this does not at all account for the firm deletion of the first *together* and

And on her hair a glory like a Saint's —
She seem'd ~~like an immortal agel drest~~
silvery angel newly drest,
Save wings for heaven — Porphyro grew faint
She knelt too pure a thing, too free from motal taint —

page 152 /

And the stanza is tidied up by the deletion of the final *s* of *Saint's*. In the second draft Keats reverted to the much happier first thought of *warm*, and changed the rather inhuman and metallic silver angel to *a splendid angel*.

26

But soon his heart revives —

(Porphyro, like Fleury, "reprit vigueur")

her prayers said

And now Keats addresses himself to the delicate business of getting Madeline undressed. He probably, as Mr. W. T. Arnold pointed out, called to his aid a passage in Browne's *Britannia's Pastorals:*

And as a lovely maiden, pure and chaste,
With naked ivory neck, a gown unlaced
Within her chamber, when the day is fled,
Makes poor her garments to enrich her bed:
First she puts off her lily-silken gown,
That shrinks for sorrow as she lays it down;
Her breasts all bare, her kirtle slipping down,

. . . .

Prepares for sweetest rest.

though I am not clear that there is anything very specific there

---

I cannot make any combination of the words before us that will make a line with *together* omitted. And one cannot help wondering, though it would upset the idea that Keats was wanting more varied colour, whether *rose* did not start life as a verb, in contrast to *down she kneeld*.

There is one interesting small point, which indicates the rapidity with which Keats wrote when composing. In line 7 as altered there is clearly an *a* wanted before *silvery*. And Keats omitted it because he thought it was there. The *d* of *seem'd* is not only badly made, but widely spaced from the rest of the word, and Keats' eye was caught by it as he re-wrote the line and took it for the *a* that was needed.

by way of parallel except the *unlaced* and the *slipping down* and the latter could at least as well have been derived from a visual as from a literary memory. However, with whatever memories, Keats begins:

> She lays aside her veil

page 153 /

But this is the first that we have heard of a veil, and anyway it is not important, so cut it out and try

> She strips her hair of all its wreathed pearl

and then try this the other way round,

> its pearled wreath

and go on

> Unclasps her bosom jewels

but this (apart from the awkwardness of *bosom* as an adjective) is going too fast and leaves the hair unfinished, so delete it and write

> And twists it one knot upon her head

But Keats now knows that he is getting well out of his depth, so the whole thing disappears and he starts again, having made up his mind we may suppose that in this unfamiliar region the only thing for it is rigorous compression:

> But soon his heart revives — her prayers done

(changed first, to avoid the awkward dissyllable, into *her prayers soon done* and then into *her praying done*)

> ~~Sh~~Of all ~~her its~~ wreathed pearl she strips her hair
> Unclasps her warmed jewels one by one

So far so good; but now comes a desperate moment which can only be indicated by an attempt to represent the agitations of the draft:

> ~~her bursting~~
> Loosens ~~her boddice from her~~
> ~~her Boddice lace~~ string
> ~~her Boddice and her bosom bare~~
> her

One can almost see Keats arriving, at the fourth attempt and with clenched teeth, at the end of the line and a rhyme for *hair*, even though grammar has been sacrificed to get there; and hear the sigh with which he writes the final and undeleted *her* but refuses to write *Boddice* for the **page 154 /** fourth time. At this point he turns the page and tries the line again, this time with happier success:

> Loosens her fragrant boddice and doth bare
> Her

But by now it is time for a new attempt, and after an idle moment of recuperation, in which he goes back and counts the stanzas he has written, he numbers this one (the first he has numbered since he started) and advances to the attack once more.

> Anon
> But soon his heart revives — her praying done
> Of all its wreathed pearl her hair she strips
> Unclasps her warmed jewels one by one
> Loosens her fragrant boddice: and down slips
> Her sweet attire

At any rate we are once for all done with the boddice; but Keats finds himself stuck in the middle of a line when he wants to be at the end of it; so he alters *and down slips* to *to her knees*, which allows him to hold the verb up as long as he wishes, make the consequential alteration of *frees* for *strips* in the second line, and takes up line 5 again. First he tries

> Her sweet attire falls light

and then

> creeps down by

which was presumably to continue

> slow degrees

when it occurs to him to put the degrees earlier and the knees here, and he arrives at

> Loosens her fragrant boddice: by degrees
> Her sweet attire creeps rusteling to her knees
> Half hidden like a Syren of the Sea
> And more melodious **page 155 /**

But he finds that associations have run away with him, since there is no point in Madeline being either more or less melodious than a Syren (unless he had for the moment intentions of making her rather than Porphyro sing like Mrs. Radcliffe's damsels); so

> Half hidden like a Mermaid in sea weed
> She stands awhile in thought; and sees

the line being then completed by the insertion of *dreaming* before *thought*,

> In fancy fair Saint Agnes in her bed
> But dares not look behind or all the charm is ~~fled~~ dead

In the second draft the *praying* is specified as *vespers*, the attire becomes *rich* instead of *sweet*, the seventh line opens

> Pensive awhile she dreams awake

and *fled* comes in again for *dead*.

There at last, after all the difficulties, is Madeline rather summarily undressed, and she is left shivering in the midst of her discarded raiment with no hint of Mother Bunch's clean shift or any other shift. But all the King's horses and men will not drag Keats back over this stricken field again, and, nightdress or no nightdress, Madeline must be got safely into bed as rapidly as may be.

27

> Then stepping forth she slips

deleted at once;

> The charm fled not — she did not look behind;
> Soon trembling in her soft and chilly nest

("chilly"; no wonder).
At this point it seems better to give up the first line altogether, so it is cancelled and we start with the second, and go on

> She lay and had not seen her

also cancelled;

> She lay ~~and as~~ and till the poppied warmth of sleep **page 156 /**

also cancelled; but it has contained an idea which is retained:

> She lay, in sort of wakeful swoon perplext

and this only requires transposition to serve

> In sort of wakeful swoon perplext she lay
> Until the poppied warmth of sleep opprest
> Her soothed Limbs, and Soul fatigued away;
> Flown like a thought until the morrow day;
> Blissfully havend both from joy and pain
> Shut like a Missal where swart paynims pray —

Several alternatives are tried, *Like a shut Missal, Like a clasp'd Missal, and finally*

> Clasp'd like a Missal where swart paynims pray —
> ~~Dead to~~ Blinded alike from Sunshine and from rain
> As though a rose should ~~shut close~~ shut and be a bud again.

The source of the missal has not been satisfactorily explained, but an interesting suggestion about it, which may be the solution and is certainly worth recording, was made by Professor F. N. Scott, of the University of Michigan:

> If a certain missal was much written and talked about in literary circles at this time, and if further it was a missal that had been used by Christians dwelling among the swart paynims (all of whom, as good Mohammedans, are pretty regular in their praying), there is a chance that this was the book that touched the poet's imagination and supplied the simile.
>
> As it happens, a copy of a missal which meets these conditions is now in the British Museum. It appears in the catalogue as *Missale mixtum secundum regulam beati Isidori dictum Mozarabes. . . . In regali civitate Toleti* 1500. The character of the missal, and its repute among book fanciers of Keats's time, are indicated by notes upon Lord Spencer's copy at Althorp, in T. F. Dibdin's *Bibliotheca Spenceriana.*

The account of the missal is in vol. i, pp. 135–144 of Dibdin's work; it is a printing of the "Gothic" ritual, as page 157 / emended by St. Isidore, in the seventh century; and the significant sentence in Dibdin is:

> The overthrow of the Goths, by the Moors and Arabs, succeeded in the four following centuries: but although many of the former preferred exile to the Moorish government, yet a great many of them, having a few churches granted them for the free exercise of their worship, continued to be mingled and domesticated with the conqueror; still using, but in a form probably somewhat corrupted, their Gothic ritual of worship.

28

This stanza was as it were written backwards. The idea with which it opens is ultimately deferred till the fourth line, and the idea which occurs to Keats' mind last is ultimately chosen to open with. Keats starts *in medias res* with

> Her slumbrous breathing

and deletes it; then

> The listning Porphyro her breathing heard
> And when

and deletes that, and remembering the hero of the *Romance of the Forest* who heard the breathing, and Vivaldi in *The Italian* who as he listened was entranced and felt himself in Paradise, he writes

> The entranced Porphyro stol'n to Paradise

and deletes that; but by this experimental method, and by allowing association to work, the material has been assembled and it can now be arranged.

> **Stoln to this Paradize and so entrance'd**
> **Porphyro gazed upon her empty dress**
> **And listen to her breathing, if it chanc'd**
> **To wake into a slumbrous tenderness**
> **Which when he heard ~~he breath'd himself~~**
> **that minute did he bless**
> **And breath'd himself: then from the closet crept**
> **Silent as Fear, and ? not with** **page 158 /**

But he decides to elaborate the simile of Fear, so that whatever he did not do disappears (the word is illegible from heavy deleting), and we have first

> Silent as Fear amid a wilderness

then he experiments with *Noiseless* for *Silent* and goes back to *Silent* again but leaves both standing; then deletes *amid* and writes *in a wild* and then alters *wild* to *wide*, so that the line stands

> Silent
> Noiseless as Fear in a wide wilderness
> And o'er the silent carpet hushing

changed to

A PAGE OF THE HOLOGRAPH OF

The Eve of St. Agnes

IN THE HARVARD UNIVERSITY LIBRARY

As though a tongueless nightingale should swell
Her ~~baseless~~ throat ~~in vain~~ in vain and die heart-
stifled in her dell.

~~A Casement ~~ach'd~~ tripple arch'd and ~~diamonded~~ diamonded~~
~~With many coloured glass fronted the Moon~~
~~In midst ~~of which~~ whereof a shielded scutcheon shed~~
~~High blushing gules; ~~upon~~ ~~she kneeld saintly~~ down~~
~~And inly prayed for grace and heavenly boon;~~
~~The blood red gules fell on her silver cross~~
~~And ~~her~~ white hands devout~~

There was
A Casement tripple arch'd and high
All garlanded with carven imageries
Of fruits ~~&~~ ~~trailing~~ flowers and sunny corn
ears parched

A Casement high and tripple arch'd there was
All garlanded with carven imageries
Of fruits and flowers and bunches of knot grass;
And diamonded with panes of quaint device
Innumerable of stains and splendid dies.
~~As is the tiger moth's ~~rich~~ deep ~~damasked~~~~ damasked wings
~~As is the wing of evening tiger moths;~~
~~And~~ And in ~~the~~ the midst 'mong ~~man~~ thousand heraldries
And ~~dim~~ ~~twilight~~ twilight saints and dim emblasonings

A shielded scutcheon blush'd with Blood of Queens & Kings—

Full on this Casement shone the ~~wintry moon~~
And threw ~~red~~ ~~warm~~ rich gules on Madeline's fair ~~face~~ breast
As down she knelt for heavens grace and boon
~~Rose~~ rose ~~with red~~ bloom fell on her hands together
~~Tinging her pious~~ hands ~~together~~ prest
And on her silver cross soft Amethyst.
And on her hair a glory like a Saint
She seem'd a ~~like an immortal agel drest~~
silvery angel newly drest,
Save wings for heaven — ~~Porphyro~~ Lionel grew faint
She knelt too pure a thing, too free from mortal taint—

~~But soon his heart revives — her prayers said~~
~~She lays aside her veil~~
~~Strips her hair of all its wreathed pearl~~
~~Unclasps her bosom jewels~~
~~And twists it in one knot upon her head~~

But soon his heart revives — her praying done,
Of all its wreathed pearl she strips her hair
Unclasps her warmed jewels one by one
Loosens ~~her~~ fragrant ~~boddice~~ ~~from~~ her
her ~~Boddice lace~~ string
~~her~~ ~~Boddice~~, ~~and her bosom bare~~
her

And over the hush'd carpet silent stept
And tween the Curtains peep'd, and lo! how fast she slept

The second draft reads *where lo!* for *and lo!*

29

Then by the bed side where the fading Moon
Made an illumed twilight soft he set
A Table light, and stilly threw theron
A Cloth of woven crimson gold and jet—

The third line is re-written as

A Table, and with anguish spread theron

and he continues:

O for some drowy morphean amulet
The boisterous midnight Clarions of the feast
~~Sounded though faint and far away~~
~~Came Sound in his ears~~
And kettle drums and far heard clarinet
Reach'd his scar'd ears.

But something now has to be done about the rhymes for the end of the stanza; so he goes back to the line about the Clarions, and first tries

Clarions of the Ball

and then

The boisterous midnight festive Clarions page 159 /

and then returns to the line that he was engaged with and writes it as

in
Affray'd his ears though but ~~with~~ faintest tones:
The Hall door shuts again and all the noise is gone

which means going back, making both the Clarions and the tones singular and then playing about with tenses, first making the last line past to suit *affray'd* and then making it present again and altering *affray'd* to suit it.

This stanza continued to exercise him more than most in his

final revision. The moon becomes *faded*, and the illumed twilight becomes *a dim silver twilight; with anguish* becomes *half anguished*, and *faintest* becomes *dying;* and there is an extremely interesting alteration of *midnight* as an epithet of Clarion to *braying*. I suggested that as early as the first stanza Keats had *Hamlet* in his mind; and here again surely he is at Elsinore, hearing

> The *Kettle-drum* and trumpet thus *bray* out
> The triumph of his pledge.

That this passage was running in his head will become clear beyond any reasonable doubt when we come to stanza 39, but this reading of *braying*, which only George Keats records, seems to me decisive, since, though trumpets no doubt bray in other places in Shakespeare, they do not elsewhere bray in connexion with both Kettledrums, and wassailers, and a bloated King, and Rhenish.

30

This stanza starts with deceptive facility, but when we get to the feast of fruits there is as vexatious a time as with either the window or the undressing.

> ~~But~~
> ~~And still she slept:~~
> And still she slept an azure-lidded sleep
> In blanched linen, smooth and lavender'd;
> While he from frorth the closet brough a heap
> Of candied ~~sweets~~ sweets with **page 160 /**

then the sweets become first *fruits* and then specified fruits. For some of them he goes to *Romeo and Juliet*,

> *Lady Cap.* Hold, take these keys and fetch more spices, Nurse.
> *Nurse.* They call for *dates* and *quinces* in the pastry

for some to *The Arabian Nights* passim, and for Samarcand and Fez pretty certainly to the great gazetteer in the eleventh book of *Paradise Lost* (it is worth noticing that he keeps Milton's spelling of Samar*ch*and), and for the creamed curd perhaps to *The Winter's Tale*, "The queen of curds and cream" though the collocation is common enough.

> Of candied apple Quince and plumb and gourd
> With jellies soother than the dairy curd
> And lucent syrups smooth with ?

dairy gets altered to *creamed* and *smooth* (if it is *smooth*) to *tinct*, but what the syrups were originally smooth with is a matter of conjecture. The word was clearly not at first *cinnamon*, even if there were any reason to suppose that cinnamon would make a syrup smooth. The word as it stands is *ciannamon* or, more probably, *crannamon* and one cannot help wondering whether Keats started with his cream here and then transferred it more appropriately to the curd in the line above.

But the complications increase when we get on to the more recondite confectionery. Keats starts

> And sugar'd dates ~~from~~ that o'er Euphrates fard

but after this there is such a welter of writing and re-writing and deletion in the draft that it is difficult to give any ordered notion of it. Keats is determined that he is going to have manna and dates; the dates are sometimes sugared and sometimes not; they are going to be (for rhyme) *transferred* from somewhere in something, but whether in Brigantine or Bragantine or Argosy is for long uncertain (the faring across Euphrates is given up almost as **page 161 /** soon as thought of). I fancy too that in the obscurity of the heaped fruit and the interlinear deletions there lurk some hitherto unsuspected peaches, though they had only a short life. There is no question that the provenance of the dates is to be Fez from the outset, and of the spiced dainties Samarchand; but there is a deal of hesitation as to what kind of Samarchand it is to be. First it was *wealthy*, and finally it was *silken*, but in the intermediate or cocoon stage heaven knows what it was. Buxton Forman thinks that the word is either *quilted* (with the surprising explanation that if silk is rich quilted silk is richer) or *guilded* (for *gilded*); I should read the word as *glutted*, which seems to me just possible for Keats, though not satisfactory. At any rate, after all the trouble, a feast of fruits is prepared to make the mouth water, and much more luscious than that repast about whose cooling there was no fear, which had been supposed, rightly or not, to be the model for it.

> And still she slept an azure-lidded sleep
> In blanched linen smooth and lavender'd;

While he from forth the closet brough a heap
  Of candied apple Quince and plumb and gourd
  And lucent syrups tinct with cinnamon
  Manna and daites in Argosy transferrd
  From fez — and spiced danties every one
From silken Samarchand to cedard lebanon

The second draft reads *brought from the cabinet* and *creamy*. And also, it will be remembered, adds the stanza which makes this one, which otherwise is no better than an ill-attached adornment, an integral part of the story.

31

These Delicates with glowing hand he

but *heap'd* is going to be troublesome, so delete *he* and insert *he heap'd* before *with*; that at least is what Keats intended; but being in a hurry he inserts the words first page 162 / between *glowing* and *hand*, sees that it is wrong, and deletes the caret, but even so is too impatient to go back far enough, and inserts the new caret after *with*.

he heap'd
These Delicates with ^ glowing hand
  On golden salvers and in baskets bright
Of ~~twisted~~ wreathed silver — sumptuous they stand
  Amid the quiet of St. Agnes' night,
  And now saith he my seraph

But this is getting on too fast and besides is not going to provide a rhyme for *night*, so delete and elaborate on the fruit and the cold:

Filling the chilly room with perfume light
~~Teeming~~
And now saith he my Seraph may awake,

which is weak, and at once emended to

And now my Love, my Seraph fair awake!
Thou art my heaven and I thine Eremite
Open thine eyes for meek St. Agnes' sake
Or I shall drowse beside thee, so my Soul doth ache.

32

We have had enough of Porphyro standing by his dessert; it is time he acted;

> ~~Thus~~ So whispering, his warm unnerved arms
> Sunk in her pillow. Shaded was her sleep
> By the dusk curtains; dreamless of alarms
> And

Then all this is deleted and a fresh start made:

> Thus whispering his warm unnerved arm
> Sunk in her pillow. Shaded ~~were~~ was her dreams
> By the dusk Curtains. 'Twas a midnight charm
> Impossible to melt as iced stream!
> The lustrous salvers ~~on~~ in the moonlight gleam
> Broad golden fringe lies wealthy on the f
> It seems he never neve can redeem
> From such a stedfast spell his Lady's eyes **page 163 /**

So back two lines and secure the rhyme, and make a change of tense in the next line:

> Broad golden fringe upon the carpet lies
> It seemd he never neve could redeem
> From such a stedfast spell his Lady's eyes
> And ~~stood~~ mus'd awhile entoild in woofed Phantasies.

In the second draft the salvers become dishes, and the reading of the printed text *in the retired quiet of the night* is given by *X* [an unknown emender] in pencil in Woodhouse's second transcript.

The reminiscences of *The Arabian Nights* in these last four stanzas are I think quite unmistakable. In the introduction to Scott's edition Keats would find syrups, creams, and confections; he would also find very exactly the broad gold fringe; "cotton mattresses . . . over these a covering of *broadcloth* trimmed with *gold* lace and *fringes hanging over to the ground*." And he would find not only the supposedly anachronistic carpet on which the fringe lies, but also perhaps the matting of an earlier stanza; "the terrace floor below the platform being first matted is covered with the finest carpets." In the tales themselves he would find apples, peaches, quinces, and gourds (though not plums), and spices. He would find, in a passage quoted earlier, the "baskets" of fruits, and the setting of the table in others, e.g. "the slave in a little time brought a collation of fruits upon a small silver table, which she set down." He would find innumerable carpets, and more fringes, here connected with the cloth for the table, "He had an eating cloth bordered with rich fringe, and whenever any person was present about mealtime he used to call out to his black servant, "Lay the fringed cloth!" He would also find here, as well as in Milton, Euphrates and Samarcand. **page 164 /**

33

Now, pursuing the ordinary sequence of *The Arabian Nights*, music is needed.

> Awakening up, he took her hollow Lute,
> Tumultuous, and in chords that tenderest be
> He play'd an ancient ditty long since mute
> In Provence call'd 'La belle dame sans mercy'
> Close to her ear he held the Melody;

altered first to *he touch'd the Melody* and then to *touching the Melody*:

> Wherewith disturb'd she uttered a soft moan
> He ceas'd — her breathing ceas'd — and suddenly
> Her blue half-frayed eyes wide open shone: —
> Upon his knees he sunk pale as smooth sculpturd stone.

Her breathing ceas'd is changed to *she panted quick;* and in the second draft *half-frayed* is changed to the straightforward *affrayed* and *smooth* to *fair.* There is an interesting small point in the last line. The line actually stands

> Upon his knees he sunk pale, ~~as~~ as smooth sculpturd stone

with the comma deleted. I think that there can be no doubt that Keats first wrote *he sunk pale, as* . . . where *as* was not the preposition but the beginning of another word, probably *ashen*, and then deleted both this and the comma and completed the line as we have it.

Of the probable sources of this stanza so far as it is concerned with Madeline's frightened awakening enough has already been said, and in one of the passages from Mrs. Radcliffe we have the sinking to the knees. But for the rest of the last line there is another passage in Mrs. Radcliffe, which seems to me much the most **page 165 /** significant of all as evidence of Keats' memories of her works:

> his countenance became fixed, and touched as it now was by the silver whiteness of the moonlight, he resembled one of those marble statues of a monument which seem to bend, in hopeless sorrow, over the ashes of the dead, shewn
>
> by the blunted light
> That the dim moon through painted casements lends
>
> *The Emigrants.*

34

The next stanza moves easily:

Her eyes were open but she still beheld
Now wide awake, the vision of her sleep:
There was ~~some~~ a painful change, — that nigh expell'd
The Blisses of her dream so pure and deep:
At which ~~she~~ ? [a deleted word, probably a jumble of a repeated *she* and *sighd*]
fair Madeline began to weep
And moan forth little words with many a sigh
While still her gaze on Porphro would keep
Who with an aching brow and piteous eye
Feared to move or speak she look'd so dreamingly —

In the second draft *witless*, which was written in the margin of the first draft, is substituted for *little*, and the last two lines read

Who knelt with joined hands and piteous eye
Fearing to move. . . .

35

~~At length~~ she speaks, "Ah Porpyro but
'~~Ah Porphyro, saith she but~~ even now
Thy voice was at sweet tremble ~~by~~ in mine ear
Made tuneable by every sweetest vow
And thy kind eyes were spiritual and clear
How chang'd at thou how pallid, chill and drear **page 166 /**
Give me that voice again my Porphiro!
Those looks immortal ~~and that~~
—— those complainings dear
O leave me not in this eternal woe
Ah! if thou diest my love I know not where to go!

Here I think he had in mind for the fourth line a line and a half which he had underlined in his Shakespeare

> your tongue's sweet air
> More tuneable than lark to shepherd's ear

but this is altered in the second draft to

> And tun'd devout with every softest vow.

And from this as well as one or two other instances one may guess that Keats was more keenly aware of his direct borrowings from Shakespeare than of those from others and took deliberate steps to modify them. The second draft opens the stanza with *Ah Porphyro said she*, makes Porphyro *cold* instead of *chill*, and his eyes *sad* instead of *kind*. In Woodhouse's first transcript a gap is left after *again* in the sixth line, and *X* has filled the gap with the remarkable reading *sweet Prospero*, and Buxton Forman notes, with even less explicability, that the insertion was probably made by Keats himself. On the opposite page *X* "indulges the Muse" (one feels that that would have been his own phrase) on his own account, with

> Give me again that voice's warbling flow

but this effort mercifully got no further than a pencilled note.

36

And now after the breathing-space of one or two stanzas which have more or less written themselves Keats comes to the climax of the action, which he knows must be handled with a rare combination of perfect delicacy and perfect firmness. And it is not going to be too easy. For the opening of the stanza he has recollections of Hippolitus who was tenderly *impassioned* by his lady's voice; and page 167 / Fleury who seemed "passer en joye les regions des dieux"; and perhaps a passage in which "in the *deep serene* of the heavens . . . the *stars* now seemed to *tremble*, and now to emerge with purer splendour." But for the conclusion of the stanza he has to rely on his own imagination and his own taste.

> Impassion'd far beyond a mortal man
> At these voluptuous ~~words~~ accents he arose
> Ethereal, ~~fulshd~~ flush'd and

At this point, *ethereal* having suggested a star, he goes back and transposes the two halves of line 1, and goes on

like a throbbing star
~~Was either~~
(a most mysterious opening, but I cannot make anything else of the second word)
Seen 'mid the sapphire heaven's deep repose
With her bright dream he m

Followed by

In her bright dream he m

and then

Into her dream he melted as the rose
Blendeth her ~~p~~ its perfume with the violet.

and then *perfume* deleted and *odour* substituted.

~~A ? as one~~
Solution sweet.

and this too deleted and nothing put in to fill the gap, and the line completed

Meantime the frost wind blows
~~Darkness~~
Like ? alarum pattering the sharp ?
Against the Casement gloom — St. Agnes moon had set.

Then he tries *Window's gloom* and then tries making first the casement and then *windows* dark, so that the line finally stands

Against the windows dark — St. Agnes moon had set. page 168 /

The second word in the eighth line was certainly not *Love's* at first and it would be interesting to find what it was. It appears to have begun *Lot*, but then *Love's* was so heavily written over it that conjecture is precarious. And the word at the end of the line is not in the least degree like *sleet*, though I see nothing else that it can have been meant to be.

Almost miraculously successful as this may seem to us, in giving the picture which Keats wanted to give, and yet not breaking the tone of the poem, it did not satisfy him, and in the second draft he changes the last two lines of the preceding stanza and recasts most of this, as follows:

> (Give me that voice again my Porphyro
> Those looks immortal those complainings dear)
> See while she speaks his arms encroaching slow
> Have zon'd her, heart to heart — loud, loud the dark winds blow.
>
> For on the midnight came a tempest fell.
> More sooth for that his close rejoinder flows
> Into her burning ear: — and still the spell
> Unbroken guards her in serene repose.
> With her wild dream he mingled as a rose
> Marryeth its odour to a violet.
> Still, still she dreams. — louder the frost wind blows,

(Woodhouse II reads *quick* for *close.*)

This alteration Keats showed to Woodhouse, as well as probably some more drastic ones of which we have no record; and the board of censors got to work. Some of the correspondence is worth giving, showing as it does the kind of temper in which Keats was working at the time of the revisions.

Woodhouse writes to Taylor on the 20th of September 1819, and says that a week earlier Keats had come to see him in town.

> He wanted I believe to publish The Eve of St. Agnes & Lamia *immediately:* but Hessey told him it could not answer to do so page 169 / now. I wondered why he said nothing of Isabella: & assured him it would please more than the Eve of St. Agnes — He said he could not bear the former now. It appeared to him mawkish. This certainly cannot be so. The feeling is very likely to come across an author on review of a former work of his own, particularly where the objects of his present meditations are of a more sobered & unpassionate character. The feeling of mawkishness seems to me to be that which comes upon us where anything of great tenderness & excessive simplicity is met with when we are not in a sufficiently tender & simple frame of mind to bear it: when we experience a sort of revulsion, or resiliency (if there be such a word) from the sentiment or expression. Now I believe there is nothing in the most passionate parts of Isabella to excite this feeling. It may, as may Lear, leave the sentiment far behind: but there is none of that sugar & butter sentiment, that cloys & disgusts.

To us there is an odd irony in Woodhouse's innocent supposition that Keats' dissatisfaction with *Isabella* was in part due to the objects of his present meditations being of a more sobered and unpassionate character. When Keats wrote *Isabella* he did not know what passionate love was; when he came to revise *The Eve of St. Agnes* he knew all too bitterly well. No wonder that he felt as he did about *Isabella.* And how cynically amused he would have been at the mention in one breath of *Isabella* and *Lear.*

Woodhouse continues:

> He had the Eve of St. A. copied fair. He has made trifling alterations, inserted an additional stanza early in the poem to make the *legend* more intelligible, and correspondent with what afterwards takes place, particularly with respect to the supper and the playing on the Lute — he retains the name of Porphyro — has altered the last 3 lines to leave on the reader a sense of pettish disgust by bringing old Angela in (only) dead stiff & ugly. He says he likes that the poem should leave off with this change of sentiment — it was what he aimed at, & was glad to find from my objections to it that he had succeeded. — I apprehend he had a fancy for trying his hand at an attempt to play with his reader, and fling him off at last — I sho'd have thought he affected the "Don Juan" style of mingling up sentiment and sneering: but that he had before asked Hessey if he page 170 / co'd procure him a sight of that work, as he had not met with it, and if the E. of St. A. had not in all probability been altered before his Lordship had thus flown in the face of the public. There was another alteration, which I abused for "a full hour by the *Temple* clock." You know if a thing has a decent side I generally look no further — As the Poem was orig'y written, *we* innocent ones (ladies & myself) might very well have supposed that Porphyro, when acquainted with Madeline's love for him, & when "he arose, Etherial flush'd &c. &c. (turn to it) set himself at once to persuade her to go off with him, & succeeded & went over the "Dartmoor black" (now changed for some other place) to be married in right honest chaste & sober wise. But, as it is now altered, as soon as M. has confessed her love, P. winds by degrees his arm round her, presses breast to breast, & acts all the acts of a bonafide husband, while she fancies she is only playing the part of a Wife in a dream. This alteration is of about 3 stanzas; and tho' there are no improper expressions but all is left to inference, and tho' profanely speaking, the Interest on the reader's imagination is greatly heightened, yet I do apprehend it will render the poem unfit for ladies, & indeed scarcely to be mentioned to them among the "things that are." He says he does not want ladies to read his poetry: that he writes for men — & that if in the former poem there was an opening for a doubt what took place, it was

> his fault for not writing clearly & comprehensibly — that he sho'd despise a man who would be such an eunuch in sentiment as to leave a maid, with that character about her, in such a situation: & sho'd despise himself to write about it &c. &c. &c. — and all this sort of Keats-like rhodomontade.

Now Woodhouse's account of the alterations where it refers to what we have in front of us is precisely correspondent with it, both in the comment on the last three lines, and the alteration of Dartmoor, and the insertion of an additional stanza (which it will be noticed he differentiates from "alterations"), and in the "winds by degrees his arm round her, presses breast to breast." And this makes us the more surprised when we read, "This alteration is of page 171 / about three stanzas." The "alterations" as we have them cover no more than the last two lines of one stanza and the first half of the next, and the second stanza as altered, moving as it does even farther in the direction of "inference" and away from plain statement than the original, would surely have caused Woodhouse less rather than more distress. The conclusion is then that either Woodhouse meant three lines when he wrote three stanzas, and was quarrelling with the last two lines of stanza 35 as altered, both of which seem improbable, or that there were at least two completely new (not altered) stanzas of which we have no trace. But this supposition when we come to look at it is not much more satisfactory, since to write two stanzas which shall describe the hero "acting all the acts of a bonafide husband," and yet write them so that there "are no improper [in Woodhouse's sense] expressions but all is left to inference" seems to be a task whose difficulty amounts to impossibility. It looks at first sight as though the connexion between the corrected stanzas as we have them told against the supposition that there were at one stage two completely new stanzas inserted at that point; but further consideration at least leaves room for doubt. It is true that the mention of the loud winds at the end of stanza 35 is immediately followed by the explanatory "For on the midnight rose a tempest fell" at the beginning of 36. But there is an extremely abrupt transition from the slowly encroaching arms to the loud winds, there seems no very good reason why the tempest should make his *close rejoinder* more sooth, as *for that* implies, and the close rejoinder itself is more puzzling still, since none has yet been made, and before one is made, in the next stanza, there is a further reference to the winds. So that the transition which seemed at first so natural appears at least possibly to have been the result of a neat short-circuit operation, with the excision of the offending portion. In view of the fact that Woodhouse's account of the alterations corresponds so exactly to the alterations that we have down to the description of the encroaching arms, but then **page 172 /** contains a phrase which corresponds if anything more accurately to the unoffending first draft than to the second as we have it, one would have little doubt that Keats in his anti-mawkish, anti-Isabella mood, being determined that this poem at least was not going to be "weak-sided" and that a touch of realism would stiffen it, a touch let us say more in the vein of Boccaccio than he had permitted himself in the first draft, wrote two explicit stanzas that would put his meaning beyond doubt, and that he then in deference to Woodhouse destroyed them and patched things up as best he could, flinging, I cannot help feeling, a half-contemptuous sop to the rather mild Cerberus, who was insisting on the position being regularized without delay, in the shape of the odd alteration of the *blendeth* of the first draft to the *marryeth* of the second. Woodhouse could at least have the word if he could not have the fact. But Woodhouse's description of the stanzas as leaving all to inference still presents a difficulty which I suggested earlier; and in the upshot one must leave the matter open to conjecture. **page 173 /**

. . . .

CHAPTER TWO

More Explanations by Manuscript Versions

STEPHEN SPENDER

The Express

The Funeral

Seascape

The Express

STEPHEN SPENDER

After the first powerful, plain manifesto
The black statement of pistons, without more fuss
But gliding like a queen, she leaves the station.
Without bowing and with restrained unconcern
She passes the houses which humbly crowd outside,
The gasworks, and at last the heavy page
Of death, printed by gravestones in the cemetery.
Beyond the town, there lies the open country
Where, gathering speed, she acquires mystery,
The luminous self-possession of ships on ocean.
It is now she begins to sing — at first quite low
Then loud, and at last with a jazzy madness —
The song of her whistle screaming at curves,
Of deafening tunnels, brakes, innumerable bolts.
And always light, aerial, underneath,
Retreats the elate metre of her wheels.
Steaming through metal landscape on her lines,
She plunges new eras of white happiness,
Where speed throws up strange shapes, broad curves
And parallels clean like trajectories from guns.
At last, further than Edinburgh or Rome,
Beyond the crest of the world, she reaches night
Where only a low stream-line brightness
Of phosphorus on the tossing hills is light.
Ah, like a comet through flame, she moves entranced,
Wrapt in her music no bird song, no, nor bough
Breaking with honey buds, shall ever equal.

The Funeral

STEPHEN SPENDER

Death is another milestone on their way.
With laughter on their lips and with winds blowing round them
They record simply
How this one excelled all others in making driving belts.

This is festivity, it is the time of statistics.
When they record what one unit contributed:
They are glad as they lay him back in the earth
And thank him for what he gave them.

They walk home remembering the straining red flags,
And with pennons of song still fluttering through their blood
They speak of the World State
With its towns like brain centres and its pulsing arteries.

They think how one life hums, revolves and toils,
One cog in a golden singing hive:
Like spark from fire, its task happily achieved,
It falls away quietly.

No more are they haunted by the individual grief
Nor the crocodile tears of European genius,
The decline of a culture
Mourned by scholars who dream of the ghosts of Greek boys.

The Meaning of the Discarded Poem

KARL SHAPIRO

Any reaction to stimulus may be causally explained; but the creative act, which is the absolute antithesis of mere reaction, will for ever elude the human understanding.[1]

To C. G. Jung we are indebted for what must be one of the most discouraging statements concerning the creative activity ever written. I use it as the epigraph to this paper as a suggested motto for the student of manuscripts. If we must enter this ground, let us first abandon hope of making a discovery. Nevertheless, I do not feel that the mystery can be shut up so concisely and finally as the psychologist asserts; and, at any rate, as long as there is poetry there will be curiosity about its genesis. Consider how much more is known today about the behavior of the mind than was known a century ago. Dreams, at least by the initiated, are no longer considered nonsense; may not poems yet be found to express some undiscovered language of the spirit? The current unpopularity of the Freudian contribution to this end is perhaps a symptom of resistance to such a true discovery. We are told by the objectors that if art is a symptom of mental sickness then both its validity as art and its morality must suffer in the eyes of a healthy world. It is also suggested that Freud was a victim of a

[1] C. G. Jung, *Modern Man in Search of a Soul*, Harcourt, Brace, p. 177.

nineteenth-century delusion that the creative function implies a disability in the creator. Let us look at this argument briefly.

The disability theory, or what I would call the clubfoot theory of art, has by no means been disestablished. Of course, it would be priggish and absurd for the poet to coddle a monster of the mind or to live up to a deformity of the body, although it is common knowledge that these defects are often the mark of the artist. To say they do not exist is to conceal perfectly good evidence. Some effort must still be made to solve the question of sickness and creativity.

We must first understand that by "sick" we really mean page 85 / only "different" or what the clinician would call abnormal. What is abnormal is thought to be beyond the needs of nature, or in excess of nature. The sick man finds it necessary to concentrate on some activity in his body or his mind that obliterates all other activities. But "sick" also implies an injury to some part of the body or mind. A child who is in pain because it is cutting a tooth is not said to be sick, as is an adult with an abscessed tooth, the difference being that in one case the pain will be beneficial and in the other malignant. Few people contend that poetry is anything but beneficent, but many believe that the "symptoms" of creation are abnormal, diseased and dangerous. I am not as interested in the outcome of this question as I am in another: Whether the artist is more different ("sicker") than, say, a philosopher, a scientist or a man of business. I believe he is, for this reason. It is the nature of the creative mind to familiarize itself with depths of memory, desire, a sensation and all the remote quadrants of its being that the speculative or the commercial mind has no need of, and indeed shuns for its own safety. It is certainly true that a great deal — perhaps most — poetry also shuns these subterranean places, and that at a certain level of creativity a poet can compose without seriously ruffling the composure of his spirit. But it is the activity below this level that is most apt to tell us something about itself.

Let us agree, then, that the poet is different from the nonpoet in that he makes greater demands on his own Unknown than anyone else, and that he brings to light certain riches which are accorded a universal value. "Rimbaud stole his diamonds, but where?" asks Cocteau. "That is the puzzle."

Anyone who attempts literary criticism must sooner or later come to the point at which he is forced to use terms that designate levels of inspiration, sources of material, kinds of inventiveness, and so on. In general, no effort is made to define these terms, but the reader knows, by the context and from page 86 / his own experience, what is implied. We are accustomed to find such language as the following in the most scrupulous criticism. "It is only when the ideas become more automatic, come more freely and are less manipulated, that we begin to suspect their origin, to suspect that they spring from a shallower source."[2] The words *ideas, manipulated, origin, shallower source* certainly indicate a theory of composition which we do not know, and do not need to know. This is because it is "our" theory, or what everyone interested in writing thinks is the way writing happens.

The critic's recognition of various levels of creativity points to the existence of a scale or ladder of poetic methods. Just as the expression "a shallower source" indicates other, deeper sources, so are we ultimately led to believe that there is a "top" and a "bottom" to the poetic psyche; and that, if one had insight enough, he could define the functions of the poem-making activity at any level of the scale. It is always interesting to see how these levels are labeled and what functions the investigator attributes to them. Nietzsche, for instance, spoke of the Apollonian, or static principle of art, in distinction to the Dionysian, or dynamic principle, and made the latter stand for the nobler and more life-producing strain.[3] Shelley speaks of the principle of analysis and the principle of synthesis, the first referring to the reason and the second to the imagination. Poetry is a thing of the imagination, although, even at its most glorious, a poem is probably only a pale reflection of the original conception of the poet.[4] Herbert Read uses the terms *organic* and *abstract* to denote a similar correspondence between the truly inventive act and that which represents a fixation of a particular form.[5] Jung discovers a page 87 / dichotomy in the process of artistic creation which he calls the psychological and the visionary modes. The former deals with always intelligible, always familiar material: the resultant art does not disturb the charted currents of the society that sees its birth. Such works, indeed, do not transcend the conscious life of man at all, and it is works of this category that account for the bulk

[2] T. S. Eliot, *Selected Essays,* Harcourt, Brace, p. 277.
[3] F. W. Nietzsche, *The Birth of Tragedy.*
[4] P. B. Shelley, *Defence of Poetry.*
[5] Herbert Read, *Form in Modern Poetry,* Sheed and Ward.

of all literature, music and art. The visionary modes of creation reverses these conditions of composition completely. It is a "primordial experience" from which it derives its power, an experience "foreign and cold, many-sided, demonic and grotesque." The whole process involves a mystic participation in the collective unconscious[6] — and it is there that Jung lets the matter rest.

I would like to mention one more instance of this dualism that crops up when the critic speaks of the origins of poetry, this one the most interesting because, despite its great age, it is the fullest expression of the idea of the double principle of creativity I know of. Speaking of the poet who has no touch of the Muse's madness in his soul, Socrates says, "The sane man disappears and is nowhere when he enters into rivalry with the madman." Madness here is meant as insanity, not as a figurative expression for the creative excitement. What is important in this passage from the *Phaedrus* is that the philosopher makes a distinction between prophecy and madness, including both as aspects of the poetic activity. For the time being, we can use these designations of Plato as the most inclusive we have. *Mantic* or prophetic poetry can stand for the cool, scientific method of creation which relies on fixed rules, signs and traditions to produce its art: *Manic* or insane poetry would be that uttered under supernatural suggestion, like the oracles of the Pythoness. One might extend these definitions to include mystical poetry as the highest form of the manic art — that which makes a direct contract with a deity. We would page 88 / then have a closed circle, the complete circuit, as it were, of the entire poetic process. Socrates takes pains to point out that the "ancients" had only the one word to define both prophecy and madness.

These definitions, of course, would not tell us what happens to the poem after the initial inspiration is given, and, as we shall see in a moment, the poetic material given under supernatural or sub-natural suggestion can scarcely be termed poetry until it has been worked upon by the poet.

I think it would be of value to purely scientific inquiry if poets would now and then try to describe what they felt about the levels of inspiration and the terrain of the poetic psyche. A remarkable letter written by Schiller to a friend who complained of his lack of creative power is quoted by Freud as an example of

[6] C. G. Jung, *op. cit.*

insight into "freely rising" ideas. It is encouraging to come upon an observation as keen as this:

> The reason for your complaint lies, it seems to me, in the constraint which your intellect imposes upon your imagination. . . . Apparently it is not good — and indeed it hinders the creative work of the mind — if the intellect examines too closely the ideas already pouring in, as it were, at the gates. Regarded in isolation, an idea may be quite insignificant, and venturesome in the extreme, but it may acquire importance from an idea which follows it; perhaps, in a certain collocation with other ideas, which may seem equally absurd, it may be capable of furnishing a very serviceable link. The intellect cannot judge all these ideas unless it can retain them until it has considered them in connection with these other ideas. In the case of a creative mind . . . the intellect has withdrawn its watchers from the gates, and the ideas rush in pell-mell, and only then does it review and inspect the multitude. You worthy critics . . . are ashamed or afraid of the momentary and passing madness which is found in all real creators. . . .[7] page 89 /

Once again the dualism of the intellect and the imagination is posed, with the characteristic emphasis on madness as the helpmate of poetry.

I would like to give my own impression of the poetic psyche and try to apply this picture to a study of the manuscripts of certain contemporary poets. My impression is based in part on those of the foregoing critics and on my own experience.

The poetic psyche I compare with a tree. To the roots belong the demonic principle, or that which cannot see, but works belowstairs, searching out and down in all directions for anchorage and food. It is probably the first part of the psyche to appear. The trunk and limbs I would identify with the metaphysical principle; this stands in and out of the earth at the same time and is simultaneously interested in being and knowing. The leaves, by far the most populous equipment of the tree, I would identify with the literary principle: only the leaves are millionfold; they flourish, manufacture food and die, some to enrich the earth, most to become dust. Last, the mystical principle, which I would place in the flower, fruit and seed of the tree.

This description, despite its obvious faults, also suggests the

[7] S. Freud, "The Method of Dream Interpretation," *Basic Writings of Freud*, Modern Library.

biological cycle. When the tree has done its work, our attention is turned to the ground: poetry reproduces itself on the broadest scale by flowering, bearing, and then running to seed. In periods of revolt we are always back to first principles. Now it should not be concluded because of location alone that the demonic principle is inferior to the mystical principle or that one extreme stands for evil and the other for good. The most we can say about the two extremes of the poetic psyche is that in the demonic principle the poetic material arrives, whereas in the mystical principle it is arrived at. The one begins in frenzy, the other achieves frenzy. And about the relative greatness of these four principles, I think it would be page 90 / unsafe to say anything more than that the greatest poets use several or all four of the principles, in turn or together. Jung, in keeping with his definition of the visionary art, cites three works as among the highest examples, *The Divine Comedy*, the second part of Goethe's *Faust*, and *The Shepherd of Hermas.*[8]* The first two I would place among the foremost poems, that is, those that duplicate the life-cycle of the tree, but the third, which is a work of literature only by assumption, I would not include at all. Plato's differentiation of prophetic from poetic madness is useful here. I cannot believe that apocalyptic literature is poetry, if poetry is to have any meaning of its own. This is not a quibble; *The Shepherd of Hermas* is part of the primitive Christian literature almost included in the final *New Testament.* As such, it is free of the strictures of literary aims.

The question now rises, when do we know who is a true demonic or mystical poet and who is not. What is the difference, say, between the mysticism of Gerard Manley Hopkins and that of Augustus Montague Toplady? Or what is the difference between the demonism of Arthur Rimbaud and that of André Breton? Is vision enough or must we have the fruit of the vision in terms of poetry? Is madness enough or must we have the poem that emerges from the frenzy? Merely to write about heaven or hell is insufficient, if the writing lacks the intuitive genius of form. And merely to be mad or prophetic is not enough, unless the madness or the mysticism be of the prophetic variety. There is no good surrealist poetry because surrealism merely imitates the conditions of madness; because it violates the genius of form by trying to make form insane! Compare such a technique with

[8] C. G. Jung, *op. cit.* *Jung, however, is speaking of vision and not of poetry.

that of a true demonic poet, Rimbaud or Poe, who is almost classical in his craftsmanship. Notice also that the majority page 91 / of English hymns are inferior and even abominable poems. The same is true of national anthems, political verse, and other hortatory branches of the art. We need not look to the asylum or the monastery for poetry.

Literary poetry, the bulk of all poetry that lies between the blossoms and the roots, escapes analysis for hidden elements; by and large, it is simply human poetry, full of the foibles and tricks of wit that belong to wide-awake life. But frequently we come upon the poet who gravitates toward mysticism or toward the depths, but who nevertheless does not quite rise from the literary foliage. I think two such poets are Yeats and Rilke; both seem to possess everything except the conviction of their own visions, and almost deliberately they give us the impression of make-believe. Hart Crane, one of the poets whose manuscripts I want to discuss, suffered the opposite fate. Crane was that rare thing, a true demonic poet, who, when his demon deserted him, failed into wretched literary pretense.

It seems, then, that the final test of validity, the final means of discovering the level of inspiration of a particular poet, lies nowhere but in the form. And if that is so, we are back where we started from — as Jung threatened. There is nothing to do but try to break through the poem from another side. We have seen that conviction (vision or madness) does not count for much when it comes to producing a good poem, for if that were so, the greatest sufferers and the greatest visionaries would be the greatest poets. We have seen also that the will to be a poet doesn't count for much either. For to vision or madness or the poetic desire must be added the indispensable element of the knowledge of form. *Genius in poetry is probably only the intuitive knowledge of form.* The dictionary contains all words and a textbook on verse contains all meters, but nothing can tell the poet which words to choose and in what rhythms to let them fall except his own intuitive knowl- page 92 / edge of form. It is thus that form, or style, to use the more common term, becomes the instrument of interpretation and the measure of the poet's gift. Form, indeed, most override any other consideration in the criterion of the true poem. The form is the intelligence of the poem, and upon the form hangs the very life of the poem. One might add, parenthetically, that a great quantity of literary criticism today overlooks this tenet, with the result that inferior works are judged side by side with the best on the grounds that both have "just as much to say." This practice, I think, will eventually invalidate a whole corpus of our criticism.

Can the study of form under construction give evidence of the level of inspiration on which the poet stands at the time he composes a particular work? Or is the final evidence the finished work, in which so many of our clues are buried? I think we are now constrained to use the former method if we are to storm the gates at all, for even experts admit defeat in the other field. What we must do is to tear the poem down, unless we are fortunate enough to have rescued the records of its creation. From working-drafts, marginalia, personalia, and the like, we can proceed to the external form (psychology of imagery), to the materials of form (language and metric), to the sources of form (personality, tradition and the Unknown). We will then be as close to the place of the creative act as we can hope to get. In the case of the literary poem we can probably learn no more than the particular psychology of imagery but we do not expect this kind of poem to conceal anything from our view. The literary poem is written off the top of one's head, as the humorous saying goes. But the poem of any of the other levels might well reveal that concealable material which will lead to the portals of discovery.

Before examining the manuscripts I would like to make one further observation about the peculiarities of this kind of research. In many cases the most difficult preliminary stages of **page 93 /** composition seem to have been accomplished mentally, that is, without the poet's knowledge of how many trials and errors he has overcome before his pen has touched paper. The habitual poet perhaps has learned a technique of discard of which he is no longer aware. Therefore much valuable materials will always be missing from the record. During the process of the poem we often come upon a "semi-final" version of a verse or stanza which is so inferior to the final version that any question of establishing the relationship seems impossible. These are probably moments of the greatest importance to the poet and to us.

Study of *The Express*, by Stephen Spender

The author at the time of composition is a young man with certain identifiable ideas about progress, justice, and social change.

He is, however, a poet and an optimist who is making a search in himself for a new iconography which will implement his poetry as well as the beliefs he has adopted. Alternately he is tossed up to heights of happiness by his optimism and his poetic genius, and thrown down into despondency by his "social" despair and his inability to assist in the rebirth. Like Whitman, another poet with a sweeping political philosophy, he fuses the love of comrades with a personal eros, and saturates his verses with symbols of masculinity. One interpretation of *The Express* must suggest the masculine image of sexuality as one interpretation of *The Landscape Near an Aerodrome* must suggest the opposite, the destroyed image of feminine creativity, with its ikons of grief-stricken woman, and the church. The more conscious stimulus which would evoke the theme of the poem about the train is the barely latent idea of progress and change, with its corollary idea of escape ("further than Edinburgh or Rome"). The page 94 / overt theme, of course, is praise of the beauty of this machine and the ecstasy of its motion.

There are in the Lockwood Library's Spender notebook six sequential, incremented versions, which may be called drafts *A*, *B*, *C*, *D*, *E*, and *F*. The initial draft is almost the completed poem in itself, except for the four final moving verses which lift the express from the rails and plunge it into a garden of nightsky, birdsong and boughs. But there is a good deal of interference before this transitional miracle can be effected. The opening lines of this draft contain minor textual changes and two possibly significant ones. (By a minor change I mean one that moves only a negligible distance toward a different level. Thus "the clear statement of pistons" in becoming "the black statement of pistons" merely clarifies the metaphor of "plain manifesto." A plain manifesto makes a clear statement, but a plain manifesto, to put it in headlines, makes a black statement. It is extraordinary that in Spender's crowded imagery there is never any sense of confusion, even, as I shall try to show, when he switches abruptly from the physical to the mystical image.)

Here is the opening of the first draft:

> After the first powerful plain manifesto,
>   black
> The ~~clear~~ statement of pistons, without more fuss
> But gliding like a queen she leaves the station:

The first significant change is not actually a change at all, but an obliterated word (completely indecipherable) between "queen" and "she." I take it that the poet here is disturbed by the word "queen," which used in this particular meliorative connection puts up a warning signal in his mind. "Queen" is not very good socialism, and it must be remembered that Spender is forging an appropriate language as he writes. But more than this, the word probably raises the strange question page 95 / of the sex of trains. The vehicle in the poem, with its blackness, iron, bolts, pistons and power, argues for the male interpretation. The wheels, flight, song, "luminous self-possession," mystery, and of course the analogy of ships at sea, argue for the feminine interpretation. Also a decision becomes important because of the eleven subsequent *she*'s and *her*'s which would have to become *he*'s and *his*'s. The original impulse to make the symbol feminine Spender finds correct, and the poem acquires a pleasing dualism at the outset.

The second significant change occurs in the imagery of the cemetery, through which the express passes. Draft *A* stands:

> Without bowing and with restrained unconcern
> She notices the houses humbly crowding outside
> And then the gasworks and at last the printed psalm
> Of death written by gravestones in the cemetery.

Draft *B* makes the final alterations:

> Without bowing and with restrained unconcern
> She passes the houses which humbly crowd outside,
> The gasworks, and at last the heavy page
> Of death printed by gravestones in the cemetery.

"Psalm" is the undesirable word here. Spender's whole conception of death at this period is given very full treatment in *The Funeral*, which we will examine in a moment. In keeping with the imagery of the manifesto, printing and change, the psalm is altered to "the heavy page of death," that is to say, a mere statement of death, without religious overtones. This consistency of aim contributes to the enormous force in the poem.

A third change is of possible interest. The express is now in open country and

> It is now she begins to sing — at first quite low
> And then loud and at last with a jazzy madness —

page 96 /

"With a jazzy madness" stood originally as "with mad joy," a phrase almost devoid of tone. The substitution of "jazzy" with its good-bad (modern-decadent) associations is a piece of extreme cleverness, and in a sense would be the turning-point of the poem, or a lead to the departure of the train into the soft ecstasy of the closing lines: but it is still too early for that. There is this one seductive suggestion of the slattern and then a quick tightening "of tunnels, of brakes, of innumerable bolts." It is not yet time to leave the train.

Another brilliant minor change occurs in the development of the verses:

> And always light, aerial, under~~neath~~ this
> Is the tapping metre of her wheels. (Draft *A*)

Draft *C* reads:

> And always light, aerial, underneath
>   racing
> Is (Goes) the ~~tapping~~ metre of her wheels.

which emerges in Draft *D* in the final form:

> And always light, aerial, underneath
>   elate
> Goes the ~~racing~~ metre of her wheels.

Here again the perfect solution has been found to describe sensorially and emotionally the condition of the train at top speed. By repeating the word "elate" by itself very rapidly one even awakens in the car the characteristic music of the train.

The poem, according to Draft C, is now at the half-way mark. The express has been put into full speed, and the poet's problem is what to do with it. There are two possible directions the express can take: one toward the poet, down, as it were, toward the depths of his psyche; and up, away from the poet and people, into the night of comet, flame and the page 97 / bodiless world of the spirit. Some such struggle is evident in the following Drafts *C* and *D*, which should be shown in full.

Draft *C*:

> After the first powerful plain manifesto
> The black statement of pistons, without more fuss

But gliding like a queen, she leaves the station.
Without bowing and with restrained unconcern
She passes the houses which humbly crowd outside,
The gasworks, and at last the heavy page
Of death printed by gravestones in the cemetery.
Beyond the town there lies the open country
Where, gathering speed, she acquires mystery,
at
The luminous self-possession of ships ~~on~~ ocean.
It is now she begins to sing — at first quite low,
~~And~~ Then loud, and at last with a jazzy madness —
The song of her whistle screaming at corners,
Of ~~blindi~~ deafening tunnels, brakes, innumerable bolts;
And always light, aerial, underneath
racing
~~Is~~ (Goes) the ~~tapping~~ metre of her wheels.
Her passengers (further than Edinburgh or Rome)
Explore new eras ~~of wild~~ happiness
At night when dark flags ~~touch the glass~~ knock the glass
~~And~~ only the low stream-line brightness
Of moonlight on the tossing hills is white.
Rapt ~~in~~ what
~~Entranced by a~~ symphony (ies) they dream
tapping
Of ~~gleaming~~ metals: ~~and~~ sharp strange shapes entrance
lines
Them in their rigid ~~folds;~~ Not bird song, no nor bough
Breaking with honey~~ed~~ buds, nor dreams of India
hunting jeweled
And ~~tracing~~ through thick leaves the ~~rare jewelled~~ tiger,
So rules with stamped and iron image ~~Can build~~
The strange world where they turn, as this
Of jetting steam and rods . . . She stops

page 98 /

In Draft *D* the first ten lines remain unaltered. Then:

It is now she begins to sing — at first quite low
Then loud and at last with a jazzy madness —
The song of her whistle screaming at corners,
Of deafening tunnels, brakes, innumerable bolts:
And always light, aerial, underneath
elate
Goes the ~~racing~~ metre of her wheels.

Her passengers, (further than Edinburgh or Rome),
Explore new eras of wild happiness
At night when dark flags knock the glass
And only the low stream-line brightness
Of moonlight on the tossing hills is white
~~Oh,~~ They are wrapt in music no bird song nor bough
Breaking with honey buds, nor tale from India
~~Of~~ hunting through dripping boughs the precious tiger,
Can build iron
~~Creates~~ ~~They are~~ ruled round with lines
builds
~~And stamped with imagery which makes new worlds~~
~~This strange new world~~
And strange new forms of rods and jets of steam
Stamp on their brains an image of new worlds
~~Their brains are stamped pressed on by with forms poured on~~
~~by steam~~
They watch
The images of power stamp their brain
~~And of works whose fires~~
~~And of metals moulten to create new works worlds~~
And hear
Ruled round with iron lines
They watch the images of power that stamp their brain
Impressed by thunder of waters & tearing steam
And roar of furnace(s) that mould machines.

It is probably the idea of travelers and passengers that awakens the complexity of dark associations in the poet's mind, and as we shall see, it is only by eliminating people altogether page 99 / that unity is maintained in the poem, and the express freed to establish itself in the cosmos. Meanwhile the poem is beset with active and malignantly beautiful objects, dark gusts, flags of wind that knock the glass, dreams of India, and a jeweled tiger. Rapt in symphonies, the mind begins to dream, then awakens, for the dreams become tales. The question is how this irrelevant material got as far as these two versions of the poem, and what this material signifies. I will attempt a guess. "And tracing through thick leaves the rare jeweled tiger" and "of hunting through dripping boughs the precious tiger" are not even Spenderian images. In poem 13, however, of Spender's first published book, we come upon something of interest:

I feared more than tigers their muscles like iron
And their jerking hands and knees tight on my arms . . .
They were light, they sprang out behind hedges . . .

The poet is here speaking of children "who were rough." Again,

> We lacked the Spring-like resources of the tiger.

which comes from a political poem in which the poet begs that the future will never say that Spender's generation lacked the resources to build a new world. Without knowing the sequence of composition of the three poems it is possible to see that the rough boys who sprang out at the boy Spender like tigers have a dual significance. They hunted him and yet he chooses to identify himself with them; he is the hunter and the hunted at once. The rare jeweled tiger, the precious tiger, the tiger with Spring-like resources (the pun is self-explanatory) is possibly Spender's hound of heaven.

There is one further problem of the transit of Spender's symbol of the express which I do not know where to locate. It occurs in the seemingly child-like verse "At last, further page 100 / than Edinburgh or Rome" and occurs in all six drafts of the poem. The only thing I am sure of here is that the names are not simply place-names. The obvious connections would be Edinburgh, the actual destination of the train (?) and Rome, the past. But in examining the verses that immediately follow the six Edinburgh and Rome configurations, it seems that the names are only a springboard for the final destination of the express and the poem, namely, "beyond the crest of the world" where both train and poem reach the destination "night." This establishes the resolution of the poem; the express is to be merged in darkness, in flame, in song, in boughs breaking with honey buds.

> Ah, like a comet through flame, she moves entranced
> Wrapped in her music no bird song, no, nor bough
> Breaking with honey buds shall ever equal.

The mystical melting together of sight, sound and smell in these verses dispels the jazzy madness, the mechanical elate meter of wheels, and leaves us in a trance of excitement that is happy and acceptable.

Study of *The Funeral*, by Stephen Spender

The second Spender poem I want to examine is *The Funeral*, which bears some relationship to *The Express* and does, in fact, directly precede it in the first published edition. In the notebook it occupies two pages and consists of two versions, the first incomplete, the second virtually finished. A moral consideration of the poem is out of place here, but it would be of help to remember that this work pleads an extreme case in an extreme manner, and pursues its point to a mercilessly logical conclusion. The argument is that grief for death is dead. A worker has passed away, but one who has given his life for the "hive" (the state). Therefore rejoice; page 101 / read lists of projects for building over his grave, and be thankful for what this man contributed. A deleted line at the top of the second draft reads, "No more are they haunted by the individual grief." *Haunted* I think is the real key in which the poem is written.

In the initial quatrain of the first draft we get a preliminary exercise of thought which is absent in *The Express* manuscript.

> On the little hill at the edge of the town
> They stand amongst stiff grass and the breeze lifts their hair,
> The strange cause of rejoicing that lightens their eyes
> Is the death of a hero of labour.

This preparatory work the poet finds unsatisfactory. It is too obvious, too sentimental, despite the curious theme it announces. The weakness of this beginning nevertheless leads immediately into the almost final and very arresting opening

> For death is ~~only~~ another milestone on their way

In the second draft the weak quatrain is obliterated and the conjunctive "for" free to drop out.

> Death is another milestone on their way

is a typically powerful Spenderian beginning. But, for the moment, it is the rejected material that is of interest. First, there is the setting of the poem, the locale, which a few stanzas down we learn is London! Second, there is the time, which from "the little hill" phrase I would adduce to be soon, just after the world revolution. The little hill presumably denoted a little cemetery, a new one, not one of those infinite hideous and sprawling affairs where the pre-revolutionary dead are buried. Finally, we are made to know that instead of grief there is rejoicing; the poet still finds this "strange," for everything has become different quite suddenly. page 102 /

In the succeeding quatrain the poet discusses with himself the relative merits of jobs in the new world — or so it seems from the change in the text. The hero "excelled all others in making, say, driving belts." "Say" is eventually thought superfluous, as is the moral question for which it stands. Both the verse and the argument are strengthened by this simple deletion. The stanza shows numerous textual revisions, mostly pertinent to the political meaning of the poem.

> For death is ~~the last~~ festivity; it is the time for statistics
> one
> When they record how much ~~this~~ atom contributed ~~to the state,~~
> are glad as they him whence
> They ~~laugh as we~~ lay ~~him back~~ in the earth ~~from which~~ he came
> And thank him for what he gave them.

Stanza four is the "London" stanza and is of interest because it expresses what is *exactly* in the poet's mind, but not what will help create the poem.

> Then follow the speeches and the songs of the new life
> And lists are read out of projects to build ~~new~~ steel-works
> And to pull down
> The worst of the slums around London.

"Steel-works" falls by the way in the next version and becomes "projects for building." In steel-works we sense a militancy to which the poet probably objects. (There is now no further need of militancy; we are in the immediate future, but we are already safe. "The worst of the slums around London" becomes "The last of the slums around London.")

The fifth quatrain ends this version, and the poem is begun again "on the little hill at the edge of the town." It now proceeds smoothly, almost finally, through all its seven quatrains, the first and fourth of which are later struck out. Both of these are local, political stanzas; poetically they bear no page 103 / relationship to the rest of the poem, but are rather the stimuli that excite the creation in its development. The closing stanza, the most exciting of all, appears in the second version in finished form.

> No more are they haunted by the individual grief
> Nor the crocodile tears of European genius
> The decline of a culture
> Mourned by scholars who dream of the ghosts of Greek boys.

This is the only moment when one feels a tremor of motion below the surface of the poem; until this final quatrain we are standing in the near future. Then the sudden look behind into the present. I have never been sure what is meant by "the crocodile tears of European genius" though probably it has a political meaning for the initiated. At any rate, this quatrain is the only one that *appeared* without having to undergo development. Can we presume from this that it is the "inspired" stanza, or that it contains the real substance of the poem? If so, what does it mean and what light does it throw on the rest of the creation? Probably only this. That Spender at this period experiences the individual grief and is haunted by it; it is the one thing he must submerge in order to become a better socialist and a more effective revolutionary. *He* is the individual grief upon which his scorn is showered. In other works in this collection Spender constantly makes it clear that he is not "using" his revolutionary material for his own "singing tree" (his own aims). No doubt it is the enthusiasm of the political visionary that enables him to dismiss the heritage of European genius with such finality. Everything must go, what is held most dear, even oneself.

The Funeral carries a tremendous shock in its quiet lines. What in the notebook threatens to become merely a piece of boyish pettishness, turns out to be a brilliant experiment in nihilism. Anyone who has followed Spender's poetry closely will have recognized an integral struggle between himself and page 104 / his idea of justice, a struggle I think that is between Spender's mysticism and his socialism. The poems about Beethoven and the truly great do not spring from the same psyche as the poems about comrades and the need for destruction. The direction of the express train is not accidental but is a symptom of this poet's psychical direction. There is, in fact, a sizeable mystical vocabulary in Spender, which is most of the time overlooked but is now and then miscalled "romantic." "As iron heated red hot loses its own appearance and glows like fire" is a typical Spenderian form; it was written, however, by St. Bernard. Spender is a first-rate language maker, and it is therefore doubly interesting to notice the ease with which he draws upon the vocabulary of the ecstatics. "Cross, rose, pilgrimage, missionary, love, wheel, death, distance, the mystic One, heaven, peace, trumpeter, sun spirit, edge of being, moth, worms," and others taken out of context would not appear to rise from the Spenderian vocabulary. Some of the same words used by Yeats, for example, would carry only a literary force or a pseudo-mystical beauty. Spender's mysticism, it can be argued, must be real because he has to fight it back and because he has to find a weapon, political materialism, with which to render it harmless. In his hand that weapon itself grows flowers, in the manner of an ancient miracle. page 105 /

Seascape

STEPHEN SPENDER

In Memoriam, M. A. S.

There are some days the happy ocean lies
Like an unfingered harp, below the land.
Afternoon gilds all the silent wires
Into a burning music for the eyes.
On mirrors flashing between fine-strung fires
The shore, heaped up with roses, horses, spires,
Wanders on water, walking above ribbed sand.

The motionlessness of the hot sky tires
And a sigh, like a woman's, from inland
Brushes the instrument with shadowing hand
Drawing across its wires some gull's sharp cries
Or bell, or shout, from distant, hedged-in shires;
These, deep as anchors, the hushing wave buries.

Then from the shore, two zig-zag butterflies,
Like errant dog-roses, cross the bright strand
Spiralling over sea in foolish gyres
Until they fall into reflected skies.
They drown. Fishermen understand
Such wings sunk in rital sacrifice,

Recalling legends of undersea, drowned cities.
What voyagers, oh what heroes, flamed like pyres
With helmets plumed, have set forth from some island
And them the sea engulfed. Their eyes,
Contorted by the cruel waves' desires
Glitter with coins through the tide scarcely scanned,
While, above them, that harp assumes their sighs.

The Making of a Poem

STEPHEN SPENDER

Apology

It would be inexcusable to discuss my own way of writing poetry unless I were able to relate this to a wider view of the problems which poets attempt to solve when they sit down at a desk or table to write, or walk around composing their poems in their heads. There is a danger of my appearing to put across my own experiences as the general rule, when every poet's way of going about his work and his experience of being a poet are different, and when my own poetry may not be good enough to lend my example any authority.

Yet the writing of poetry is an activity which makes certain demands of attention on the poet and which requires that he should have certain qualifications of ear, vision, imagination, memory, and so on. He should be able to think in images, he should have as great a mastery of language as a painter has over his palate, even if the range of his language be very limited. All this means that, in ordinary society, a poet has to adapt himself, more or less consciously, to the demands of his vocation, and hence the peculiarities of poets and the condition of inspiration which many people have said is near to madness. One poet's example is only his adaptation of his personality to the demands of

---

poetry, but if it is clearly stated it may help us to understand other poets, and even something of poetry.

Today we lack very much a whole view of poetry, and have instead many one-sided views of certain aspects of poetry which page 45 / have been advertised as the only aims which poets should attempt. Movements such as free verse, imagism, surrealism, expressionism, personalism and so on, tend to make people think that poetry is simply a matter of not writing in metre or rhyme, or of free association, or of thinking in images, or of a kind of drawing room madness (surrealism) which corresponds to drawing room communism. Here is a string of ideas: Night, dark, stars, immensity, blue, voluptuous, clinging, columns, clouds, moon, sickle, harvest, vast camp fire, hell. Is this poetry? A lot of strings of words almost as simple as this are set down on the backs of envelopes and posted off to editors or to poets by the vast army of amateurs who think that to be illogical is to be poetic with that fond question. Thus I hope that this discussion of how poets work will imply a wider and completer view of poets.

Concentration

The problem of creative writing is essentially one of concentration, and the supposed eccentricities of poets are usually due to mechanical habits or rituals developed in order to concentrate. Concentration, of course, for the purposes of writing poetry, is different from the kind of concentration required for working out a sum. It is a focusing of the attention in a special way, so that the poet is aware of all the implications and possible developments of his idea, just as one might say that a plant was not concentrating on developing mechanically in one direction, but in many directions, towards the warmth and light with its leaves, and towards the water with its roots, all at the same time.

Schiller liked to have a smell of rotten apples, concealed beneath the lid of his desk, under his nose when he was composing poetry. Walter de la Mare has told me that he must smoke when writing. Auden drinks endless cups of tea. Coffee is my own addiction, besides smoking a great deal, which I hardly ever do except when I am writing. I notice also that as I attain a greater concentration, page 46 / this tends to make me forget the taste of the cigarette in my mouth, and then I have a desire to smoke two or even three cigarettes at a time, in order that the sensation from the outside may penetrate through the wall of concentration which I have built round myself.

For goodness sake, though, do not think that rotten apples or cigarettes or tea have anything to do with the quality of the work of a Schiller, a de la Mare, or an Auden. They are a part of a concentration which has already been attained rather than the cause of concentration. De la Mare once said to me that he thought the desire to smoke when writing poetry arose from a need, not of a stimulus, but to canalize a disturbing leak of his attention away from his writing towards the distraction which is always present in one's environment. Concentration may be disturbed by someone whistling in the street or the ticking of a clock. There is always a slight tendency of the body to sabotage the attention of the mind by providing some distraction. If this need for distraction can be directed into one channel — such as the odour of rotten apples or the taste of tobacco or tea — then other distractions outside oneself are put out of competition.

Another possible explanation is that the concentrated effort of writing poetry is a spiritual activity which makes one completely forget, for the time being, that one has a body. It is a disturbance of the balance of body and mind and for this reason one needs a kind of anchor of sensation with the physical world. Hence the craving for a scent or taste or even, sometimes, for sexual activity. Poets speak of the necessity of writing poetry rather than of a liking for doing it. It is spiritual compulsion, a straining of the mind to attain heights surrounded by abysses and it cannot be entirely happy, for in the most important sense, the only reward worth having is absolutely denied: for, however confident a poet may be, he is never quite sure that all his energy is not misdirected nor that what he is writing is great poetry. At the moment when art achieves its highest attainment it reaches beyond its medium of page 47 / words or paints or music, and the artist finds himself realizing that these instruments are inadequate to the spirit of what he is trying to say.

Different poets concentrate in different ways. In my own mind I make a sharp distinction between two types of concentration: one is immediate and complete, the other is plodding and only completed by stages. Some poets write immediately works which, when they are written, scarcely need revision. Others write their poems by stages, feeling their way from rough draft to rough draft, until finally, after many revisions, they have produced a result which may seem to have very little connection with their early sketches.

These two opposite processes are vividly illustrated in two examples drawn from music: Mozart and Beethoven. Mozart thought out symphonies, quartets, even scenes from operas, entirely in his head — often on a journey or perhaps while dealing with pressing problems — and then he transcribed them, in their completeness, on to paper. Beethoven wrote fragments of themes in notebooks which he kept beside him, working on and developing them over years. Often his first ideas were of a clumsiness which makes scholars marvel how he could, at the end, have developed from them such miraculous results.

Thus genius works in different ways to achieve its ends. But although the Mozartian type of genius is the more brilliant and dazzling, genius, unlike virtuosity, is judged by greatness of results, not by brilliance of performance. The result must be the fullest development in a created aesthetic form of an original moment of insight, and it does not matter whether genius devotes a lifetime to producing a small result if that result be immortal. The difference between two types of genius is that one type (the Mozartian) is able to plunge the greatest depths of his own experience by the tremendous effort of a moment, the other (the Beethovenian) must dig deeper and deeper into his consciousness, layer by layer. What counts in either case is the page 48 / vision which sees and pursues and attains the end; the logic of the artistic purpose.

A poet may be divinely gifted with a lucid and intense and purposive intellect; he may be clumsy and slow; that does not matter, what matters is integrity of purpose and the ability to maintain the purpose without losing oneself. Myself, I am scarcely capable of immediate concentration in poetry. My mind is not clear, my will is weak, I suffer from an excess of ideas and a weak sense of form. For every poem that I begin to write, I think of at least ten which I do not write down at all. For every poem which I do write down, there are seven or eight which I never complete.

The method which I adopt therefore is to write down as many ideas as possible, in however rough a form, in notebooks (I have at least twenty of these, on a shelf beside my desk, going back over fifteen years). I then make use of some of the sketches and discard others.

The best way of explaining how I develop the rough ideas which I use, is to take an example. Here is a notebook begun in 1944. About a hundred pages of it are covered with writing, and from this have emerged about six poems. Each idea, when it first occurs is given a number. Sometimes the ideas do not get beyond one line. For example No. 3 (never developed) is the one line:

A language of flesh and roses

I shall return to this line in a few pages, when I speak of inspiration. For a moment, I turn to No. 13, because here is an idea which has been developed to its conclusion. The first sketch begins thus:

(*a*) There are some days when the sea lies like a harp
Stretched flat beneath the cliffs. The waves
Like wires burn with the sun's copper glow
(*all the murmuring blue every silent*)
page 49 /
Between whose spaces every image
Of sky (*field and*) hedge and field and boat
Dwells like the huge face of the afternoon.
(*Lies*)

When the heat grows tired, the afternoon
Out of the land may breathe a sigh
(*Across these wires like a hand. They vibrate
With*)
Which moves across those wires like a soft hand
(*Then the vibration*)
Between whose spaces the vibration holds
Every bird-cry, dog's bark, man-shout
And creak of rollock from the land and sky
With all the music of the afternoon.

Obviously these lines are attempts to sketch out an idea which exists clearly enough on some level of the mind where it yet eludes the attempt to state it. At this stage, a poem is like a face which one seems to be able to visualize clearly in the eye of memory, but when one examines it mentally or tries to think it out, feature by feature, it seems to fade.

The idea of this poem is a vision of the sea. The faith of the poet is that if this vision is clearly stated it will be significant. The vision is of the sea stretched under a cliff. On top of the cliff there are fields, hedges, houses. Horses draw carts along lanes, dogs bark far inland, bells ring in the distance. The shore seems laden with hedges, roses, horses and men, all high above the sea, on a very fine summer day when the ocean seems to reflect and absorb the shore. Then the small strung-out glittering waves of the sea lying under the shore are like the strings of a harp which catch the sunlight. Between these strings lies the reflection of the shore. Butterflies are wafted out over the waves, which they mistake for the fields of the chalky landscape, searching them for flowers. On a day such as this, the land, reflected in the sea, appears to enter into the sea, as though it lies under it, like Atlantis. The wires of the harp are like a seen music fusing seascape and landscape. page 50 /

Looking at this vision in another way, it obviously has symbolic value. The sea represents death and eternity, the land represents the brief life of the summer and of one human generation which passes into the sea of eternity. But let me here say at once that although the poet may be conscious of this aspect of his vision, it is exactly what he wants to avoid stating, or even being too concerned with. His job is to recreate his vision, and let it speak its moral for itself. The poet must distinguish clearly in his own mind between that which most definitely must be said and that which must not be said. The unsaid inner meaning is revealed in the music and the tonality of the poem, and the poet is conscious of it in his knowledge that a certain tone of voice, a certain rhythm, are necessary.

In the next twenty versions of the poem I felt my way towards the clarification of the seen picture, the music and the inner feeling. In the first version quoted above, there is the phrase in the second and third lines

The waves
Like wires burn with the sun's copper glow.

This phrase fuses the image of the sea with the idea of music, and it is therefore a key-phrase, because the theme of the poem is the fusion of the land with the sea. Here, then, are several versions of these one and a quarter lines, in the order in which they were written:

(*b*) The waves are wires
Burning as with the secret song of fires

(*c*) The day burns in the trembling wires
With a vast music golden in the eyes

(*d*) The day glows on its trembling wires
Singing a golden music in the eyes

(*e*) The day glows on its burning wires
Like waves of music golden to the eyes.

page 51 /

(*f*) Afternoon burns upon its wires
Lines of music dazzling the eyes

(*g*) Afternoon gilds its tingling wires
To a visual silent music of the eyes

In the final version, these two lines appear as in the following stanza:

(*h*) There are some days the happy ocean lies
Like an unfingered harp, below the land.
Afternoon gilds all the silent wires
Into a burning music of the eyes.

On mirroring paths between those fine-strung fires
The shore, laden with roses, horses, spires,
Wanders in water, imaged above ribbed sand.

Inspiration

The hard work evinced in these examples, which are only a fraction of the work put into the whole poem, may cause the reader to wonder whether there is no such thing as inspiration, or whether it is merely Stephen Spender who is uninspired. The answer is that everything in poetry is work except inspiration, whether this work is achieved at one swift stroke, as Mozart wrote his music, or whether it is a slow process of evolution from stage to stage. Here again, I have to qualify the word "work," as I qualified the word "concentration": the work on a line of poetry may take the form of putting a version aside for a few days, weeks or years, and then taking it up again, when it may be found that the line has, in the interval of time, almost rewritten itself.

Inspiration is the beginning of a poem and it is also its final goal. It is the first idea which drops into the poet's mind and it is the final idea which he at last achieves in words. In between this start and this winning post there is the hard race, the sweat and toil. page 52 /

Paul Valéry speaks of the "une ligne donnée" of a poem. One line is given to the poet by God or by nature, the rest he has to discover for himself.

My own experience of inspiration is certainly that of a line or a phrase or a word or sometimes something still vague, a dim cloud of an idea which I feel must be condensed into a shower of words. The peculiarity of the key word or line is that it does not merely attract, as, say, the word "braggadocio" attracts. It occurs in what seems to be an active, male, germinal form as though it were the centre of a statement requiring a beginning and an end, and as though it had an impulse in a certain direction. Here are examples:

A language of flesh and roses

This phrase (not very satisfactory in itself) brings to my mind a whole series of experiences and the idea of a poem which I shall perhaps write some years hence. I was standing in the corridor of a train passing through the Black Country. I saw a landscape of pits and pitheads, artificial mountains, jagged yellow wounds in the earth, everything transformed as though by the toil of an enormous animal or giant tearing up the earth in search of prey or treasure. Oddly enough, a stranger next to me in the corridor echoed my inmost thought. He said: "Everything there is man-made." At this moment the line flashed into my head

A language of flesh and roses

The sequence of my thought was as follows: the industrial landscape which seems by now a routine and act of God which enslaves both employers and workers who serve and profit by it, is actually the expression of man's will. Men willed it to be so, and the pitheads, slag-heaps and the ghastly disregard of anything but the pursuit of wealth, are a symbol of modern man's mind. In other words, the world which we create — the world of slums and telegrams and newspapers — is a kind of language of our inner wishes and thoughts. Although this is so, it is obviously a language page 53 / which has got outside our control. It is a confused language, an irresponsible senile gibberish. This thought greatly distressed me, and I started thinking that if the phenomena created by humanity are really like words in a language, what kind of language do we really aspire to? All this sequence of thought flashed into my mind with the answer which came before the question: *A language of flesh and roses.*

I hope this example will give the reader some idea of what I mean by inspiration. Now the line, which I shall not repeat again, is a way of thinking imaginatively. If the line embodies some of the ideas which I have related above, these ideas must be further made clear in other lines. That is the terrifying challenge of poetry. Can I think out the logic of images? How easy it is to explain here the poem that I would have liked to write! How difficult it would be to write it. For writing it would imply living my way through the imaged experience of all these ideas, which here are mere abstractions, and such an effort of imaginative experience requires a lifetime of patience and watching.

Here is an example of a cloudy form of thought germinated by the word *cross*, which is the key word of the poem which exists formlessly in my mind. Recently my wife had a son. On the first day that I visited her after the boy's birth, I went by bus to the hospital. Passing through the streets on the top of the bus, they all seemed very clean, and the thought occurred to me that everything was prepared for our child. Past generations have toiled so that any child born today inherits, with his generation, cities, streets, organization, the most elaborate machinery for living. Everything has been provided for him by people dead long before he was born. Then, naturally enough, sadder thoughts colored this picture for me, and I reflected how he also inherited vast maladjustments, vast human wrongs. Then I thought of the child as like a pin-point of present existence, the moment incarnate, in whom the whole of the past, and all possible future *cross*. This word *cross* somehow suggested the whole situation to me of a page 54 / child born into the world and also of the form of a poem about his situation. When the word *cross* appeared in the poem, the idea of the past should give place to the idea of the future and it should be apparent that the *cross* in which present and future meet is the secret of an individual human existence. And here again, the unspoken secret which lies beyond the poem, the moral significance of other meanings of the word "cross" begins to glow with its virtue that should never be said and yet should shine through every image in the poem.

This account of inspiration is probably weak beside the accounts that other poets might give. I am writing of my own experience, and my own inspiration seems to me like the faintest flash of insight into the nature of reality beside that of other poets whom I can think of. However, it is possible that I describe here a kind of experience which, however slight it may be, is perhaps truer to the real poetic experience than Aldous Huxley's account of how a young poet writes poetry in his novel *Times Must Have a Stop*.

Memory

If the art of concentrating in a particular way is the discipline necessary for poetry to reveal itself, memory exercised in a particular way is the natural gift of poetic genius. The poet, above all else, is a person who never forgets certain sense-impressions which he has experienced and which he can re-live again and again as though with all their original freshness.

All poets have this highly developed sensitive apparatus of memory, and they are usually aware of experiences which happened to them at the earliest age and which retain their pristine significance throughout life. The meeting of Dante and Beatrice when the poet was only nine years of age is the experience which became a symbol in Dante's mind around which the *Divine Comedy* crystallized. The experience of nature which forms the subjects of Wordsworth's poetry was an extension of a childhood **page 55 /** vision of "natural presences" which surrounded the boy Wordsworth. And his decision in later life to live in the Lake District was a decision to return to the scene of these childhood memories which were the most important experiences in his poetry. There is evidence for the importance of this kind of memory in all the creative arts, and the argument certainly applies to prose which is creative. Sir Osbert Sitwell has told me that his book *Before the Bombardment*, which contains an extremely civilized and satiric account of the social life of Scarborough before and during the 1914–18 war, was based on his observations of life in that resort before he had reached the age of twelve.

It therefore is not surprising that although I have no memory for telephone numbers, addresses, faces and where I have put this morning's correspondence, I have a perfect memory for the sensation of certain experiences which are crystallized for me around certain associations. I could demonstrate this from my own life by the overwhelming nature of associations which, suddenly aroused, have carried me back so completely into the past, particularly into my childhood, that I have lost all sense of the present time and place. But the best proofs of this power of memory are found in the odd lines of poems written in notebooks fifteen years ago. A few fragments of unfinished poems enable me to enter immediately into the experiences from which they were derived, the circumstances in which they were written, and the unwritten feelings in the poem that were projected but never put into words.

> . . . Knowledge of a full sun
> That runs up his big sky, above
> The hill, then in those trees and throws
> His smiling on the turf.

That is an incomplete idea of fifteen years ago, and I remember exactly a balcony of a house facing a road, and, on the other side of the road, pine trees, beyond which lay the sea. Every morning the sun sprang up, first of all above the horizon of the sea, then it climbed to the tops of the trees and shone on my window. And page 56 / this memory connects with the sun that shines through my window in London now in spring and early summer. So that the memory is not exactly a memory. It is more like one prong upon which a whole calender of similar experiences happening throughout years, collect. A memory once clearly stated ceases to be a memory, it becomes perpetually present, because every time we experience something which recalls it, the clear and lucid original experience imposes its formal beauty on the new experiences. It is thus no longer a memory but an experience lived through again and again.

Turning over these old notebooks, my eye catches some lines, in a projected long poem, which immediately reshape themselves into the following short portrait of a woman's face:

> Her eyes are gleaming fish
> Caught in her nervous face, as if in a net.
> Her hair is wild and fair, haloing her cheeks
> Like a fantastic flare of Southern sun.
> There is madness in her cherishing her children.
> Sometimes, perhaps a single time in years,
> Her wandering fingers stoop to arrange some flowers —
> Then in her hands her whole life stops and weeps.

It is perhaps true to say that memory is the faculty of poetry, because the imagination itself is an exercise of memory. There is nothing we imagine which we do not already know. And our ability to imagine is our ability to remember what we have already once experienced and to apply it to some different situation. Thus the greatest poets are those with memories so great that they extend beyond their strongest experiences to their minutest observations of people and things far outside their own self-centredness (the weakness of memory is its self-centredness: hence the narcissistic nature of most poetry).

Here I can detect my own greatest weakness. My memory is defective and self-centred. I lack the confidence in using it to create situations outside myself, although I believe that, in theory, page 57 / there are very few situations in life which a poet should not be able to imagine, because it is a fact that most poets have experienced almost every situation in life. I do not mean by this that a poet who writes about a Polar expedition has actually been to the North Pole. I mean, though, that he has been cold, hungry, etc., so that it is possible for him by remembering imaginatively his own felt experiences to know what it is like to explore the North Pole. That is where I fail. I cannot write about going to the North Pole.

Faith

It is evident that a faith in their vocation, mystical in intensity, sustains poets. There are many illustrations from the lives of poets to show this, and Shakespeare's sonnets are full of expressions of his faith in the immortality of his lines.

From my experience I can clarify the nature of this faith. When I was nine, we went to the Lake District, and there my parents read me some of the poems of Wordsworth. My sense of the sacredness of the task of poetry began then, and I have always felt that a poet's was a sacred vocation, like a saint's. Since I was nine, I have wanted to be various things, for example, Prime Minister (when I was twelve). Like some other poets I am attracted by the life of power and the life of action, but I am still more repelled by them. Power involves forcing oneself upon the attention of historians by doing things and occupying offices which are, in themselves, important, so that what is truly powerful is not the soul of a so-called powerful and prominent man but the position which he fills and the things he does. Similarly, the life of "action" which seems so very positive is, in fact, a selective, even a negative kind of life. A man of action does one thing or several things because he does not do something else. Usually men who do very spectacular things fail completely to do the ordinary things which fill the lives of most normal people, and which would be far more heroic and spectacular perhaps, if they did not happen to be done page 58 / by many people. Thus in practice the life of action has always seemed to me an act of cutting oneself off from life.

Although it is true that poets are vain and ambitious, their vanity and ambition is of the purest kind and attainable in the world, for the saint renounces ambition. They are ambitious to be accepted for what they ultimately are as revealed by their inmost experiences, their finest perceptions, their deepest feelings, their uttermost sense of truth, in their poetry. They cannot cheat about these things, because the quality of their own being is revealed not in the noble sentiments which their poetry expresses, but in sensibility, control of language, rhythm and music, things which cannot be attained by a vote of confidence from an electorate, or by the office of Poet Laureate. Of course, work is tremendously important, but, in poetry, even the greatest labor can only serve to reveal the intrinsic qualities of soul of the poet as he really is.

Since there can be no cheating, the poet, like the saint, stands in all his works before the bar of a perpetual day of judgment. His vanity of course is pleased by success, though even success may contribute to his understanding that popularity does not confer on him the favorable judgment of all the ages which he seeks. For what does it mean to be praised by one's own age, which is soaked in crimes and stupidity, except perhaps that future ages, wise where we are foolish, will see him as a typical expression of this age's crimes and stupidity? Nor is lack of success a guarantee of great poetry, though there are some who pretend that it is. Nor can the critics, at any rate beyond a certain limited point of technical judgment, be trusted.

The poet's faith is therefore, firstly, a mystique of vocation, secondly, a faith in his own truth, combined with his own devotion to a task. There can really be no greater faith than the confidence that one is doing one's utmost to fulfil one's high vocation, and it is this that has inspired all the greatest poets. At the same time this faith is coupled with a deep humility because one knows that, ultimately, judgment does not rest with oneself. page 59 / All one can do is to achieve nakedness, to be what one is with all one's faculties and perceptions, strengthened by all the skill which one can acquire, and then to stand before the judgment of time.

In my notebooks, I find the following Prose Poem, which expresses these thoughts:

> Bring me peace bring me power bring me assurance. Let me reach the bright day, the high chair, the plain desk, where my hand at last controls the words, where anxiety no longer undermines me. If I don't reach these I'm thrown to the wolves, I'm a restless animal wandering from place to place, from experience to experience.
>
> Give me the humility and the judgment to live alone with the deep and rich satisfaction of my own creating: not to be thrown into doubt by a word of spite or disapproval.
>
> In the last analysis don't mind whether your work is good or bad so long as it has the completeness, the enormity of the whole world which you love.

Song

Inspiration and song are the irreducible final qualities of a poet which make his vocation different from all others. Inspiration is an experience in which a line or an idea is given to one, and perhaps also a state of mind in which one writes one's best poetry. Song is far more difficult to define. It is the music which a poem as yet unthought of will assume, the empty womb of poetry for ever in the poet's consciousness, waiting for the fertilized seed.

Sometimes when I lie in a state of half-waking half-sleeping, I am conscious of a stream of words which seem to pass through my mind, without their having a meaning, but they have a sound, a sound of passion, or a sound recalling poetry that I know. Again sometimes when I am writing, the music of the words I am trying to shape takes me far beyond the words, I am aware of a rhythm, a dance, a fury, which is as yet empty of words.

In these observations, I have said little about headaches, midnight oil, pints of beer or of claret, love affairs, and so on, which page 60 / are supposed to be stations on the journeys of poets through life. There is no doubt that writing poetry, when a poem appears to succeed, results in an intense physical excitement, a sense of release and ecstasy. On the other hand, I dread writing poetry, for, I suppose, the following reasons: a poem is a terrible journey, a painful effort of concentrating the imagination; words are an extremely difficult medium to use, and sometimes when one has spent days trying to say a thing clearly one finds that one has only said it dully; above all, the writing of a poem brings one face to face with one's own personality with all its familiar and clumsy limitations. In every other phase of existence, one can exercise the orthodoxy of a conventional routine: one can be polite to one's friends, one can get through the day at the office, one can pose, one can draw attention to one's position in society, one is — in a word — dealing with men. In poetry, one is wrestling with a god.

Usually, when I have completed a poem, I think "this is my best poem," and I wish to publish it at once. This is partly because I only write when I have something new to say, which seems more worth while than what I have said before, partly because optimism about my present and future makes me despise my past. A few days after I have finished a poem, I relegate it to the past of all my other wasted efforts, all the books I do not wish to open.

Perhaps the greatest pleasure I have got from poems that I have written is when I have heard some lines quoted which I have not at once recognized. And I have thought "how good and how interesting," before I have realized that they are my own.

In common with other creative writers I pretend that I am not, and I am, exceedingly affected by unsympathetic criticism, whilst, praise usually makes me suspect that the reviewer does not know what he is talking about. Why are writers so sensitive to criticism? Partly, because it is their business to be sensitive, and they are sensitive about this as about other things. Partly, because every serious creative writer is really in his heart concerned with reputation and not with success (the most successful writer I have known, page 61 / Sir Hugh Walpole, was far and away the most unhappy about his reputation, because the "highbrows" did not like him). Again, I suspect that every writer is secretly writing for *someone*, probably for a parent or teacher who did not believe in him in childhood. The critic who refuses to "understand" immediately becomes identified with this person, and the understanding of many admirers only adds to the writer's secret bitterness if this one refusal persists.

Gradually one realizes that there is always this someone who will not like one's work. Then, perhaps, literature becomes a humble exercise of faith in being all that one can be in one's art, of being more than oneself, expecting little, but with a faith in the mystery of poetry which gradually expands into a faith in the mysterious service of truth.

Yet what failures there are! And how much mud sticks to one; mud not thrown by other people but acquired in the course of earning one's living, answering or not answering the letters which one receives, supporting or not supporting public causes. All one can hope is that this mud is composed of little grains of sand which will produce pearls. page 62 /

CHAPTER THREE

An Explanation by Literary Origins

SAMUEL TAYLOR COLERIDGE

Kubla Khan

Kubla Khan

SAMUEL TAYLOR COLERIDGE

In Xanadu did Kubla Khan
A stately pleasure-dome decree:
Where Alph, the sacred river, ran
Through caverns measureless to man
   Down to a sunless sea.
So twice five miles of fertile ground
With walls and towers were girdled round:
And here were gardens bright with sinuous rills,
Where blossomed many an incense-bearing tree,
And here were forests ancient as the hills, 10
Enfolding sunny spots of greenery.

But oh! that deep romantic chasm which slanted
Down the green hill athwart a cedarn cover!
A savage place; as holy and enchanted
As e'er beneath a waning moon was haunted
By woman wailing for her demon-lover!
And from this chasm, with ceaseless turmoil seething,
As if this earth in fast thick pants were breathing,
A mighty fountain momently was forced;
Amid whose swift half-intermitted burst 20
Huge fragments vaulted like rebounding hail,
Or chaffy grain beneath the thresher's flail:
And 'mid these dancing rocks at once and ever
It flung up momently the sacred river.
Five miles meandering with a mazy motion

Through wood and dale the sacred river ran,
Then reached the caverns measureless to man,
And sank in tumult to a lifeless ocean:
And 'mid this tumult Kubla heard from far
Ancestral voices prophesying war! 30
The shadow of the dome of pleasure
Floated midway on the waves;
Where was heard the mingled measure
From the fountain and the caves.
It was a miracle of rare device,
A sunny pleasure-dome with caves of ice!

A damsel with a dulcimer
In a vision once I saw:
It was an Abyssinian maid,
And on her dulcimer she played, 40
Singing of Mount Abora.
Could I revive within me
Her symphony and song,
To such a deep delight 'twould win me,
That with music loud and long,
I would build that dome in air,
That sunny dome! those caves of ice!
And all who heard should see them there,
And all should cry, Beware! Beware!
His flashing eyes, his floating hair! 50
Weave a circle round him thrice.
And close your eyes with holy dread,
For he on honey-dew hath fed,
And drunk the milk of Paradise.

The Sleeping Images

JOHN LIVINGSTON LOWES

Coleridge's own account of the genesis of "Kubla Khan" is as follows. It was first published in 1816, with the poem.

> In the summer of 1797, the Author, then in ill health, had retired to a lonely farm-house between Porlock and Linton, on the Exmoor confines of Somerset and Devonshire. In consequence of a slight indisposition, an anodyne had been prescribed, from the effects of which he fell asleep in his chair at the moment that he was reading the following sentence, or words of the same substance in "Purchas's Pilgrimage": "Here the Khan Kubla commanded a palace to be built, and a stately garden thereunto. And thus ten miles of fertile ground were inclosed with a wall." The Author continued for about three hours in a profound sleep, at least of the external senses, during which time he has the most vivid confidence, that he could not have composed less than from two to three hundred lines; if that indeed can be called composition in which all the images rose up before him as *things*, with a parallel production of the correspondent expressions, without any sensation or consciousness of effort. On awaking he appeared to himself to have a distinct recollection of the whole, and taking his pen, ink, and paper, instantly and eagerly wrote down the lines that are here preserved. At this moment he was unfortunately called out by a person on business from Porlock, and detained by him above an hour, and on his return to his room, found, to his no small surprise and mortification, that though he still retained some vague and dim recollection of the

Reprinted, by permission, from *The Road to Xanadu*, by John Livingston Lowes (Boston: Houghton Mifflin Company, 1927).

> general purport of the vision, yet, with the exception of some eight or ten scattered lines and images, all the rest had passed away like the images on the surface of a stream into which a stone has been cast, but, alas! without the after restoration of the latter!

That is all we know. The year 1797, as Ernest Hartley Coleridge has clearly shown, is wrong. The one thing which Coleridge seems to have been constitutionally incapable of remembering correctly was a date that concerned himself. The visit to the farm-house between Porlock and Linton took place in the **page 356 /** early summer of *1798*, and "Kubla Khan," instead of preceding "The Ancient Mariner," closely followed it. That is important, as we shall see.

For "the images [which] rose up before him as *things*," rose up from somewhere. And our study of "The Ancient Mariner" has revealed the fact that Coleridge's memory was tenanted by throngs of visual images derived from books. If, then, we can reconstruct, for the moment when Coleridge fell asleep over *Purchas His Pilgrimage*, the elements, even in part, of that subliminal chaos, we shall have taken a long step towards the clarification of our problem. Those elements, on Coleridge's own testimony, were images with the objective distinctness of *things* — the "ocular spectra," in a word, of his favourite terminology. But they had, in the first instance (to employ that terminology once more), "flashed from *words*. And it is only through those words that we, in our turn, can arrive at them. Our sole hope, accordingly, of reconstituting any portion of the sleeping imagery which at the moment of the dream was susceptible of movement towards the light, lies again in an examination of the books which Coleridge had been reading. And as in the case of "The Ancient Mariner" that avenue is open. But before we enter on it, I wish to guard against a misunderstanding which may easily arise — the assumption, namely, that the passages which I shall quote are, in themselves and as they stand, the constituents, or even (in the stock sense of the term) the "sources" of "Kubla Khan." They are not that. Their very words, undoubtedly, were now and then remembered. But that is incidental. What they did for Coleridge was to people the twilight realms of consciousness with *images*. And the thing they enable *us* to do is to gain some inkling of what those subliminal "atomes crochus" were — those mysterious elements out of whose confluences and coalescences suddenly emerged the poem. If, then, in this chapter the poem itself should seem far away, it is because we must, as Drayton has it, "adventure upon desperate untrodden ways" — must pass, indeed, in very truth

> From the presence of the sun,
> Following darkness like a dream.

page 357 /

I

Most fortunately we know, from Coleridge himself, what it was that struck down into the dark and waked the sleeping images to an intense activity. For he tells us what was before his eyes at the instant when he fell asleep, and the poem begins with the actual words on which his eyes had closed. It would be hard to come closer than that to the point at which waking slips over the verge into sleep. The last conscious impressions had been communicated by these lines:

> *In Xamdu did Cublai Can* build *a stately* Palace, encompassing sixteene *miles of* plaine *ground with a wall*, wherein are *fertile* Meddowes, pleasant springs, delightfull Streames, and all sorts of beasts of chase and game, and in the middest thereof a sumptuous house of *pleasure*, which may be removed from place to place.

The images which first rose up "as *things*" had taken on this correspondent form:

> *In Xanadu did Kubla Khan*
> *A stately pleasure*-dome decree:
> Where Alph, the sacred river, ran
> Through caverns measureless to man
> Down to a sunless sea.
> So twice five *miles of fertile ground*
> *With Walls* and towers were girdled round:
> And there were gardens bright with sinuous rills,
> Where blossomed many an incense-bearing tree;
> And here were forests ancient as the hills,
> Enfolding sunny spots of greenery.

And there, for the moment, we may pause.

Into those thronged precincts, then, "just on the vestibule of consciousness," where the sleeping images maintain their "shadowy half-being," there had sunk, at the very instant when conscious control had been suspended, a new and richly suggestive concourse of impressions. That, at least, is clear. But page 358 / so is something else. Once granted that conjunction, it was inevitable that flashes of association should dart in all directions, and that images endowed with the potentiality of merging should stream together and coalesce. I know that these are "goings-on" (to use Coleridge's phrase) which "matter-moulded forms of speech" are hard put to it to express. But something not wholly remote from what they adumbrate certainly took place.

For even in the few lines of "Kubla Khan" which I have quoted are details which by no farthest stretch of fancy can be thought of as implicit in the sentence from the *Pilgrimage*.

> Where Alph, the sacred river, ran
> Through caverns measureless to man
> Down to a sunless sea.

The images, for instance, which underlie that startling metamorphosis of Purchas's "delightful streames" had obviously flashed from other pages than the one which Coleridge was reading when he fell asleep. So, with no less certainty, had most of the vividly distinct and concrete imagery of the remainder of the poem. What the impressions from Purchas had done, in a word, was to summon up other images, and set swift trains of association interweaving. And the enterprise before us now is the attempt to reconstruct in part those evanescent operations, which yet builded of their fleetingness a fabric beside which

> . . . rocks impregnable are not so stout,
> Nor gates of steel so strong.

No mortal can hope to call back all that insubstantial pageant which once moved through a long-vanished dream. Most of it faded on the instant, and left not a track behind. But some of page 359 / the elements which streamed together are yet traceable, nor is it impossible even to gather, sometimes, how and why they merged. The sequence, however, in which their coalescences occurred is something which I am not so reckless as to attempt to guess. And so the order which we shall follow in the sequel is simply the order which clarity in setting forth the facts demands.

II

Let us return to the sentence in Purchas which Coleridge was reading. Obviously something else — perhaps even before unconsciousness descended — had flashed back to his memory. For Coleridge knew well not merely *Purchas His Pilgrimage,* but *Purchas His Pilgrimes* too. It was in the third volume of the *Pilgrimes* that he had read of William Barents and of the ice-fields of the North. And in this same volume was another and more detailed account of Kubla Khan. Whether this consciousness lapsed is immaterial; in some form or other it was there. For it betrays its presence. I do not know what edition of the *Pilgrimage* Coleridge was reading. If by any chance he had taken Wordsworth's copy with him to his retreat, he had before him the edition of 1617. In that event the name of Kubla's city as it would meet his eye had the cacophanous form "Xamdu" — as was also the case if his edition were that of either 1614 or 1626. If, on the other hand, it was the first, of 1613, the form he saw was "Xaindu." But the name which lends its euphony to the poem's opening line is neither; it is "*Xanadu.*" And that is the form which he knew in the *Pilgrimes,* "Xandu" — now "unfurled to music suddenly."

At or after the moment, then, when Coleridge fell asleep, recollections of the *Pilgrimes* had been stirred to life by the reading of the *Pilgrimage.* Anything else, indeed, when (as here) the two narratives ran parallel, would have been, even disregarding "Xandu," well nigh incredible. Let us see what that involves. In the account of Xamdu (or Xaindu) which Coleridge was reading in the *Pilgrimage* was a "*house of pleasure,*" in the midst of "fertile Meddowes, pleasant springs, delightfull Streames." But in the *Pilgrimes,* in the marginal gloss to the page 360 / parallel account of Kubla's palace, was a "house of pleasure" too. And just eight pages before this remembered account of Xandu in the *Pilgrimes* is one of the most unforgettable passages in the book. And in it also are "*houses of pleasure,*" in the midst of "a goodly Garden, furnished with the best trees and fruits." There was, then, between the two narratives a palpable associative link. What happened?

The passage in the *Pilgrimes* is the famous account of the Old Man of the Mountain. I shall first quote a couple of sentences from the beginning of it:

> His name was Aloadine, and was a Mahumetan. Hee had in a goodley Valley betwixt two Mountaynes very high, made *a goodly Garden, furnished with the best trees* and fruits he could find,

> adorned with divers Palaces and *houses of pleasure*, beautified with gold Workes, Pictures, and Furnitures of silke.

That the sentence which Coleridge read in the *Pilgrimage* brought back this definitely linked passage in the *Pilgrimes*, and that the images which rose up from the two of them blended in the dream, it is difficult to doubt. The "fertile Meddowes, pleasant springs, delightfull Streames" and the "goodly Garden, furnished with the best trees" have slipped together, like Martens' snow and Father Bourzes' rainbow in the spray, into an exquisitely lucid whole compact of both — and, as we shall see, of something else:

> And there were *gardens bright with sinuous rills,*
> Where blossomed *many an* incense-bearing *tree.*

But the spell of the Old Man of the Mountain was more potent far than that. And its presence now becomes unmistakable.

For now I shall take up again the account of Aloadine's house of pleasure at the exact point where I broke it off, and shall then set down at once the wonderful last paragraph of "Kubla Khan." What gave Coleridge the two vivid figures — the damsel with a dulcimer and the youth with flashing eyes and floating hair — who appear in the poem out of nothing, with a dream-like suddenness and a dream's serene oblivion of **page 361 /** their inconsequence? Here, at all events, are the inmates of Aloadine's Paradise:

> There by divers Pipes answering divers parts of those Palaces were seene to runne Wine, *Milke, Honey*, and cleer Water. In them hee had placed goodly *Damosels skilfull in Songs and Instruments of Musicke* and Dancing, and to make Sports and Delights unto men whatsoever they could imagine. They were also fairely attyred in Gold and Silke, and were seene to goe continually sporting in the Garden and Palaces. He made this Palace, *because Mahomet had promised such a sensuall Paradise to his devout followers . . .*
>
> Aloadine had *certaine Youthes* from twelve to twentie yeares of age, such as seemed of a bold and undoubted disposition, *whom hee instructed daily touching Mahomets Paradise*, and how hee could bring men thither. And when he thought good, *he caused a certaine Drinke to bee given unto* ten or twelve of *them*, which cast them in a dead sleepe: and then he caused them to be carryed into divers Chambers of the said Palaces, *where they saw the things aforesaid* as soone as they awaked: *each of them having those*

Damosels to minister Meates and excellent Drinkes, and all varieties of pleasures to them; *insomuch that the Fooles thought themselves in Paradise indeed.* When they had enjoyed those pleasures foure or five dayes, they were againe cast in a sleepe, and carryed forth againe. After which, hee . . . questioned where they had beene, which answered, by your Grace, *in Paradise.* . . . Then the old man answered, This is the commandment of our Prophet, that *whosoever defends his Lord, he make him enter Paradise:* and if thou wilt bee obedient to mee, thou shalt have this grace. And having thus animated them, *hee was thought happie whom the old man would command, though it cost him his life: so that other Lords and his Enemies were slaine by these his Assasines, which exposed themselves to all dangers, and contemned their lives.*

Now let us return to the poem:

A damsel with a dulcimer
In a vision once I saw:
It was an Abyssinian maid,
And on her dulcimer she played,
Singing of Mount Abora.
Could I revive within me
Her symphony and song,
To such a deep delight 'twould win me,
That with music loud and long,
I would build that dome in air,
That sunny dome! those caves of ice!
And all who heard should see them there,
And all should cry, Beware! Beware!
His flashing eyes, his floating hair!
Weave a circle round him thrice,
And close your eyes with holy dread,
For he on honey-dew hath fed,
And drunk the milk of Paradise.

page 362/

There can be little question of what has happened. Behind the strange and haunting beauty of the dream's imagery recollected fragments of the striking picture of the pleasure-houses flash and fade and cross and interweave: "goodly Damosels" with "Songs and Instruments of Musicke," seen between sleep and sleep; the milk and honey of Paradise, drunk and eaten at the singing, playing damsels' hands; the desire on waking out of sleep to live again the lost delights ("Could I revive within me Her symphony and song"); the duped inmates of the palace, fired, that so they may regain a Paradise once tasted and now withdrawn, with a fanatic zeal to kill:

> And all who heard, should see them there,
> *And all should cry, Beware! Beware!*
> His flashing eyes, his floating hair! . . .
> For he on honey-dew hath fed,
> And drunk the milk of Paradise.

They are at once the same and not the same, as you and I have known their like to be a hundred times in dreams. Nobody in his waking senses could have fabricated those amazing eighteen lines. For if anything ever bore the infallible marks of authenticity it is that dissolving panorama in which fugitive hints of Aloadine's Paradise succeed each other with the vivid incoherence, and the illusion of natural and expected sequence, and the sense of an identity that yet is not identity, which are the distinctive attributes of dreams. Coleridge's statement of his experience has more than once been called in question. These lines alone, in their relation to the passage which suggested them, should banish doubt.

Whence, however, slipped into the dream — like journeying stars which enter unannounced — Abyssinia, and Mount Abora, and the dome in air, and the caves of ice, and Alph the sacred **page 363 /** river with its caverns and its sunless sea? They are all, I think, distinctly traceable. But to reach them we must first meander with a mazy motion through regions already traversed in our earlier quest.

III

Is it possible to repeople with its vanished images another corner of Coleridge's unconscious mind into which may have flashed those associations which are the stuff of dreams? With the aid of the Note Book I believe it is.

In April, 1798, Coleridge, who had been suffering from an infected tooth, wrote as follows, in a letter to his brother George:

> Laudanam gave me repose, not sleep; but you, I believe, know how divine that repose is, *what a spot of enchantment, a green spot of fountain and flowers and trees* in the very heart of a waste of sands!

Now when Coleridge wrote that, he was recalling and echoing, consciously or unconsciously, something else. For in the Note Book (which, as we know, belongs to this same period) appears this memorandum:

> —*some wilderness-plot, green and fountainous* and unviolated by Man.

Is it possible to discover what lies behind this note?

The entry is sandwiched in, together with Hartley's tumble and his tears which glittered in the moonlight, between the two parts of the long note on Bartram's crocodiles. That note, in turn, is transcribed from pages 127–30 of Bartram's *Travels.* The next entry in the Note Book is from Bartram's 140th page; the next from pages 161–62; the next from pages 132–33. And on page 157, flanked on one side by our old friends the crocodiles and snake-birds, and on the other by the Gordonia lasianthus, stands the following:

> I was however induced to . . . touch at the inchanting little Isle of Palms. This delightful spot, planted by nature, is almost an entire grove of Palms, with a few pyramidal Magnolias, Live Oaks, golden Orange, and the animating Zanthoxilon; what a beautiful retreat is here! *blessed unviolated spot of earth!* rising page 364 / from the limpid waters of the lake; its fragrant groves and blooming lawns invested and protected by encircling ranks of the Yucca gloriosa; a fascinating atmosphere surrounds this blissful garden; the balmy Lantana, ambrosial Citra, perfumed Crinum, perspiring their mingled odours, wafted through Zanthoxilon groves. I at last broke away from *the enchanting spot* . . . then traversing a capacious semi-circular cove of the lake, verged by low, extensive grassy meadows, I at length by dusk made a safe harbour.

And two pages earlier "the dew-drops twinkle and play . . . on the tips of the lucid, green savanna, sparkling" beside a "serpentine rivulet, meandering over the meadows."

Those lines from Bartram, then, are in the very thick of the pages which Coleridge was ardently transcribing in his Note Book, and the picture which they painted made a profound impression on his mind. For he twice came back to it. It inspired the memorandum in the Note Book, for the "wilderness-plot, green and fountainous and *unviolated* by Man" is unmistakably the "blessed *unviolated* spot of earth" on which Bartram lavished such a wealth of words. It no less clearly underlies the passage in the letter, whose "*spot of enchantment*" is Bartram's "*enchanting spot*," and whose "green spot of fountain" is the "plot, green and fountainous" of the Note Book. And in the letter it becomes the symbol of the "divine repose" induced by opium, and the letter was written not more than a month or two before "Kubla Khan." Of one thing, then, we may be certain: impressions of Bartram's "inchanting little Isle of Palms" were among the sleeping images in Coleridge's unconscious memory at the time when "Kubla Khan" emerged from it.

But a thousand other impressions coexisted with them there. Did this particular cluster constitute what we have called an *atome crochu?* Had it, in other words, hooks-and-eyes which might draw it into the extraordinary complex which was taking form? If it *were* so equipped, its attraction within the circle was almost inevitable. For it lay, so to speak, just over the threshold of consciousness. Twice already its imagery had recurred to memory and clothed itself with words. And recurrence to memory soon becomes a habit. Conspicuous, now, among its details were "grassy meadows," a "blissful garden," "fragrant groves," and multitudes of trees. And at the moment of the page 365 / dream, by way of Purchas, impressions of "fertile Meddowes," conjoined with a "goodly Garden" furnished with trees, were stirring actively in Coleridge's brain. Clearly, then, there were sufficient links between the images from Purchas which were sinking into the Well, and the images from Bartram which were already there.

And they *did* coalesce. Here are the lovely lines of the fragment once again:

> And there were *gardens bright with sinuous rills,*
> Where *blossomed* many an *incense-bearing* tree;
> *And here were forests* ancient as the hills,
> *Enfolding sunny spots of greenery.*

"As I bent my head," wrote Coleridge to Godwin in words which I have quoted once before, "there came a distinct, vivid spectrum upon my eyes; it was one little picture — a rock, with birches and ferns on it, a cottage backed by it, and a small stream. Were I a painter I would give an outward existence to this, *but it will always live in my memory*." Even so into the dream had come remembered ocular spectra from Bartram — images which rose up before the dreamer "as *things*." There were Bartram's "*balmy*

Lantana, *ambrosial* Citra, *perfumed* Crinum, *Perspiring their mingled odours*." But the dreamer was Coleridge, not Bartram, and so the mass of particulars melted into a single line, redolent of the odours of all spicy shores: "Where blossomed *many an incense-bearing tree*." Into the dream, moreover, had slipped the image of an image of an image — that luminous visualization in the letter (still only a few weeks old) of the same scene as it came up through the Note Book from Bartram: "a spot of enchantment, *a green spot* of fountain and flowers and trees." And so in the dream there are "forests ancient as the hills, Enfolding sunny *spots of greenery*." And the "*serpentine rivulet*" meandering through "the *lucid, green savanna*" sparkling with sunlit dew — that too, merged with another recollection, rose up in the dream as "one little picture," to which were fitted, "without consciousness of effort," perfect words: "And there were gardens *bright with sinuous rills*." Even "enfolding" is a transmuted flash of memory. For in Bartram's "enchanting spot" are "blooming lawns *invested . . .* page 366 / *by encircling* ranks" of towering flora. And these "blooming" forest-glades are seen in the blossoming of the incense-bearing trees. Every detail in the four lines which recollections of Purchas leave wanting or incomplete, reminiscences of Bartram have supplied. But neither *Travels*, nor *Pilgrimage*, nor *Pilgrimes*, nor all of them combined, supplied the resultant beauty.

IV

We have by no means finished, however, with the Isle of Palms. For the images which rose from Bartram were furnished with still other powerful links. It will be remembered that in the Note Book Bartram's "blessed unviolated spot of earth" appeared as a "wilderness-plot, green and fountainous," and that in the letter it reappeared as "a green spot of *fountain* and flowers and trees." But there were no fountains in Bartram's Isle of Palms. Yet even before the dream fountains had somehow become fixed in Coleridge's mental picture. How had they entered it?

The account of the Isle of Palms is on Bartram's 157th page. The Gordonia lasianthus is on page 161–62. Coleridge, then, was still intently reading on. And the entry in the Note Book touching the "Siminoles," which draws on pages 212–13, and the footnote to "This Lime-Tree Bower my Prison," which quotes verbatim a sentence from page 221, afford ample evidence that he had read still farther. Now on page 165, just three pages beyond the Gordonia lasianthus, is this:

> I seated myself upon *a swelling green knoll*, at the head of the chrystal bason. Near me, on the left, was a point or projection of an entire grove of the aromatic Illisium Floridanum; on my right and all around behind me, was a fruitful *Orange grove*, with *Palms* and *Magnolias* interspersed; in front, just under my feet was the *enchanting and amazing chrystal fountain.*

The fountain and the Isle of Palms are separated by eight pages only, and a passage entered in the Note Book lies between. They may easily have been read at the same sitting, and the associative links between the two — green knoll, aromatic groves, oranges, palms, magnolias — are patent at a glance. At all events, the Note Book and the letter are evidence that before the dream was dreamed the two green and fragment spots page 367 / of trees and flowers had coalesced in Coleridge's memory. And into the picture which was later to haunt the dream had been carried the imagery suggested by "the inchanting . . . chrystal fountain."

Now let us see a little more of this amazing fountain. The account of it proceeds:

> Just under my feet was the inchanting and amazing chrystal fountain, *which incessantly threw up, from dark, rocky caverns below, tons of water every minute, forming* a bason, capacious enough for large shallops to ride in, and *a creek* of four or *five* feet depth of water, and near twenty yards over, *which meanders six miles through green meadows*, pouring its limpid waters into the great Lake George. . . . About twenty yards from the upper edge of the bason . . . is a *continual and amazing ebullition, where the waters are thrown up in such abundance and amazing force*, as to jet and swell up two or three feet above the common surface: *white sand and small particles of shells are thrown up with the waters . . . when they . . . subside* with the expanding flood, and gently *sink again.*

That, then, before the dream, Coleridge had seen in his mind's eye. What did he see in the dream?

> And from this chasm, *with ceaseless turmoil seething,*
> As if this earth in fast thick pants were breathing,
> *A mighty fountain momently was forced:*

> Amid whose swift half-intermitted burst
> Huge *fragments vaulted* like rebounding hail,
> Or chaffy grain beneath the thresher's flail:
> And 'mid these dancing rocks at once and ever
> *It flung up momently the sacred river.*
> *Five miles meandering* with a mazy motion.
> *Through wood and dale* the sacred river ran,
> *Then reached the caverns* measureless to man,
> *And sank* in tumult to a lifeless ocean.

The images which rose up in the dream, in conjunction with "sunny spots of greenery," were images which had risen up before, in similar conjunction, when Coleridge, with that preternatural visualizing faculty of his, was eagerly devouring Bartram. They are that beyond the shadow of a doubt. But they are also, as so often happens in a dream, simultaneously something else. That something else must wait its turn, however, since we have still to do with Bartram.

For Bartram was inordinately fond of letting himself go on page 368 / the subject of ebullient fountains — which were, indeed, in all conscience, remarkable enough. And certain striking details from one or two of these other lively descriptions had fixed themselves in Coleridge's memory. Ernest Hartley Coleridge, who saw so much that has enriched us, missed the "inchanting and amazing chrystal fountain" which reappears in such startling fashion in the dream. But he calls attention, in a footnote to the lines of "Kubla Khan" before us, and more fully in a paper read before the Royal Society of Literature in 1906, to "William Bartram's description of the "Alligator Hole.' " Now that description is only seventeen pages beyond the account of the savanna crane, of which Coleridge quotes half a dozen lines, and we may be certain that he read it. And what he read included the story, as told by an eye-witness, of the last eruption from the vast orifice. Here is enough of it to serve our purpose:

> On a sudden, he was astonished by an inexpressible rushing noise, like a mighty hurricane or thunder storm, and looking around, he saw the earth overflowed by torrents of water . . . *attended with a terrific* noise and *tremor of the earth*. . . . He immediately resolved to proceed for the place from whence the noise seemed to come, and soon came in sight of *the incomparable fountain*, and saw, with amazement, *the floods rushing upwards many feet high*, and the expanding waters . . . spreading them-

> selves far and near. . . . It continued to *jet* and flow in this manner for several days, *forming a large* . . . *river*, descending and following the various . . . *windings* of the valley, for the distance of seven or eight miles, emptying itself into a vast savanna, where there was a . . . *sink which received* . . . *its waters*. . . . At places, where ridges or a swelling bank . . . opposed its course and fury, are *vast heaps of fragments of rocks*, white chalk, stones and pebbles, *which were* . . . thrown into the lateral vallies.

The two descriptions could not but recall each other, and in the dream their images coalesced. The sense of a tremendous force is heightened: the "white sand and small particles of shells . . . thrown up" by "the inchanting fountain" give place to "fragments of rocks . . . thrown" in vast heaps into the vallies; the "terrific tremor of the earth" now pulsates through the dream, "As if this earth in fast thick pants were breathing." But the concourse of the hooked atoms is not yet complete. **page 369 /**

Just eight pages earlier Coleridge had read of still another "grand fountain," "the admirable Manate Spring":

> The ebullition is astonishing, and continual, *though its greatest force or fury intermits*, regularly, *for the space of thirty seconds of time* . . . the ebullition is perpendicular upwards, from *a vast ragged orifice through a bed of rocks* . . . *throwing up small particles or pieces of white shells*, which subside with the waters, at the moment of *intermission* . . . yet, before the surface becomes quite even, the fountain vomits up the waters again, and *so on perpetually*.

And so there is added, with fresh emphasis on the "*ceaseless* turmoil," the suggestion of the "*swift half-intermitted* burst." The imagery of the "mighty fountain" in the vision is an amazing confluence of images from these separate yet closely linked reports of actual fountains which Coleridge had read. Yet in another sense the confluence is not "amazing"; it is the normal mechanism of a dream.

V

And now among the elements which blended in the panorama appears a train of imagery stranger and more startling than any which has gone before. For through the dream, mysteriously flooding and subsiding, flows "the sacred river."

One of the books most widely read at the close of the century was James Bruce's *Travels to Discover the Source of the Nile.* And Coleridge knew it well. He made use of it (as we have seen) in his "Religious Musings," dated "on the Christmas Eve of 1794," and in a footnote to the poem he quotes Bruce's graphic description of the Simoom. In 1801 he makes a memorandum of his intention to use, in a comparison after the manner of Jeremy Taylor, the idea of "seeking the fountains of the Nile." And in 1807 he recommends the last edition of the *Travels* to Lady Beaumont as "a book that [she] ought by all means to have." It was no wonder that he did so. Bruce, in Richard Garnett's words, "will always remain the poet, and his work the epic, of African travel." And as the tale of an attempt to penetrate the mystery which had veiled for centuries the sources of the most venerable of all historic streams, the narrative was and is one to stir imagination. Nor should we expect a superb contemporary chapter in the romance of discovery to leave Coleridge's tenacious memory bare of images. **page 370 /**

Certainly no one who ever read it would forget the dramatic climax of the story. Bruce, baffled and annoyed by the shifts and evasions of his native guide, lost his temper:

> Come, come, said I . . . no more words; it is now late, lose no more time, but carry me to Geesh, and the head of the Nile directly, without preamble, and shew me the hill that separates me from it. He then carried me round to the south side of the church, out of the grove of trees that surrounded it. "This is the hill, says he, looking archly, that . . . was between you and *the fountains of the Nile;* there is no other; look at *that hillock of green sod* in the middle of that watery spot, it is in that the two *fountains of the Nile* are to be found: Geesh is on the face of the rock where *yon green trees* are: if you go the length of the fountains pull off your shoes . . . for these people are all Pagans . . . and they believe in nothing that you believe, but only in this river, *to which they pray every day as if it were God.*" . . . Half undressed as I was by loss of my sash, and throwing my shoes off, I ran down the hill towards *the little island of green sods;* . . . the whole side of the hill was *thick grown over with flowers*, the large bulbous roots of which appearing above the surface of the ground, and their skins coming off on treading upon them, occasioned two very severe falls before I reached the brink of the marsh; I after this came to *the island of green turf,* which was in form of an altar, apparently the work of art, *and I stood in rapture over the principal fountain which rises in the middle of it.*

> It is easier to guess than to describe the situation of my mind at that moment — standing in that spot which had baffled the genius, industry, and inquiry of both ancients and moderns, for the course of near three thousand years.

We need not pursue Bruce's meditation farther; but in that thrilling moment the "little island of green sods" held, both for him and for his readers, the answer to a question older than the riddle of the sphinx. And for two long chapters this other "wilderness-plot, green and fountainous," is in the foreground of the narrative.

Now Bruce, in his attempt to prove himself the first European to reach the sources of the Nile, discusses at great length the narrative of Father Peter Paez, who claimed to have discovered the two fountains on April 21, 1618. And he quotes, on the authority of Athanasius Kircher, Paez's description of the fountains, in which, after declaring that he "saw, with the greatest delight [summaque animi mei voluptate], what neither Cyrus **page 371 /** king of the Persians, nor Cambyses, nor Alexander the Great, nor the famous Julius Cæsar, could ever discover," he mentions certain striking details which have for us peculiar interest:

> The second fountain lies about a stone-cast west from the first: the inhabitants say that *this whole mountain is full of water*, and add, that the whole plain about the fountain is floating and unsteady, a certain mark that there is water concealed under it; for which reason, the water does not overflow at the fountain, but *forces itself with great violence out* at the foot of the mountain. The inhabitants . . . maintain that that year it trembled little on account of the drought, but other years, that *it trembled and overflowed so as that it could scarce be approached without danger*.

It would be hard to imagine "hooks-and-eyes of the memory" more effective than those which link the description of that fountain with the accounts of its congeners in Florida. The "hillock of green sod," like the "swelling green knoll" by the "inchanting fountain"; the hillside "thick grown over with flowers"; the plain about the fountain that "trembled"; the water that "forced itself out with great violence": every detail recalls some parallel in Bartrum. But there is a further correspondence so close as to verge on the uncanny. The Nile, just after it has left the fountain, "makes so many sharp, unnatural *windings*, that it differs," says Bruce, "from any other river I ever saw, making above twenty sharp angular peninsulas *in the course of five miles.*" The stream thrown up by Bartram's "amazing chrystal fountain" "*meanders six miles* through green meadows." Coleridge being Coleridge, with that prehensile associative faculty of his, it was really the inevitable which happened. "*Five miles meandering* with a mazy motion" — so ran the sacred river which the mighty fountain in the dream flung up. And that is Bartram and Bruce in one. The vivid images of fountains in Florida and Abyssinia, with their powerfully ejected streams, have coalesced in the deep Well and risen up together, at once both and neither, in the dream. And by virtue of that incomprehensible juggling with identities which is the most familiar trick of dreams, "the sacred river" *is* the Nile — while at the same time it is *not*. Only in a dream, I once more venture to believe, could the phantasmagoria which now for the first time it is possible to estimate, have risen up. page 372 /

VI

And now certain other mysterious features of the dream fall into place. Why was the damsel with a dulcimer "an Abyssinian maid"? The answer is not far to seek. The fountains of the sacred river are in Abyssinia; almost from beginning to end the scene of Bruce's narrative is laid in Abyssinia; and Abyssinia hovered in the background of the vision, to become suddenly explicit in this seemingly unaccountable detail. And for still another instant Abyssinia held the foreground of the dream:

> It was an Abyssinian maid,
> And on her dulcimer she played,
> *Singing of Mount Abora.*

What was Mount Abora, unknown to any map, I think, since time began?

The account which I have quoted of Bruce's rapturous plunge down the flowery hillside to the fountains of the Nile is on pages 596–97 of his third volume. Between pages 580 and 588 occurs fifteen times — six times on page 587 alone — a name which has not appeared before. It is that of the river, or valley, or plain of *Abola*. "The river Abola" — a tributary of the Nile — "comes out of the valley between [the] two ridges of mountains of

Litchambra and Aformasha," which Bruce at once identifies with "the Mountains of the Moon, or the *Montes Lunæ* of antiquity, at the foot of which the Nile was said to rise." No reader of Bruce could reach the story of the fountains of the Nile without "Abola" ringing in his ears. And "Abola" was itself amply sufficient to suggest the dream-word "Abora," as "Xamdu" or "Xaindu" suggested "Xanadu." But there was another name in Bruce which with little doubt blended in Coleridge's memory with "Abola," to bring about the metamorphosis.

Only eight pages beyond Bruce's account of his thrilling discovery is a description of the island of Meroë: "That island . . . having a twilight of short duration" (a remark peculiarly adapted to catch Coleridge's eye) "was placed between the Nile and *Astaboras.*" In the next chapter (still the "Description of the Sources of the Nile") the name turns up repeatedly again. "It seems very clear that the *Atbara* is the *Astaboras* of the **page 373 /** ancients"; "Meroë . . . was inclosed between the *Astaboras* and the Nile"; "Pliny says, Meroë . . . is called Astaboras. . . . '*Astabores* lævo alveo dictus.' " Moreover, the first appearance of the Astaboras in the narrative is not without suggestion: "this prodigious body of water . . . *tearing up rocks* and large trees in its course, and *forcing down their broken fragments* scattered on its stream, with a noise like thunder echoed from a hundred hills . . . is very rightly called the 'terrible.' " "Astaboras," then, can scarcely have failed to print itself on Coleridge's memory, and the accented element of the name is "*abora.*" And the obvious relation between the modern "Atbara" and the ancient "Astaboras" would serve to fix attention on this central element. Between "*Abola*" and "*Astaboras,*" accordingly, Coleridge's "Abora" seems to have slipped into the dream.

But why should hints from the names of two *rivers* have contributed a *mountain* to the dream? Whatever the suggestion, it doubtless flashed for an instant and was gone, "impalpable as the wind, fleeting as the wings of sleep"—*par levibus ventis volucrique simillima somno.* Yet to recapture it (if recapture it we can) we must traverse with heavy feet the labyrinth through which it fled like light. But we have long been doing that.

Some years ago, Professor Lane Cooper suggested, in an article on "The Abyssinian Paradise in Coleridge and Milton," that Coleridge's "Mount Abora" was really Milton's "Mount Amara."

In the sense in which "the sacred river" at the same time is and is not the Nile, I think he is right; and in the light of the facts already presented in this chapter his suggestion takes on new significance. Mount Amara closes the bead-roll of those enticing earthly Paradises which Milton, in the fourth book of *Paradise Lost,* sets over against his glowing account of the true Paradise of Eden:

> Not that fair field
> Of Enna, where Proserpin gathering flowers,
> Herself a fairer flower, by gloomy Dis
> Was gathered — which cost Ceres all that pain
> To seek her through the world — nor that sweet grove
> Of Daphne by Orontes, and the inspired
> Castalian spring, might with this Paradise
> Of Eden strive . . .
> Nor, *where Abassin kings their issue guard,*
> *Mount Amara* (though this by some supposed
> True Paradise) under the Ethiop line
> *By Nilus' head*, enclosed with shining rock,
> A whole day's journey high.

page 374/

No one will doubt that Coleridge, who knew his Milton through and through, and who believed that "in the description of Paradise itself . . . [Milton's] descriptive powers are exercised to the utmost," was thoroughly conversant with the lines on Amara, in their passingly lovely context. Had they, however, associations which might blend some fugitive recollection of them with the dream?

The links are there, not single spies, but in battalions. The setting of Mount Abora in the dream is a flashing stream of reminiscences of that Paradise of the Old Man of the Mountain wherein "Fooles thought themselves in Paradise indeed"; Milton's Mount Amara is such another pseudo-Paradise, like Aloadine's, "by some supposed True Paradise." Through the imagery of the dream ebbs and flows the sacred river, and the sacred river, as we now know, is the Nile; Mount Amara is "under the Ethiop line by Nilus' head" — these fountains which by way of Bruce flung up the sacred river in the dream. And by way of Bruce Mount Amara itself might have found, together with the fountains, ready entrance. For Bruce writes of Amhara too, as one of the geographical divisions of Abyssinia:

> It is a very mountainous country, full of nobility; the men are reckoned the handsomest in Abyssinia, as well as the bravest. . . . What, besides, added to the dignity of this province, was the high mountain of Geshen, or the grassy mountain, *whereon the king's sons were formerly imprisoned.*

"Nor, *where Abassin kings their issue guard*, Mount Amara"! It would be hard for Coleridge to read the first without a flash of recollection, on the very threshold of the sacred river, to the second. Into the dream, moreover, had poured the imagery of that enchanting spot in Bartram, where balmy trees "perspir[ed] their mingled odours"; "Groves whose rich trees wept odorous gums and balm" precede by only thirty lines the Miltonic Amara. And in the "*fertile ground*" of Eden, and its "many a *rill*" page 375 / that rolled "with *mazy* error," and its river which "through the shaggy hill *Passed underneath ingulfed*," are correspondences which compel belief that Milton's Paradise, and with it his Mount Amara, lent fleeting touches to the panorama of the dream. And in that phantasmagoria "Amara" (well worthy of commemoration in an Abyssinian damsel's symphony and song) has passed, under the spell of sounds more closely associated with the sacred river, through "Abola" and "Astaboras," into "Abora."

All this is enhanced by the further fact (to which Professor Cooper also calls attention) that Purchas has an entire chapter in his *Pilgrimage* entitled "Of the Hill Amara," and it was this chapter which inspired Milton's lines. It is one of the most memorable purple patches of the book, and nobody who knew the *Pilgrimage* would be likely to forget it. Coleridge, certainly, in that quest of materials for his "Hymns to the Sun, Moon, and the Elements" which led him to Maurice and Quintus Curtius, could not well have overlooked it, for on the hill "there are two Temples, built before the Raigne of the Queene of Saba, one in honour of the Sunne, the other of the Moone, the most magnificent in all Ethiopia." And its links with the dream are as obvious as Milton's. It is difficult to believe that Coleridge did not know it; and through it, or through both (I think we may be sure), Mount Amara — its name merged with the name of the river that flowed by the Mountains of the Moon — was drawn into that concourse of impressions which, as Coleridge sat sleeping over Purchas, was slipping through the ivory gate.

VII

I am aware that to some of my readers all this ado about a name will be regarded as the veriest trifling. But I beg such readers to remember that nothing is trivial which contributes to our understanding, on the one hand, of the strange workings of the mind in dreams, and on the other, of the waking operations of the creative faculty. There is not, in my judgment, among all existing records of the human mind, an opportunity of study- page 376 / ing the two together which is comparable to that afforded by "The Ancient Mariner" and "Kubla Khan." We shall see, I hope, when the materials which it is the formidable business of this chapter to elucidate are all before us, that the workings of the dream throw welcome light upon the waking processes. If that be so, no clue is too slight to follow where it leads. And there are more for us to follow.

For still other reminiscences of Bruce seem to have blended with the dream — recollections which

> Stream'd onward, lost their edges, and did creep
> Roll'd on each other, rounded, smooth'd, and brought
> Into the gulfs of sleep.

Let me set down in Bruce's words a few glimpses of the Abyssinian landscape caught as the little caravan approached the fountains of the Nile:

> The [whole mountain] was covered with thick wood, which often occupied the very edge of the precipices on which we stood. . . . Just above this almost impenetrable wood, in a very *romantic* situation, stands St. Michael, in a hollow space like a nitch between two hills. . . . The Nile here is not four yards over . . . [The whole company] were sitting in the shade of *a grove of magnificent cedars*. . . . The banks [of the Nile] . . . are covered with black, dark, and thick groves . . . a very rude and awful face of nature, *a cover* from which our fancy suggested a lion should issue, or some animal or monster yet more *savage* and ferocious. . . . "Strates," said I, "be in no such haste; remember the water is *inchanted*." . . . In the middle of this cliff [at Geesh], in a direction straight north towards the fountains, is a *prodigious cave*. . . . From the edge of the cliff of Geesh . . . *the ground slopes* with a very easy descent due north. . . . On the east

> *the ground descends* likewise with a very easy . . . slope. . . . From [the] west side of it . . . the ascent is very easy and gradual . . . all the way covered with good earth, *producing fine grass.*

And here is the landscape of the dream:

> But oh! that deep *romantic chasm* which *slanted*
> *Down the green hill* athwart a *cedarn cover!*
> *A savage place!* as holy and *enchanted*
> As e'er beneath a waning moon was haunted
> By woman wailing for her demon-lover!

Other impressions, to be sure, after the fashion of the sleeping page 377 / images, have merged in the dream with the ocular spectra which had flashed from Bruce's panoramic pages. But allowing for the wizardry of sleep, the "deep romantic chasm" of "the sacred river" is essentially the setting of the fountains of the Nile.

One other picture seems to owe its startling vividness to Bruce. Few images in the dream can have risen up more thrillingly as *things* than that apparition from the "bewitched enclosure" of Aloadine's Paradise:

> And all should cry, Beware! Beware!
> *His flashing eyes, his floating hair!*

And as one of Aloadine's Tartar damsels becomes, thanks to Bruce, an Abyssinian maid, so through the same influence, one of Aloadine's fanatic devotees is visualized (it would seem) as an Abyssinian king.

One of the most dramatic scenes in Bruce occurs a few pages after the fountains of the Nile are left behind. Bruce has joined the king of Abyssinia, Tecla Haimanout, who is fighting for his throne. And now the following extraordinary incident takes place:

> [The king] had desired me to ride before him, and shew him the horse I had got from Fasil. . . . It happened that, crossing the deep bed of a brook, a plant of the kantuffa hung across it. I had upon my shoulders a white goat-skin, of which it did not take hold; but the king, who was dressed in the habit of peace, *his long hair floating all around his face,* wrapt up in his mantle, or thin cotton cloak, *so that nothing but his eyes* could be seen, was paying more attention to the horse than to the branch of kantuffa beside him;

> it took first hold of his hair, and the fold of the cloak that covered his head . . . in such a manner that . . . no remedy remained but he must throw off the upper garment, and appear . . . with his head and face bare before all the spectators.
>
> This is accounted great disgrace to a king, who always appears covered in public. However, he did not seem to be ruffled . . . but with great composure, and in rather a low voice, he called twice, Who is the Shum of this district? Unhappily he was not far off. A thin old man of sixty, and his son about thirty, came trotting, as their custom is, naked to their girdle, and stood before the king. . . . The king asked if he was Shum of that place? he answered in the affirmative, and added . . . that the other was his son.
>
> There is always near the king, when he marches, an officer called Kanitz Kitzera, the executioner of the camp; he has upon page 378 / the tore of his saddle a quantity of thongs made of bull's hide . . . this is called the *tarade*. The king made a sign with his head, and another with his hand, without speaking, and two loops of the tarade were instantly thrown round the Shum and his son's neck, and they were both hoisted upon the same tree, the tarade cut, and the end made fast to a branch. They were both left hanging. . . .

That is not the sort of tale which one forgets. And with images of Tartary and Abyssinia already freely telescoping in the dream, it seems highly probable that some leap of association from Aloadine's assassins called up that sharp-etched picture of the ruthless Abyssinian king whose floating hair precipitated such a tragedy.

And now, with the kaleidoscopic swiftness of a dream, the scene shifts from Abyssinia to Cashmere. But even that surprising shift is not fortuitous. For Abyssinia and Cashmere were linked, for Coleridge, through a circumstance which we have now to see.

VIII

I said "for Coleridge," since Coleridge's associations of ideas are all that count in Coleridge's dream. And among the sleeping images below the threshold of his consciousness there was one of Cashmere which was definitely associated with the Nile. That will be clear, if we turn back to the reading on which Coleridge was intent at the time when he was jotting down matters of interest in Bartram.

In the Note Book, it will be remembered, a few pages after the excerpts from Bartram, appears the following entry:

> Hymns Moon
>
> In a cave in the mountains of Cashmere an Image of Ice, which makes it's apearance thus — two days before the new *moon* there appears a bubble of Ice which increases in size every day till the 15th day, at which it is an ell or more in height: then as the moon decreases, the Image does also till it vanishes.
>
> Read the whole 107th page of Maurice's Indostan.

Coleridge, that is, was collecting materials for his projected "Hymns to the Sun, the Moon, and the Elements — six hymns," and was reading Maurice with an eye alert for imagery which he page 379 / could turn to account in the great work which was never to be. The five mathematicians on the lofty tower in Pekin, who were somehow to enliven the Hymn to Air, he made note of from Maurice, and Maurice, as we shall see in a moment, gave him a hint for the Hymn to the Sun. Lore associated with the Sun, Moon, or the Elements, accordingly, was unlikely at this juncture to escape a treasure-seeker's vigilant eye.

The passage which he first made note of reads, in its context, as follows:

> I have already noticed the remarkable circumstance of 360 *fountains . . . sacred to the moon*, at Kehrah, a town in Cashmere; Cashmere, probably the most early residence of the Brahmins, and the theatre of the purest rites of their theology.
>
> In a cave of the same mountainous subah a very singular phænomenon is said, in the Ayeen Akbery, at certain periods to make its appearance. . . . In this cave, says Abul Fazil, is sometimes to be seen an image of ice, called AMERNAUT, which is holden in great veneration. The image makes its appearance after the following manner —

and the rest is substantially as Coleridge sets it down.

Now the image of ice is on pages 106–07. Keeping in mind the suggestive reference to *fountains,* let us pass to the next entry in the Note Book:

> Sun
>
> Hymns —— Remember to look at Quintius [*sic*] Curtius — lib. 3. Cap. 3 and 4.

But why? On the page in Maurice (105) immediately preceding the cave with its bubble of ice are these two footnotes:

See Quinti Curtii, lib. 3. cap. 3.
Ibid. lib. 3. cap. 4.

It was Maurice, then, who was sending Coleridge to Quintus Curtius, and it is easy to see why Coleridge was anxious not to forget to look him up. For Maurice had just given, on the authority of these two passages, two highly picturesque details which were a godsend to a poet with a Hymn to the Sun obstinately hanging fire:

> He [Quintus Curtius] declares it to have been an immemorial custom among the Persians, for the army never to march before page 380 / the rising of the sun; that a trumpet, sounding from the king's pavilion, proclaimed the first appearanct of its beam, and that a golden image of its orb, inclosed in a circle of crystal, was then displayed in the front of that pavilion, which diffused so wide a splendour that it was seen through the whole camp. . . .
>
> The grooms appointed to train and conduct these horses [one of which was called THE HORSE OF THE SUN] . . . bore in their hands golden rods, or wands, pointed at the end in imitation of the solar ray.

Coleridge's mind, it is plain, was picking up like a magnet imagery associated with the sun and moon. But (since we are for the moment working backwards) he had just been reading, a couple of pages earlier, a striking account of honours paid to the sun and moon in *Egypt*. And his eye — as quick to take notice as those of any five Chinese astronomers! — would assuredly catch this:

> The whole of the annual magnificent festival of Osiris and Isis was in the most pointed manner allusive to the influence of the SUN AND MOON upon the earth. . . . To the MOON, or Isis, they were by no means ungrateful for affording, by night, her kindly ray to conduct the mariner . . . over the boundless ocean, and the benighted traveller over deserts of sands . . . as well as her immediate utility in swelling the waters of *that sacred river*, whose annual inundations were the pepetual and abundant source of plenty.

And for another page the mutations of the Nile are Maurice's theme.

This, then, is clear. The Nile and Cashmere were definitely connected, through the moon, in Maurice. The Image of Ice, accordingly, in the cave in the mountains of Cashmere, sank below the threshold as an *atome crochu.* And its particular "hook of the memory" — that potentiality of junction which it carried with it — was the sacred river. And through their association with the sacred river the caves of ice were drawn into the dream:

> Through wood and dale *the sacred river* ran,
> Then reached the caverns measureless to man . . .
> Where was heard the mingled measure **page 381/**
> From the fountain and the caves.
> It was a miracle of rare device,
> A sunny pleasure-dome with *caves of ice!*

That is no fortuitous concourse of atoms. The elements of the dream are knit together through linkages like filaments of steel.

And now it is possible to take another step. In Maurice's Preliminary Chapter occurs the following sentence:

> I have immediately directed my own and my reader's attention to the intelligent Memoir, and very accurate map of Hindostan, presented to the world by *Major Rennell,* whose unwearied efforts to lucidate her intricate geography, must secure him the applause of all those who are either interested in the commerce, or attached to the literature, of the East.

That is the sort of thing on reading which Coleridge was apt to find his heart moved more than with a trumpet, and the next entry in the Note Book is brief but pregnant:

Major Rennell.

We know Coleridge's habit of verifying references, and the memorandum is conclusive evidence of his intentions in the present case. And since at the moment he was on a hot scent of promising materials for his galaxy of Hymns, there is special reason for assuming that his purpose was carried out.*

Now the work to which Maurice had referred, the *Memoir of a Map of Hindoostan* (1793), contains an uncommonly inviting

* "I seldom read except to amuse myself, and I am almost always reading. . . . I compose very little, and I absolutely hate composition" (*Letters,* I, 181). When Coleridge meant to *read a book,* he usually read it. When he meant to *write a poem,* he generally did not.

description of the landscape of Cashmere. And in it are certain significant details:

> The valley or country of Cashmere, is celebrated throughout upper Asia for its *romantic* beauties, [and] for *the fertility of its* soil. . . . It is . . . surrounded by steep mountains, that tower above the regions of snow; and . . . its soil is composed of the mud deposited by a *capital river*, which originally formed its waters into a lake . . . until it *opened itself a passage through the mountains*. . . . The author of the Ayin Acbaree dwells with rapture on the beauties of Cashmere. . . . Only light showers fall there: these, however, are in page 382/ abundance enough to feed some thousands of cascades, which are precipitated into the valley, from every part of *the stupendous and romantic bulwark that encircles it*. . . . In a word, the whole scenery is beautifully picturesque; and a part of the *romantic* circle of mountains, makes up a portion of every landscape. The pardonable superstitution of the sequestered inhabitants, has multiplied the places of worship of Mahadeo [whose image it was that appeared in the cave], of Bishen, and of Brama. *All Cashmere is holy land; and miraculous fountains abound*. . . . To sum up the account of Cashmere, in the words of [Abul Fazil], "*It is a garden in perpetual spring*."

Now let us reread a few lines of the poem:

> But oh! that *deep romantic chasm* which slanted
> Down the green hill athwart a cedarn cover!
> A savage place! As *holy* and enchanted
> As e'er beneath a waning moon was haunted . . .

There are links in plenty to catch up Major Rennell's picture into that stream of images which were rising before the sleeping Coleridge as *things* — the miraculous fountains, and the fertile ground, and the river that opened a passage through the mountains, and the sunny garden spot. And the landscape of the deep romantic vale of Cashmere and the landscape of the valley of the upper Nile seem to have melted into one another in the dream, and the enchanted territory of the poem becomes "*holy* land."

IX

Purchas and Bartram and Bruce and Maurice we know beyond peradventure that Coleridge had read. Major Rennell we know that he meant to read, and probably did. Up to this point, whatever may be said of our conclusions, the facts on which they rest admit no question. Coleridge had read these things; and the images which we have just been calling back had sunk into those secret tracts where all that is forgotten waits, keyed to associations at the lightest touch of which the sleeping past may flash up again — like a Venetian thoroughfare — to recollection. For

> Zwar ist's mit der [Traum]-Fabrik
> Wie mit einem Weber-Meisterstück,
> Wo Ein Tritt tausend Fäden regt,
> Die Schifflein herüber hinüber schiessen,
> Die Fäden ungesehen fliessen,
> *Ein Schlag tausend Verbindungen schlägt.*

page 383)

But there are two or three other books which I cannot definitely prove that Coleridge had read, yet which, for the strongest reasons, we may be reasonably certain that he had. It is their probable contribution to the dream which I shall now present. And the first is directly connected with the *Memoir of a Map of Hindoostan.*

At the beginning of his notice of Cashmere, Major Rennell refers as follows to a famous narrative: "The reader may collect from Bernier (*the most instructive of all Indian travellers*), in what mode the emperors travelled to Cashmere; as he has written a full account of his journey, when he travelled thither in the suite of Aurungzebe, in the year 1664." Just two pages beyond the account of the image of ice, moreover, Maurice in his turn, having already whetted his reader's interest in Bernier's journey to Cashmere, devotes more than a page to an incident in his travels, "so curious and interesting, that," as he says, "I cannot use the reader so ill as to pass it over." And *Mr. F. Bernier's Voyage to Surat*, which had given Dryden the materials for *Aurenge-Zebe*, was easily accessible. The normal chances that Coleridge would look it up were heightened, moreover, by the peculiar circumstances of the moment. For (once more) it must not be forgotten that Coleridge was just then avowedly collecting data for his six Hymns; that the scope of the Hymns was appalling, with "a sublime enumeration of all the charms and Tremendities of Nature" as a single item; that their hopeful projector was striking out, as the Note Book shows, from one book to another in directions which seemed to promise contributions; and that from both Maurice and Rennell the guideposts pointed straight and enticingly to Bernier.

Now Bernier, who is as entertaining as he is instructive, and whose account of his experiences en route to Cashmere is diverting to the last degree, gives in his Ninth Letter "An exact description of the kingdom of Kachemire . . . together with an answer to five considerable questions of a friend." It is worth pausing to note that the fifth of the friend's demands is this: page 384 / "That I would at length decide unto you the old controversy touching *the causes of the increase of the Nile*." And in his answer Bernier tells, on the authority of "two ambassadors of Ethiopia" whom he met at Delhi, how the Nile "issueth out of the earth at two big bubbling springs," and how, as "a pretty river . . . it runs bending" thence. If Coleridge did read Bernier, there was curiously enough a second hook to draw Cashmere and the fountains of the Nile together in the dream.

But he would also find a lively account of Cashmere itself, set down with a wealth of picturesque detail — an account which is extraordinarily rich in its links with that other reading which we know to have poured its imagery into the dream. It is out of the question to give all the parallels. Like Aloadine's Paradise and Kubla Khan's demesnes the vale is a spot of goodly gardens, houses of pleasure, pleasant springs, delightful streams:

> Out of all these mountains do issue *innumerable sources and rivulets*. . . . All these rivulets, descending from the mountains, make the plain and all those hillocks so fair and fruitful, that one would take this whole kingdom for *some evergreen garden*. . . . The lake hath this peculiar, that 'tis full of little isles, which are as many *gardens of pleasure*, that appear all green in the midst of the water. . . . Beyond the lake, upon the side of the hills, there is nothing but *houses and gardens of pleasure* . . . *full of springs and rivulets*.

Like Bartram's Florida, the vale abounds in ebullient fountains:

> Thence I went to find out a fountain, which hath something that's rare enough in it; bubling up gently, and rising with some little impetuosity, and making small bubbles of air, and carrying with it, to the top, some small sand that is very fine, which goeth away again as it came, the water becoming still, a moment after it, without ebullition, and without bringing up sand; and soon after beginning afresh as before, and so continuing its motion by intervals, which are not regular.

That might have come straight out of Bartram. There is, moreover, a cave of ice ("a grotto of odd congelation"), which is clearly identical with the cave of the bubble of ice in Maurice; and there is a subterranean cavern; and "the wall of the world" slopes down green hills to the plain; and not far away in the story are the fountains of the Nile. There are other corre- **page 385 /** spondences, but these must serve. If Coleridge had ever read the *Voyage to Surat*, its marvels could not have linked themselves in the dream with the like "charms and Tremendities of Nature" in Purchas and Bartram and Bruce and Maurice.

All this, however, might have found its way into the dream had Coleridge never laid eyes on Bernier. But there is one group of pictures in the *Voyage* which it is well nigh impossible to believe that he had not seen. The structure which Kubla Khan decreed in Xanadu was "a stately pleasure-*dome*," and it stood, in the dream, in close proximity to the fountain which flung up the river:

> *The shadow of the dome of pleasure*
> *Floated midway on the waves;*
> Where was heard the mingled measure
> From the fountain and the caves.

There is no hint of all that in Purchas or Bartram or Bruce or Maurice. But among Bernier's pleasant little vignette sketches are these:

> Returning from Send-brary I turn'd a little aside from the road to go and lie at Achiavel, which is *an house of pleasure* of the ancient kings of Kachemire, and at present of the great Mogol. That which most adorns it is *a fountain. . . . It breaks out of the earth, as if by some violence it ascended up from the bottom of a well, and that with such an abundance as might make it to be called a river* rather than a fountain. . . . The garden itself is very fine, there being curious walks in it, and *store of fruit-bearing trees.*

> The most admirable of all these gardens is that of the king, which is called Chah-limar. From the lake, one enters into it by a great canal, border'd with great green turfs. . . . It leadeth to a great cabinet in the midst of the garden, where begins another canal far more magnificent . . . and in the midst of it there is a long row of jets of water. . . . And this canal ends at another great cabinet.
>
> These cabinets, which are in a manner *made like domes*, [are] *situate in the middle of the canal, and encompassed with water.*

> I left my way again, to approach to a great lake, which I saw afar off, through the middle whereof passeth the river that runs to

> Baramoulay. . . . In the midst of this lake there is an eremitage with its little garden, which, as they say, *doth miraculously float upon the water.* page 386 /

There, without question — together with that "*great and vast dome* of white marble" which Bernier saw with delight surmounting Shah Jehan's Taj-Mahal at Agra — are elements which might have risen up, blended and transfigured, in the lovely image of the dream. And in their light the probability that Coleridge had looked up Bernier approaches certainty.

And in the darting play of associations which called up the picture of the floating image of the dome upon the wave, Bartram's fountains (which were, merged with the Abyssinian springs, the very fountain of the dream) may well have had a part. For in the bason of his "inchanting and amazing chrystal fountain" Bartram saw "the pendant golden Orange dancing on the surface of the pellucid waters"; and the waters of the Manate Spring "appear of a lucid sea green colour . . . owing to the reflection of the leaves above." A shadow that floated on the wave was printed on the very image of the wave itself as it arose. Admit Bernier's magic touch to set the simulacrum of the *dome* beside the wave, and the images were foreordained to blend. Dreams do behave in just that fashion, and the suggestion that this dream was no exception at least strains no probabilities.

X

Our exploration of the crowded anetchambers of the vision is almost at an end. There remain but two or three cluster-points of imagery the confluence of which in Coleridge's memory we shall attempt to trace. And they are (if I am right) among the most remarkable.

They carry us back from the vale of Cashmere to the idiosyncrasies of the sacred river:

> Where *Alph,* the sacred river, ran
> *Through caverns measureless to man*
>   Down to *a sunless sea . . .*
> Through wood and dale the sacred river ran,
> Then reached *the caverns measureless to man,*
> And sank in tumult to a *lifeless ocean.*

Whence came the "caverns measureless to man," and the "lifeless ocean," and the "sunless sea"? Above all, what lost suggestion underlies that most mysterious of appellations, "Alph"? Let us take up the riddles in their order. page 387 /

From the day of the Fathers down to Coleridge's own century (and since) one of those still-vex'd questions which have stretched the *pia mater* of many a subtle brain has been the identity of two of the four rivers — Pison, Gihon, Hiddekel, and Phrath — which, on the authority of *Genesis,* went out of Eden. That the last two represent the Tigris and Euphrates has always been matter of common consent. As for the other pair, in the dispute which waxed and waned through centuries, Pison was now the Indus, now the Danube, now the Nile, but far more frequently the Ganges; whereas Gihon, in spite of scattering voices raised in favour of the Orontes, or the Araxes, or the Oxus, was almost universally believed to be the *Nile.* But between Mesopotamia (which, barring a few fantastic guesses, was the accepted site of Paradise) between Mesopotamia and the regions where admittedly the Nile, as mortal eyes behold it, takes its rise, lay the deserts of Arabia and the Red Sea. How, on the venerable and orthodox assumption, did the now doubly sacred river make its way?

There could, of course, be but one answer. It must flow under ground and under sea. And that myth of the subterranean-submarine passage of the Nile from Asia through to Africa Coleridge certainly knew. It is needless to conjecture how often, in "the wide, wild wilderness" of his early reading, he had met it. He could scarcely have escaped it in Pausanias and the Life of Appolonius of Tyana, but the book entitled "Of the Primæval Earth, and Paradise" in that *Sacred Theory* of Thomas Burnet which he twice proposed to turn into blank verse, and later bracketed with Plato — not to mention that other work of Burnet's which gave the motto to "The Ancient Mariner" — these two afford evidence enough. The ancients, says Burnet, "supposed generally, that paradise was in the other hemisphere . . . and yet they believed that Tygris, Euphrates, Nile, and Ganges, were the rivers of paradise, or came out of it; and these two opinions they could not reconcile . . . but by supposing that these four rivers had their fountain-heads in the other hemisphere, and by some wonderful trajection broke out again here." "To this sense also," he remarks again, "Moses Bar Cepha often expresseth himself; as also Epiphanius, Procopius Gazæus, and Severianus in Catena.

Which notion amongst the page 388 / ancients, concerning the trajection or passage of the paradisiacal rivers under ground, or under sea, from one continent into another, is to me, I confess, unintelligible." It is Moses bar Cepha, however, who is most explicit, and Moses bar Cepha Coleridge probably knew, if not at first-hand, at least through the learned pages of another then celebrated work.

Bruce's paragraph about the ebullience of the second fountain of the Nile, which so strikingly parallels Bartram, is quoted from his translation of pages 57 and 59 of the first volume of Athanasius Kircher's *Œdipus Ægyptiacus*. I must regretfully forego the opportunity thus afforded of dwelling on the astonishing Athanasius and his still more dumbfounding works. It is enough to say that the *Œdipus Ægyptiacus* is prefaced by dedicatory verses to its patron in Latin, Greek, Italian, Spanish, French, Portuguese, English, German, Hungarian, Bohemian, Illyrian, Old Slavonic, Serbian, Turkish, Hebrew, Syriac, Arabic, Chaldean, Armenian, Persian, Samaritan, Coptic, Ethiopic, the Brahman alphabet, Chinese, and Egyptian Hieroglyphics. It is a book after Coleridge's own heart; his old friend Dupuis has copious references to it; Bruce's long extract would be enough to send him to it, if he had not already gone. And I have no doubt (though this I cannot prove) that he read the fascinating farrago on the subject of the Nile which fills the half-dozen pages just before the account which Bruce excerpts. And Moses bar Cepha heads the list of Kircher's, as of Burnet's, authorities.

And what Moses bar Cepha states is picturesque enough:

> The name of the second river is Gihon (*which is also called the Nile*): it flows through all the land of Chus. For no sooner has it come out of Paradise than it vanishes beneath the depths of the sea and the streams of Ocean, whence, through secret passages of the earth, it emerges again in the mountains of Ethiopia. . . . But [says bar Cepha] someone will ask, how is it possible that these rivers, when once they have passed out of Paradise, should be precipitated beneath the streams of Ocean and the heart of the sea, and should then at length emerge in this our land?

The obvious answer follows: With men this is impossible, but with God all things are possible. Whereupon Moses bar Cepha takes up his parable again:

> This also we assert, that Paradise lies in a much higher region

> page 389 / than this land, and so it happens that the rivers, impelled by so mighty a force, descend thence through *huge chasms* and subterranean channels, and, thus confined, are hurried away beneath the bottom of the sea, and *boil up* in this our orb.

This is immediately followed in Kircher by an extract from the *Geographia Arabica Medicca,* in which the plain of the Nile is said to be full of *cedars* (plena *Cedris*), and the whole land cavernous within — a region of mighty abysses (est enim tota hæc terra intus cava, et abyssos habens ingentes). The Arabic geography now disposed of, Kircher cites as a further witness Odoardus Lopez Lusitanus, who declares that the inhabitants of these quarters affirm with one accord that the Nile, plunging headlong through certain horrible and impenetrable valleys, through *chasms inaccessible to man* (per præcipitia hominibus inaccessa) and pathless deserts, is swallowed up in valleys so exceedingly deep that it is, as it were, received within the very bowels of the earth, and absorbed by its abysses. After which it reappears, and passing the cataracts, flows with many meanders (multiplici gyro) into the sea. Moreover, to add the crowning touch, between the accounts of Moses bar Cepha and the Arabic geographer, Kircher inserts a "True and Genuine Topography of the Fountains of the Nile [*Vera et genuina fontium Nili topographia*], made by P. Peter Pais on the 21st of April in the year 1618 in the presence of the Emperor," in which the two fountains are depicted on the summit of a craggy hill, encompassed with a prim circle of (one hopefully conjectures) incense-bearing trees, whence the Nile, meandering with a conspicuously mazy motion, forms the boundary of a plainly labelled kingdom of Amara (Amhara Regnum). And on the maps of Odoardus and the Arabic geographer engraved on the same plate, the river's maziness rivals that of the Dædalian labyrinth. The traditional association of the Nile with mighty caverns (to say nothing of meanderings and chasms) was still plentifully current in Coleridge's day.

And once more the link with Bartram is singularly close. For again and again Bartram might almost be paraphrasing Kircher's Latin. One passage, just before the account of the page 390 / Manate Spring, will serve to bring out the curious correspondence:

> These waters . . . augment and form . . . subterraneous rivers, which wander in darkness beneath the surface of the earth, by in-

> numerable doublings, windings and secret labyrinths; no doubt in some places forming vast reservoirs and subterranean lakes . . . and possibly . . . meeting irresistable obstructions in their course, they suddenly break through these perforated fluted rocks, in high, perpendicular jets. . . . Thus by means of those subterranean courses . . . they emerge . . . in those surprising vast fountains.

Bartram's subterranean caverns and the mythical abysses of the Nile are two of a kind. It would be next to impossible for Coleridge to read of either without some reminiscence of the other. And the two were probably associated in his memory long before the moment of the dream.

As for caverns "*measureless to man*," Paez states that he twice tried the depth of the second fountain and could find no bottom — "fundum nullum invenimus . . . denuo rem tentavimus, sed nec sic fundum tener potuimus"; and Kircher, in his remarks upon Paez's account, refers to the depth of the fountain as "inexplorabilis." Lobo asserts that "we could find no Bottom, and were assured by the Inhabitants, that none ever had been found." Whatever Coleridge knew or did not know about these accounts, he knew and had long known his Herodotus. And Herodotus has a most interesting tale. He found, he says, no one who professed any knowledge of the source of the Nile, except a single person, a scribe in the city of Saïs. And the scribe's story was this:

> Between Syêné . . . and Elephantiné, there are two hills with sharp conical tops; the name of the one is Crophi, of the other, Mophi. Midway between them are the fountains of the Nile, *fountains which it is impossible to fathom*. . . . The fountains were known to be unfathomable, he declared, because Psammetichus . . . had made trial of them. He had caused a rope to be made, many thousand fathoms in length, and had sounded the fountain with it, *but could find no bottom*.*

"Caverns measureless to man" had been for twenty-three centuries associated with the legend of the Nile. It is little wonder, page 391 / given what we now know about "the sacred river," that they turned up in the dream.

The image of the sacred river, then, which rose up before Coleridge as a *thing*, was a dream-picture, foreshortened and

* Herodotus learned also that "the river wind[s] greatly, like the Mæander."

reversed as if it lay in an enchanted crystal, of the tremendous Odyssey of the legendary Nile. Visualized under the spell of Bartram's springing fountains, the river in the vision bursts from immeasurable depths, traverses mazily, its cosmic sweep diminished to a *coup d'œil*, five miles of wood and dale — then sinks in tumult to immeasurable depths again. "From the great deep to the great deep it goes" — to the "lifeless ocean" and the "sunless sea" beneath the upper lands and waters of the world.

And I suspect that with the imagery of these nether seas of ancient story there was merged a conception vaster still, which had long been hovering in Coleridge's restless head. Between the two memoranda in the Note Book in which he dallied with the project of turning the *Telluris Theoria Sacra* into verse, stand, as we have seen, certain entries which show beyond question that he had read, with kindled imagination, the whole of Burnet's "grand Miltonic romance." Now Burnet's daring cosmogony is built about the central waters and the central fires. Beneath the hollow shell of the earth lay, from the beginning, the waters of the great abyss. At the deluge the fountains of the deep were broken up, and the shattered frame of the earth sank beneath the rush of the ascending floods. Subterranean rivers still pursue their way "through the dark pipes of the earth," and beneath us still are gathered up, in subterranean lakes and seas, the cataracts of the abyss. And at the end, when the earth shall melt with fervent heat, the waters that are under the earth, pent up and turned to steam, will lend their shattering aid again, to bring about the last catastrophe. Had Coleridge ever carried out his chimerical scheme of versifying Burnet's gorgeous prose, a Hymn to Water of epic grandeur would have made his own superfluous. But while the project was stirring in his brain, the Deluge and the Conflagration were storing the cells of memory with images. And Burnet's titanic conception of a dark, illimitable ocean, lurking beneath the unmeasured gulfs and chasms of the world, was present **page 392 /** (I think we may safely assume) somewhere in the background of the dream.

XI

There was another storied river which sank beneath the earth, and flowed under sea, and rose again in a famous fountain. As was inevitable, it was constantly associated with the legendary Nile. And Coleridge, like every schoolboy, knew it:

> . . . *Alpheum* fama est huc Elidis amnem
> occultas egisse vias subter mare; qui nunc
> ore, Arethusa, tuo Siculis confunditur undis.

But his sources of information were by no means limited to Virgil.

Burnet has a delightful note about Alpheus, but for us the ancients are more to the point. No one who has followed Coleridge's reading will doubt, I think, his acquaintance with Pausanias. Were there no other reason, Thomas Taylor had translated *The Description of Greece* in 1794, professing to "have unfolded," in his highly neo-Platonic notes, "a theory which seems for many ages to have been entirely unknown." And "Taylor the English pagan" was among Coleridge's "darling studies." Here, then, are two excerpts from Taylor's translation of Pausanias:

> But the Alpheus appears to possess something different from other rivers; for it often hides itself in the earth, and again rises out of it. Thus it . . . merges itself in the Tegeatic land. Ascending from hence in Asæa, and mingling itself with the water of Eurotas, it falls a second time into the earth, emerges from hence, in that place which the Arcadians call the fountains, and running through the Pisæan and Olympian plains, pours itself into the sea. . . . Nor can the agitation of the Adriatic sea restrain its course; for running through this mighty and violent sea, it mingles itself with the water of Arethusa in Ortygia . . . retaining its ancient name Alpheus.

> From the water of Alpheus, therefore, mingling itself with that of Arethusa, I am persuaded the fable respecting the love of *Alpheus* originated. Such indeed of the Greeks or Ægyptians as have travelled to Æthiopia . . . relate that *the Nile* entering into a certain marsh, and gliding through this no otherwise than if it was page 393 / a continent, flows afterward through lower Æthiopia into Egypt, till it arrives at Pharos and the sea which it contains.

The Nile and the Alpheus, then, are immediately associated in Pausanias.

How early Coleridge knew Strabo I do not know. There is every reason to believe that the youngster who translated Synesius at the age of fifteen, and who expounded Plotinus and recited Homer and Pindar in their Greek at Christ's Hospital, had read the *Geography* during his school days. He certainly was much at home in it later for he quotes from the Greek text in a notebook of 1806–07, and again in *Omniana*, in both of which he recognizes Strabo's hand in a noble sentence of Ben Johnson's dedication to *The Fox.* At all events, here are a few remarks of Strabo, who discusses the Alpheus at great length:

> People tell the mythical story that the river Arethusa is the Alpheius, which latter, they say, rises in the Peloponnesus, flows underground through the sea as far as Arethusa, and then empties thence once more into the sea. . . . Marvellous tales of this sort are stretched still further by those who make the Inopus cross over from *the Nile* to Delos. And Zoïlus the rhetorician says . . . that *the Alpheius* rises in Tenedos.

Again, in a context of ebullient fountains and subterranean rivers disappearing in a chasm, Strabo continues:

> The territory of the Palici has craters that spout up water in a dome-like jet and receive it back again into the same recess. The cavern near Mataurus contains an immense gallery through which a river flows invisible for a considerable distance, and then emerges to the surface, as is the case with the Orontes in Syria, which sinks into the chasm [Χάσμα] . . . and rises again forty stadia away.
>
> Similar, too, are the cases both of the Tigris in Mesopotamia and of *the Nile* in Libya . . . and again, the water near the Arcadian Asea is first forced below the surface and then, much later, emerges as both the Eurotas and *the Alpheius.*

Once more, the Nile and the Alpheus are linked together as kindred streams.

That Coleridge, with his tastes, and classical training, and cormorant habits, had read Seneca's *Quæstiones Naturales* before 1798, is a reasonable assumption. It must not be forgotten that he wrote Thelwall in 1796: "I have read almost everything" **page 394 /** —a statement which few who know their Coleridge seriously doubt! His later knowledge of Seneca has ample attestation. And Seneca, whose *Quæstiones Naturales* are a veritable mine of lore about the elements, has in that remarkable treatise matter of no small interest touching the Alpheus. In the twenty-sixth chapter of Book Three—a chapter which begins with mention of the Nile—Seneca quotes a passage from Ovid's *Metamorphoses* about Lycus, swallowed up by the yawning earth, and then proceeds:

> In the East as well as the West this happens. The Tigris is absorbed by the earth and after long absence reappears at a point far

> removed, but undoubtedly the same river. . . . Thence [from the behavior of the fountain Arethusa] comes the belief that the Alpheus makes its way right from Achaia to Sicily, stealing under sea by secret sluice, and reappearing only when it reaches the coast of Syracuse.

But the most significant passage is in the Sixth Book:

> I do not, indeed, suppose that you will long hesitate to believe that there are underground rivers and *a hidden sea.* From what other cause could the rivers burst out and come to the surface? . . . And what are you to say when you see *the Alpheus* . . . sink in Achaia and, having crossed beneath the sea, pour forth in Sicily the pleasant fountain Arethuse? And don't you know that among the explanations given of the occurrence of the inundation of *the Nile* in summer, one is that it bursts forth from the ground?

Whereupon follows the story which Seneca heard himself from the lips of two non-commissioned officers sent by Nero to investigate the sources of the Nile.

But that is not all. For the preceding chapter contains a vivid picture of the "lifeless ocean" and the "sunless sea" out of which such rivers as the Nile and the Alpheus rise, and to which they return:

> Now surely a man trusts too much to the sight of the eyes and cannot launch out his imagination beyond, if he does not believe that *the depths of earth contain a vast sea* with winding shores. I see nothing to prevent or oppose the existence of a beach down there *in the obscurity*, or a sea finding its way through the hidden entrances to its appointed place. There, too, . . . the hidden regions being desert *without inhabitant* give freer scope to the waves of the nether ocean. page 395 /

Moreover, that Bernardinus Ramazzinus from whom Burnet quotes *in extenso* the Abyssinian account of the deluge, links the Nile and the Alpheus on the same page. And finally, in the *Argonauticon* of Valerius Flaccus, the two rivers share a single line:

> Ceu refluens Padus aut septem proiectus in amnes
> *Nilus* et Hesperium veniens *Alpheos* in orbem.

The traditional links between the Nile and the Alpheus are like hoops of steel.

Now some, if not all, of these passages Coleridge without doubt had read. And just as ocular spectra which "flashed" from Bartram's fountains and from the fountains of the Nile had telescoped in the dream, so there seem to have emerged linked reminiscences of the Alpheus and the Nile. And by one of those puckish freaks of the dream intelligence which are often so preternaturally apt, "Alpheus" has been docked of its syllabic excess, and dream-fashioned, as "Alph," into a quasi-equivalence with "Nile." The *artifex verborum of* the dream — witness "Xanadu" and "Abora" — was no less adept than the waking Coleridge in the metamorphisis of words. And none of us who has ever dreamed can doubt how exquisitively right and meet and natural "Alph" must in the dream have seemed — a name which sprang like a fountain from the inmost nature of the thing, rising up, like the dream-music, a "mingled measure" from the Alpheus and the Nile.

XII

The last sentence Coleridge had read before his eyes rested on the words "In Xamdu did Cublai Can build a stately Palace," was a remarkable expression of the belief among the Tartars of the survival of the dead. And he had turned the page but once since he had read another statement of that belief more striking still:
page 396 /

> When he is dead, if he be a chiefe man, hee is buried in the field where pleaseth him. And hee is buried with his Tent, sitting in the middest thereof, with a Table set before him, and a platter full of meate, and a Cup of Mares-milke. There is also buried with him a Mare and Colt, a Horse with bridle and saddle: and they eate another Horse . . . stuffing his hide with straw, setting it aloft on two or four poles, that hee may have in the other world a Tabernacle and other things fitting for his use.

And between the two passages, within less than a page of the words that slipped bodily into the dream, stands this:

> Their Priests were diviners: they were many, but had one Captaine or chiefe Bishop, who always placed his house or Tent before that of the Great Can, about a stones cast distant . . . When an Eclipse happens they sound their Organs and Timbrels, and make a great noyse. . . . They foretell holy dayes, and those which are

> unluckie for enterprises. *No warres are begunne or made without their word.*

Of this at least, then, we are sure: when Coleridge fell asleep, the last impressions which he received included images of dead warriors surviving in the other world, in their habit as they lived; of things foretold, heard through "a great noyse"; and of wars undertaken only at the diviners' word. And among the images which rose up before him in the dream was this:

> And *'mid this tumult* Kubla heard from far
> *Ancestral voices prophesying war!*

Between the sinking into Coleridge's mind of that confluence of suggestions and the rising of the magnificently phrased conception of the dream lay, it would seem, a period measured by minutes. And meantime hosts of other images had been thronging up.

For I suspect that we are once more in the presence of a cluster-point of the "hooked atoms." Recollections of Bruce, as we know, were actively astir. Now by far the most vivid personality in Bruce's narrative, except Bruce himself, is Ozoro Esther, the young wife of the old vizier of that king of Abyssinia whose floating hair, on the expedition against the rebels, got him into Absalom's predicament. And in his account of this expedition, Bruce gives a dramatic rehearsal of a talk he had with Ozoro Esther: page 397 /

> "But, pray" [says Bruce], "what is the meaning of the Ras's speech to me about both armies wishing to fight at Serbraxos? Where is this Serbraxos?" — "Why, says she, here, on a hill just by; *the Begemder people have a prophecy, that one of their governors is to fight a king at Serbraxos,* to defeat him, and slay him there: in his place is to succeed another king, whose name is Theodorus, and in whose reign all Abyssinia is to be free from war . . . and the empire of Abyssinia to be extended as far as Jerusalem." — "All this destruction and conquest without war! That will be curious indeed. I think I could wish to see this Theodorus," said I, laughing — "See him you will, replied Ozoro Esther; peace, happiness, and plenty will last all his reign, and a thousand years afterwards. Enoch and Elias will rise again, and will fight and destroy Gog and Magog, and all this without any war." "On which I again said . . . And now, why does Ras Michael choose to fight at Serbraxos?" . . . "Why, says she, *all the hermits and holy*

> *men on our side, that can prophesy, have assured him he is to beat the rebels this month at Serraxos;* and a very holy man, a hermit from Waldubba, came to him at Gondar, and obliged him to march out against his will, *by telling him his prophecy, which he knows to be true,* as the man is not like common prophets. . . . Such a man as this, you know, Yagoube, cannot lie."

Like the incident of the floating hair, that is told in a fashion which stamps it on the memory, and which may quite possibly have brought about another fusion of Tartary and Abyssinia in the dream. Both passages, at all events, had certainly slipped, with their fleeting impressions, below the threshold of Coleridge's consciousness, and of such buried treasure is the stuff of dreams.

I wish I could say, with the complete assurance which is based on evidence, that Coleridge had read *Vathek.* As it is, I have neither doubt nor proof. Henley's translation, which preceded the French original by a year, had been twelve years in circulation — since Coleridge, that is, was a school-boy of fourteen. If he did read it, he could no more than the rest of us forget it. And its earlier pages are conceived in the very spirit of the dream. There were the Palaces of the Five Senses — "pleasure-houses" *par excellence;* there was a Paradise, with cedars and incense-bearing trees; there were four fountains, like the "four sacred rivers" which watered Eden; and at the foot of the hill of the Four Fountains there was "an immense gulph" or "chasm." **page 398 /** And as Vathek, after the Giaour had disappeared in the abyss, looked over the edge,

> One while, he fancied to himself *voices arising from the depth of the gulph:* at another, he seemed to distinguish the accents of the Indian; but, all was no more than *the hollow murmur of waters, and the din of the cataracts that rushed from steep to steep,* down the sides of the mountain.

The tumult, as in the dream, is the tumult of the waters, and it rises with the voices, as in the dream, from the abyss. That a reminiscence of it flashed through the interweaving fancies of the vision is well within the bounds of possibility.

XIII

One other detail, this time a phrase, slipped into the dream from the limbo of sleeping *words,* at the touch of a determinate association. Coleridge had planned an edition of Collins and Gray, which twice appears among his projects in the Note Book. There need be, then, no question of his familiarity with Collins' exquisite though slender sheaf of verse, even had we not his outburst of ardent admiration in a letter to Thelwall of December, 1796:

> Collins's "Ode on the Poetical Character,"—that part of it, I should say, beginning with "The band (as faery legends say) Was wove on that creating day,"—has inspired and whirled *me* along with greater agitations of enthusiasm than any the most *impassioned* scene in Schiller or Shakespeare.

Now in "The Passions" occur these charming lines on Melancholy, who,

> In notes by distance made more sweet.
> Pour'd thro' the mellow horn her pensive soul:
> And, dashing soft from rocks around
> Bubbling runnels join'd the sound;
> Thro' glades and glooms *the mingled measure* stole;
> Or o'er some *haunted* stream, with fond delay
> Round an *holy* calm diffusing,
> Love of peace and lonely musing,
> In hollow murmurs died away.

And in the dream, just after the tumult of the river's fall, **page 399 /**

> . . . was heard *the mingled measure*
> From the fountain and the caves.

The ceaseless tumult of the sacred river recalled the mellower tumult of the bubbling runnels dashing soft from rocks around, as Coleridge's "Through wood and dale," but eight lines earlier, had echoed Collins's "Thro' glades and glooms." And "haunted" and "holy," still in successive lines, had already stolen into the measures of the dream:

> A savage place! as *holy* and enchanted
> As e'er beneath a waning moon was *haunted* . . .

"Kubla Khan" is the fabric of a vision, but every image that rose up in its weaving had passed that way before. And it would seem that there is nothing haphazard or fortuitous in their return.

XIV

There are other elements of the dream which refuse to divulge their secrets, and which "sweetly torment us" (as Emerson, quoted by William James, felicitously puts it) "with invitations to their inaccessible homes." How could it possibly be otherwise? About some of these teasing phantoms of association I confess, of course, to cherishing more or less colourable conjectures. But if this chapter possess any worth, that value lies, not in its conjectures, but in its evidence — the evidence which it offers of the amazing power of association in the dream. Beyond that evidence, which can at least be weighed and tested, I do not for the present care to go.* page 400 /

But I do wish, before leaving this huge phantasmagoria, to direct attention to an implication of material importance. I have emphasized, throughout the discussion of "The Ancient Mariner," the profoundly significant part played in imaginative creation by the associations of ideas — whether those associations wrought their synthesis before the impressions so combined sank into the subliminal reservoir, or during their submergence there, or at the instant of their flashing back to consciousness. And I have offered no little evidence of their activity. But in "The Ancient Mariner" a determining will was constructively at work, consciously manipulating and adjusting and refashioning the associated images of memory into conformity with a design. And

* I wish to state with emphasis that I am dealing in this study with what psychoanalysts call the material content of the dream, and with that alone. With its so-called latent content — its possible symbolism of wish-fulfillment or conflict or what not — I have nothing whatever to do. Even granting one or another of the conflicting assumptions of modern dream psychology, I do not believe that after the lapse of one hundred and twenty-seven years the intimate, deep-lying, personal facts on which alone such an analysis must rest are longer discoverable, and I doubt whether any trained psychoanalyst would venture an interpretation. "I believe," wrote one of the most brilliant and withal most sane of recent investigators in this field, the late Dr. W. H. R. Rivers, "I believe that a really satisfactory analysis of a dream is only possible to the dreamer himself or to one who knows the conflicts and experiences of the dreamer in a most unusual way" (*Conflict and Dream*, p. 149). An essay at such an analysis of "Kubla Khan," regarded as a dream, has just been made, however, by Mr. Robert Graves. . . . Incidentally, it may be worth while to suggest, without prejudice, that the facts which this investigation has disclosed, with reference to both "The Ancient Mariner" and "Kubla Khan," counsel caution in the prevalent pursuit of so-called Freudian complexes in everything.

through that conscious imaginative moulding the links of association, as was inevitable, were often obliterated, or at least obscured. Yet sufficient traces of them still remain, as our scrutiny of Coleridge's reading soon disclosed, to establish their enormous influence. Do the facts before us contribute any further light?

I think they do. For in "Kubla Khan" the complicating factor — will as a consciously constructive agency — was in abeyance. "All the images rose up before him as *things*, with a parallel production of the correspondent expressions, without any sensation or consciousness of effort." The dream, it is evident, was the unchecked subliminal flow of blending images, and the dreamer merely the detached and unsolicitous spectator. And so the sole factor that determined the form and sequence which the dissolving phantasmagoria assumed, was the subtle potency of the associative links. There was this time no intervention of a waking intelligence intent upon a plan, to obliterate or blur them. And it is largely that absence of deliberate manipulation which has made it possible to disengage, to a degree unattainable in our study of "The Ancient Mariner," the bewildering hooks-and-eyes of the memory which were the irresponsible artificers of the dream.

But the facts thus established carry with them, as I have said, an important consequence. For we have only to recall those passages in "The Ancient Mariner" in which the formative associations have been traceable, to recognize that their operations are essentially the same. The mass of evidence now before page 401 / us corroborates with singular cogency our earlier conclusions. The subliminal blendings and fusings from which springs the insubstantial architecture of the dream are also latent beneath the complex workings of design. And that is no less essential to our understanding of the creative process than the further fact that in the one case the "streamy" associations are unruddered, whereas in the other they are masterfully curbed.

The linked images, then, which are now before us are, with little question, constituent elements of the dream. But the dream itself is another matter. And it is high time that we pass from the crowded vestibule of consciousness to the winged wonder which emerged into the light. page 402 /

The Frontiers of Criticism

T. S. ELIOT

A good deal of contemporary criticism, originating at that point at which criticism merges into scholarship, and at which scholarship merges into criticism, may be characterized as the criticism of explanation by origins. To make clear what I mean I shall mention two books which have had, in this connection, a rather bad influence. I do not mean that they are bad books. On the contrary: they are both books with which everyone should be acquainted. The first is John Livingston Lowes's *The Road to Xanadu*—a book which I recommend to every student of poetry who has not yet read it. The other is James Joyce's *Finnegans Wake*—a book which I recommend every student of poetry to read—at least some pages of. Livingston Lowes was a fine scholar, a good teacher, a lovable man and a man to whom I for one have private reasons to feel very grateful. James Joyce was a man of genius, a personal friend, and my citation here of *Finnegans Wake* is neither in praise or dispraise of a book which is certainly in the category of works that can be called *monumental*. But the only obvious common characteristic of *The Road to Xanadu* and *Finnegans Wake* is that we may say of each: one book like this is enough.

For those who have never read *The Road to Xanadu*, I will explain that it is a fascinating piece of detection. Lowes ferreted out all the books which Coleridge had read (and Coleridge was

Reprinted from *On Poetry and Poets* by T. S. Eliot, by permission of Farrar, Straus & Cudahy, Inc., and of Faber and Faber Ltd.

an omnivorous and insatiable reader) and from which he had borrowed images or phrases to be found in *Kubla Khan* and *The* page 8 / *Ancient Mariner.* The books that Coleridge read were many of them obscure and forgotten books — he read, for instance, every book of travels upon which he could lay his hands. And Lowes showed, once and for all, that poetic originality is largely an original way of assembling the most disparate and unlikely materials to make a new whole. The demonstration is quite convincing, as evidence of how material is digested and transformed by the poetic genius. No one, after reading this book, could suppose that he understood *The Ancient Mariner* any better; nor was it in the least Dr. Lowes's intention to make the poem more intelligible as poetry. He was engaged on an investigation of process, an investigation which was, strictly speaking, beyond the frontier of literary criticism. How such material as those scraps of Coleridge's reading became transmuted into great poetry remains as much of a mystery as ever. Yet a number of hopeful scholars have seized upon the Lowes method as offering a clue to the understanding of any poem by any poet who gives evidence of having read anything. "I wonder," a gentleman from Indiana wrote to me a year or more ago, "I wonder — it is possible that I am mad, of course" (this was his interjection, not mine; of course he was not in the least mad, merely slightly touched in one corner of his head from having read *The Road to Xanadu*) "whether 'the dead cats of civilisation,' 'rotten hippo' and Mr. Kurtz have some tenuous connection with 'that corpse you planted last year in your garden'?" This sounds like raving, unless you recognize the allusions: it is merely an earnest seeker trying to establish some connection between *The Waste Land* and Joseph Conrad's *Heart of Darkness.*

Now while Dr. Lowes has fired such practitioners of hermeneutics with emulative zeal, *Finnegans Wake* has provided them with a model of what they would like all literary works to be. I must hasten to explain that I am not deriding or denigrating the labors of those exegetists who have set themselves to unravel all the threads and follow all the clues in that book. If *Finnegans Wake* is to be understood at all — and we cannot judge it without such labor — that kind of detection must be pursued; and Messrs. Campbell and Robinson (to mention the authors of one such page 9 / piece of work) have done an admirable job. My grievance if any is against James Joyce, the author of that monstrous masterpiece, for writing a book such that large stretches of it are, without elaborate explanation, merely beautiful nonsense (very beautiful indeed when recited by an Irish voice as lovely as that of the author — would that he had recorded more of it!). Perhaps Joyce did not realize how obscure his book is. Whatever the final judgment (and I am not going to attempt a judgment) of the place of *Finnegans Wake* may be, I do not think that most poetry (for it is a kind of vast prose poem) is written in that way or requires that sort of dissection for its enjoyment and understanding. But I suspect that the enigmas provided by *Finnegans Wake* have given support to the error, prevalent nowadays, of mistaking explanation for understanding. After the production of my play *The Cocktail Party*, my mail was swollen for months with letters offering surprising solutions of what the writers believed to be the riddle of the play's meaning. And it was evident that the writers did not resent the puzzle they thought I had set them — they liked it. Indeed, though they were unconscious of the fact, they invented the puzzle for the pleasure of discovering the solution.

Here I must admit that I am, on one conspicuous occasion, not guiltless of having led critics into temptation. The notes to *The Waste Land!* I had at first intended only to put down all the references for my quotations, with a view to spiking the guns of critics of my earlier poems who had accused me of plagiarism. Then, when it came to print *The Waste Land* as a little book — for the poem on its first appearance in *The Dial* and in *The Criterion* had no notes whatever — it was discovered that the poem was inconveniently short, so I set to work to expand the notes, in order to provide a few more pages of printed matter, with the result that they became the remarkable exposition of bogus scholarship that is still on view today. I have sometimes thought of getting rid of these notes; but now they can never be unstuck. They have had almost greater popularity than the poem itself — anyone who bought my book of poems, and found that the notes to *The Waste Land* were not in it, would demand his money back. But I don't think page 10 / that these notes did any harm to other poets: certainly I cannot think of any good contemporary poet who has abused this same practice. (As for Miss Marianne Moore, *her* notes to poems are always pertinent, curious, conclusive, delightful and give no encouragement whatever to the researcher of origins.) No, it is not because of my bad example to other poets that I am penitent: it is because my notes stimulated the wrong kind of interest among the seekers of sources. It was just, no doubt, that I should pay my tribute to the work of Miss Jessie Weston; but I regret having sent so many enquirers off on a wild goose chase after Tarot cards and the Holy Grail.

While I was pondering this question of the attempt to understand a poem by explaining its origins, I came across a quotation from C. G. Jung which stuck me as having some relevance. The passage was quoted by Fr. Victor White, O.P., in his book *God and the Unconscious.* Fr. White quotes it in the course of exposing a radical difference between the methods of Freud and Jung.

> It is a generally recognized truth (says Jung) that physical events can be looked at in two ways, that is from the mechanistic and from the energic standpoint. The mechanistic view is purely causal: from this standpoint an event is conceived as the result of a cause. . . . The energic viewpoint on the other hand is in essence final; the event is traced from effect to cause on the assumption that energy forms the essential basis of changes in phenomena . . .

The quotation is from the first essay in the volume *Contributions to Analytical Psychology.* I add another sentence, not quoted by Fr. White, which opens the next paragraph: "Both viewpoints are indispensable for the comprehension of physical phenomena."

I take this simply as a suggestive analogy. One can explain a poem by investigating what it is made of and the causes that brought it about; and explanation may be a necessary preparation for understanding. But to understand a poem it is also necessary, and I should say in most instances still more necessary, that we should endeavor to grasp what the poetry is aiming to be; one might say — though it is long since I have employed such terms with any assurance — endeavoring to grasp its entelechy. page 11 /

Perhaps the form of criticism in which the danger of excessive reliance upon causal explanation is greatest is the critical biography, especially when the biographer supplements his knowledge of external facts with psychological conjectures about inner experience. I do not suggest that the personality and the private life of a dead poet constitute sacred ground on which the psychologist must not tread. The scientist must be at liberty to study such material as his curiosity leads him to investigate — so long as the victim is dead and the laws of libel cannot be invoked to stop him. Nor is there any reason why biographies of poets should not be written. Furthermore, the biographer of an author should possess some critical ability; he should be a man of taste and judgment, appreciative of the work of the man whose biography he undertakes. And on the other hand any critic seriously concerned with a man's work should be expected to know something about the man's life. But a critical biography of a writer is a delicate task in itself; and the critic or the biographer who, without being a trained and practicing psychologist, brings to bear on his subject such analytical skill as he has acquired by reading books written by psychologists, may confuse the issues still further.

The question of how far information about the poet helps us to understand the poetry is not so simple as one might think. Each reader must answer it for himself, and must answer it not generally but in particular instances, for it may be more important in the case of one poet and less important in the case of another. For the enjoyment of poetry can be a complex experience in which several forms of satisfaction are mingled; and they may be mingled in different proportions for different readers. I will give an illustration. It is generally agreed that the greatest part of Wordsworth's best poetry was written within a brief span of years — brief in itself, and brief in proportion to the whole span of Wordsworth's life. Various students of Wordsworth have propounded explanations to account for the mediocrity of his later output. Some years ago, Sir Herbert Read wrote a book on Wordsworth — an interesting book, though I think that his best appreciation of page 12 / Wordsworth is found in a later essay in a volume entitled *A Coat of Many Colours* — in which he explained the rise and fall of Wordsworth's genius by the effects upon him of his affair with Annette Vallon, about which information had at that time come to light. More recently still, a Mr. Bateson has written a book about Wordsworth which is also of considerable interest (his chapter on "The Two Voices" does help to understand Wordsworth's style). In this book he maintains that Annette doesn't figure nearly so importantly as Sir Herbert Read had thought, and that the real secret was that Wordsworth fell in love with his sister Dorothy; that this explains, in particular, the Lucy poems, and explains why, after Wordsworth's marriage, his inspiration dried up. Well, he may be right: his argument is very plausible. But the real question, which every reader of Wordsworth must answer for himself, is: does it matter? does this account help me to understand the Lucy poems any better than I did before? For myself, I can only say that a knowledge of the springs which released a poem is not necessarily a help toward understanding the poem: too much information about the origins of the poem may even break my contact with it. I feel no need for any light upon the Lucy poems beyond the radiance shed by the poems themselves.

I am not maintaining that there is *no* context in which such information or conjecture as that of Sir Herbert Read and Mr. Bateson may be relevant. It is relevant if we want to understand Wordsworth; but it is not directly relevant to our understanding of his poetry. Or rather, it is not relevant to our understanding *of the poetry as poetry*. I am prepared to suggest that there is, in all great poetry, something which must remain unaccountable however complete might be our knowledge of the poet, and that is what matters most. When the poem has been made, something new has happened, something that cannot be wholly explained by *anything that went before*.

The explanation of poetry by examination of its sources is not the method of all contemporary criticism by any means; but it is a method which responds to the desire of a good many readers that poetry should be explained to them in terms of something else: page 13 / the chief part of the letters I receive from persons unknown to me, concerning my own poems, consists of requests for a kind of explanation that I cannot possibly give. There are other tendencies such as that represented by Professor Richards' investigation of the problem of how the appreciation of poetry can be taught, or by the verbal subtleties of his distinguished pupil, Professor Empson. And I have recently noticed a development, which I suspect has its origin in the classroom methods of Professor Richards, which is, in its way, a healthy reaction against the diversion of attention from the poetry to the poet. It is found in a book published not long ago, entitled *Interpretations:* a series of essays by twelve of the younger English critics, each analyzing one poem of his own choice. The method is to take a well-known poem — each of the poems analyzed in this book is a good one of its kind — without reference to the author or to his other work, analyze it stanza by stanza and line by line, and extract, squeeze, tease, press every drop of meaning out of it that one can. It might be called the lemon-squeezer school of criticism. As the poems range from the sixteenth century to the present day, as they differ a good deal from one another — the book begins with "The Phoenix and the Turtle" and ends with "Prufrock" and Yeats's "Among School Children," and as each critic has his own procedure, the result is interesting and a little confusing — and, it must be admitted, to study twelve poems each analyzed so painstakingly is a very tiring way of passing the time. I imagine that some of the poets (they are all dead except myself) would be surprised at learning what their poems mean: I had one or two minor surprises myself, as on learning that the fog, mentioned early in "Prufrock," had somehow got into the drawing room. But the analysis of "Prufrock" was not an attempt to find origins, either in literature or in the darker recesses of my private life; it was an attempt to find out what the poem really meant — whether that was what I had meant it to mean or not. And for that I was grateful. There were several essays which struck me as good. But as every method has its own limitations and dangers, it is only reasonable to mention what seem to me the limitations and dangers of this one, dangers which, if page 14 / it were practiced for what I suspect should be its chief use, that is, as an exercise for pupils, it would be the business of the teacher to warn his class against.

The first danger is that of assuming that there must be just one interpretation of the poem as a whole, that must be right. There will be details of explanation, especially with poems written in another age than our own, matters of fact, historical allusions, the meaning of a certain word at a certain date, which can be established, and the teacher can see that his pupils get these right. But as for the meaning of the poem as a whole, it is not exhausted by any explanation, for the meaning is what the poem means to different sensitive readers. The second danger — a danger into which I do not think any of the critics in the volume I have mentioned has fallen, but a danger to which the reader is exposed — is that of assuming that the interpretation of a poem, if valid, is necessarily an account of what the author consciously or unconsciously was trying to do. For the tendency is so general, to believe that we understand a poem when we have identified its origins and traced the process to which the poet submitted his materials, that we may easily believe the converse — that any explanation of the poem is also an account of how it was written. The analysis of "Prufrock" to which I have referred interested *me* because it helped *me* to see the poem through the eyes of an intelligent, sensitive and diligent reader. That is not at all to say that *he* saw the poem through my eyes, or that his account has anything to do with the experiences that led up to my writing it, or to anything I experienced in the process of writing it. And my third comment is, that I should, as a test, like to see the method applied to some new poem, some very good poem, and one that was previously unknown to me: because I should like to find out whether, after perusing the analysis, I should ever be able to enjoy the poem. For nearly all the poems in the volume were poems that I had known and loved for many years; and after reading the analyses, I found I was slow to recover my feeling about the poems. It was as if someone had taken a machine to pieces and left me with the task of reassembling the parts. I suspect, in fact, that a good deal page 15 / of the value of an interpretation is — that it should be my own interpretation. There are many things, perhaps, to know about this poem, or that, many facts about which scholars can instruct me which will help me to avoid definite *mis*understanding; but a valid interpretation, I believe, must be at the same time an interpretation of my own feelings when I read it.

It has been no part of my purpose to give a comprehensive view of all the types of literary criticism practiced in our time. I wished first to call attention to the transformation of literary criticism which we may say began with Coleridge but which has proceeded with greater acceleration during the last twenty-five years. This acceleration I took to be prompted by the relevance of the social sciences to criticism, and by the teaching of literature (including *contemporary* literature) in colleges and universities. I do not deplore this transformation, for it seems to me to have been inevitable. In an age of uncertainty, an age in which men are bewildered by new sciences, an age in which so little can be taken for granted as common beliefs, assumptions and background of all readers, no explorable area can be forbidden ground. But, among all this variety, we may ask, what is there, if anything, that should be common to all literary criticism? Thirty years ago, I asserted that the essential function of literary criticism was "the elucidation of works of art and the correction of taste." That phrase may sound somewhat pompous to our ears in 1956. Perhaps I could put it more simply, and more acceptably to the present age, by saying to "promote the understanding and enjoyment of literature." I would add that there is implied here also the negative task of pointing out what should *not* be enjoyed. For the critic may on occasion be called upon to condemn the second-rate and expose the fraudulent: though that duty is secondary to the duty of discriminating praise of what is praiseworthy. And I must stress the point that I do not think of *enjoyment* and *understanding* as distinct activities — one emotional and the other intellectual. By *understanding* I do not mean *explanation* though explanation of what can be explained may often be a necessary preliminary to understanding. To offer a very simple instance: to learn the unfamiliar words, and the un- page 16 / familiar forms of words, is a necessary preliminary to the understanding of Chaucer; it is explanation: but one could master the vocabulary, spelling, grammar and syntax of Chaucer — indeed, to carry the instance a stage further, one could be very well informed about the age of Chaucer, its social habits, its beliefs, its learning and its ignorance — and yet not *understand the poetry*. To understand a poem comes to the same thing as to enjoy it for the right reasons. One might say that it means getting from the poem such enjoyment as it is capable of giving: to enjoy a poem under a misunderstanding as to what it is, is to enjoy what is merely a projection of our own mind. So difficult a tool to handle, is language, that "to enjoy" and "to get enjoyment from" do not seem to mean quite the same thing: that to say that one "gets enjoyment from" poetry does not sound quite the same as to say that one "enjoys poetry." And indeed, the very meaning of *joy* varies with the object inspiring joy; different poems, even, yield different satisfactions. It is certain that we do not fully enjoy a poem unless we understand it; and on the other hand, it is equally true that we do not fully understand a poem unless we enjoy it. And that means, enjoying it to the right degree and in the right way, relative to other poems (it is in the relation of our enjoyment of a poem to our enjoyment of other poems that *taste* is shown). It should hardly be necessary to say that this implies that one *shouldn't* enjoy bad poems — unless their badness is of a sort that appeals to our sense of humor.

I have said that explanation may be a necessary preliminary to understanding. It seems to me, however, that I understand some poetry without explanation, for instance Shakespeare's

> Full fathom five thy father lies

or Shelley's

> Art thou pale for weariness
> Of climbing heaven and gazing on the earth

for here, and in a great deal of poetry, I see nothing to be explained — nothing that is, that would help me to understand it better and therefore enjoy it more. And sometimes explanation, page 17 / as I have already hinted, can distract us altogether from *the poem as poetry*, instead of leading us in the direction of understanding. My best reason, perhaps, for believing that I am not deluded in thinking that I understand such poetry as the lyrics by Shakespeare and Shelley which I have just cited, is that these two poems give me as keen a thrill, when I repeat them today as they did fifty years ago.

The difference, then, between the literary critic, and the critic who has passed beyond the frontier of literary criticism, is not that the literary critic is "purely" literary, or that he has no other interests. A critic who was interested in nothing but "literature" would have very little to say to us, for his literature would be a pure abstraction. Poets have other interests beside poetry — otherwise their poetry would be very empty: they are poets because their dominant interest has been in turning their experience and their thought (and to experience and to think means to have interests beyond poetry) — in turning their experience and their thinking into poetry. The critic accordingly is a *literary* critic if this primary interest, in writing criticism, is to help his readers to *understand and enjoy*. But he must have other interests, just as much as the poet himself; for the literary critic is not merely a technical expert, who has learned the rules to be observed by the writers he criticizes: the critic must be the whole man, a man with convictions and principles, and of knowledge and experience of life.

We can therefore ask, about any writing which is offered to us as literary criticism, is it aimed toward understanding and enjoyment? If it is not, it may still be a legitimate and useful activity; but it is to be judged as a contribution to psychology, or sociology, or logic, or pedagogy, or some other pursuit — and is to be judged by specialists, not by men of letters. We must not identify biography with criticism: biography is ordinarily useful in providing explanation which may open the way to further understanding; but it may also, in directing our attention on the poet, lead us away from the poetry. We must not confuse knowledge — factual information — about a poet's period, the conditions of the society **page 18 /** in which he lived, the ideas current in his time implicit in his writings, the state of the language in his period — with understanding his poetry. Such knowledge, as I have said, may be a necessary preparation for understanding the poetry; furthermore, it has a value of its own, as history; but for the appreciation of the poetry, it can only lead us to the door: we must find our own way in. For the purposes of acquiring such knowledge, from the point of view taken throughout this paper, is not primarily that we should be able to project ourselves into a remote period, that we should be able to think and feel, when reading the poetry, as a contemporary of the poet might have thought and felt, though such experience has its own value; it is rather to divest ourselves of the limitations of our own age, and the poet, whose work we are reading, of the limitations of *his* age, in order to get the direct experience, the immediate contact with his poetry. What matters most, let us say, in reading an ode of Sappho, is not that I should imagine myself to be an island Greek of twenty-five hundred years ago; what matters is the experience which is the same, for all human beings capable of enjoying poetry, of different centuries and languages, the spark which can leap across those twenty-five hundred years. So the critic to whom I am most grateful is the one who can make me look at something I have never looked at before, or looked at only with eyes clouded by prejudice, set me face to face with it and then leave me alone with it. From that point, I must rely upon my own sensibility, intelligence, and capacity for wisdom.

If in literary criticism, we place all the emphasis upon *understanding*, we are in danger of slipping from understanding to mere explanation. We are in danger even of pursuing criticism as if it was a science, which it never can be. If, on the other hand, we overemphasize *enjoyment*, we will tend to fall into the subjective and impressionistic, and our enjoyment will profit us no more than mere amusement and pastime. Thirty-three years ago, it seems to have been the latter type of criticism, the impressionistic, that had caused the annoyance I felt when I wrote on "the function of criti- page 19 / cism." Today it seems to me that we need to be more on guard against the purely explanatory. But I do not want to leave you with the impression that I wish to condemn the criticism of our time. These last thirty years have been, I think, a brilliant period in literary criticism in both England and America. It may even come to seem, in retrospect, too brilliant. Who knows? page 20 /

CHAPTER FOUR

A Dubious Explanation by the Maker Himself

EDGAR ALLAN POE

The Raven

The Raven

EDGAR ALLAN POE

Once upon a midnight dreary, while I pondered, weak and weary,
Over many a quaint and curious volume of forgotten lore —
While I nodded, nearly napping, suddenly there came a tapping,
As of some one gently rapping, rapping at my chamber door.
" 'Tis some visitor," I muttered, "tapping at my chamber door —
Only this and nothing more."

Ah, distinctly I remember it was in the bleak December;
And each separate dying ember wrought its ghost upon the floor.
Eagerly I wished the morrow; — vainly I had sought to borrow
From my books surcease of sorrow — sorrow for the lost Le-
nore — 10
For the rare and radiant maiden whom the angels name Lenore —
Nameless *here* for evermore.

And the silken, sad, uncertain rustling of each purple curtain
Thrilled me — filled me with fantastic terrors never felt before;
So that now, to still the beating of my heart, I stood repeating,
" 'Tis some visitor entreating entrance at my chamber door —
Some late visitor entreating entrance at my chamber door; —
This it is and nothing more."

Presently my soul grew stronger; hesitating then no longer,
"Sir," said I, "or Madam, truly your forgiveness I implore; 20
But the fact is I was napping, and so gently you came rapping,

And so faintly you came tapping, tapping at my chamber door,
That I scarce was sure I heard you" — here I opened wide the door; —
Darkness there and nothing more.

Deep into that darkness peering, long I stood there wondering, fearing,
Doubting, dreaming dreams no mortal ever dared to dream before;
But the silence was unbroken, and the stillness gave no token,
And the only word there spoken was the whispered word, "Lenore?"
This I whispered, and an echo murmured back the word, "Lenore!"
Merely this and nothing more. 30

Back into the chamber turning, all my soul within me burning,
Soon again I heard a tapping somewhat louder than before.
"Surely," said I, "surely that is something at my window lattice;
Let me see, then, what thereat is, and this mystery explore —
Let my heart be still a moment, and this mystery explore; —
'Tis the wind and nothing more!"

Open here I flung the shutter, when, with many a flirt and flutter,
In there stepped a stately Raven of the saintly days of yore.
Not the least obeisance made he; not a minute stopped or stayed he;
But, with mien of lord or lady, perched above my chamber door — 40
Perched upon a bust of Pallas just above my chamber door —
Perched, and sat, and nothing more.

Then this ebony bird beguiling my sad fancy into smiling,
By the grave and stern decorum of the countenance it wore,
"Though thy crest be shorn and shaven, thou," I said, "art sure no craven,
Ghastly grim and ancient Raven wandering from the Nightly shore —
Tell me what thy lordly name is on the Night's Plutonian shore!"
Quoth the Raven, "Nevermore."

Much I marvelled this ungainly fowl to hear discourse so plainly,
Though its answer little meaning — little relevancy bore; 50
For we cannot help agreeing that no living human being
Ever yet was blessed with seeing bird above his chamber door —
Bird or beast upon the sculptured bust above his chamber door,
With such name as "Nevermore."

But the Raven, sitting lonely on that placid bust, spoke only
That one word, as if his soul in that one word he did outpour.
Nothing farther then he uttered — not a feather then he fluttered —
Till I scarcely more than muttered, "Other friends have flown before —
On the morrow *he* will leave me, as my Hopes have flown before."
Then the bird said, "Nevermore." 60

Startled at the stillness broken by reply so aptly spoken,
"Doubtless," said I, "what it utters is its only stock and store
Caught from some unhappy master whom unmerciful Disaster
Followed fast and followed faster till his songs one burden bore —
Till the dirges of his Hope that melancholy burden bore
Of 'Never — nevermore.' "

But the Raven still beguiling all my sad fancy into smiling,
Straight I wheeled a cushioned seat in front of bird and bust and door;
Then, upon the velvet sinking, I betook myself to linking
Fancy unto fancy, thinking what this ominous bird of yore — 70
What this grim, ungainly, ghastly, gaunt, and ominous bird of yore
Meant in croaking "Nevermore."

This I sat engaged in guessing, but no syllable expressing
To the fowl whose fiery eyes now burned into my bosom's core;
This and more I sat divining, with my head at ease reclining
On the cushion's velvet lining that the lamp-light gloated o'er,
But whose velvet-violet lining with the lamp-light gloating o'er,
She shall press, ah, nevermore!

Then, methought, the air grew denser, perfumed from an unseen censer

Swung by seraphim whose foot-falls tinkled on the tufted floor. 80
"Wretch," I cried, "thy God hath lent thee — by these angels he
hath sent thee
Respite — respite and nepenthe from thy memories of Lenore;
Quaff, oh, quaff this kind nepenthe and forget this lost Lenore!"
Quoth the Raven, "Nevermore."

"Prophet!" said I, "thing of evil! — prophet still, if bird or
devil! —
Whether Tempter sent, or whether tempest tossed thee here
ashore,
Desolate, yet all undaunted, on this desert land enchanted —
On this home by Horror haunted — tell me truly, I implore —
Is there — *is* there balm in Gilead? — tell me — tell me, I implore!"
Quoth the Raven, "Nevermore." 90

"Prophet!" said I, "thing of evil! — prophet still, if bird or devil!
By that Heaven that bends above us — by that God we both
adore —
Tell this soul with sorrow laden if, within the distant Aidenn,
It shall clasp a sainted maiden whom the angels name Lenore —
Clasp a rare and radiant maiden whom the angels name Lenore."
Quoth the Raven, "Nevermore."

"Be that word our sign of parting, bird or fiend!" I shrieked,
upstarting —
"Get thee back into the tempest and the Night's Plutonian shore!
Leave no black plume as a token of that lie thy soul hath spoken!
Leave my loneliness unbroken! — quit the bust above my door! 100
Take thy beak from out my heart, and take thy form from off my
door!"
Quoth the Raven, "Nevermore."

And the Raven, never flitting, still is sitting, *still* is sitting
On the pallid bust of Pallas just above my chamber door;
And his eyes have all the seeming of a demon's that is dreaming,
And the lamp-light o'er him streaming throws his shadow on the
floor;
And my soul from out that shadow that lies floating on the floor
Shall be lifted — nevermore!

The Philosophy of Composition

EDGAR ALLAN POE

. . . .

Let us dismiss, as irrelevant to the poem, *per se*, the circumstance — or say the necessity — which, in the first place, gave rise to the intention of composing *a* poem that should suit at once the popular and the critical taste.

We commence, then, with this intention.

The initial consideration was that of extent. If any literary work is too long to be read at one sitting, we must be content to dispense with the immensely important effect derivable from unity of impression — for, if two sittings be required, the affairs page 454 / of the world interfere, and every thing like totality is at once destroyed. But since, *ceteris paribus*, no poet can afford to dispense with *any thing* that may advance his design, it but remains to be seen whether there is, in extent, any advantage to counterbalance the loss of unity which attends it. Here I say no, at once. What we term a long poem, is, in fact, merely a succession of brief ones — that is to say, of brief poetical effects. It is needless to demonstrate that a poem is such, only inasmuch as it intensely excites, by elevating, the soul; and all intense excitements are, through a psychal necessity, brief. For this reason, at least one half of the "Paradise Lost" is essentially prose — a succession of poetical excitement interspersed, *inevitably*, with

---

From *Selected Writings of Edgar Allan Poe,* edited by Edward H. Davidson (Boston: Houghton Mifflin Company, 1956).

corresponding depressions — the whole being deprived, through the extremeness of its length, of the vastly important artistic element, totality, or unity, of effect.

It appears evident, then, that there is a distinct limit, as regards length, to all works of literary art — the limit of a single sitting — and that, although in certain classes of prose composition, such as "Robinson Crusoe," (demanding no unity,) this limit may be advantageously overpassed, it can never properly be overpassed in a poem. Within this limit, the extent of a poem may be made to bear mathematical relation to its merit — in other words, to the excitement or elevation — again, in other words, to the degree of the true poetical effect which it is capable of inducing; for it is clear that the brevity must be in direct ratio of the intensity of the intended effect: — this, with one proviso — that a certain degree of duration is absolutely requisite for the production of any effect at all.

Holding in view these considerations, as well as that degree of excitement which I deemed not above the popular, while not below the critical, taste, I reached at once what I conceived the proper *length* for my intended poem — a length of about one hundred lines. It is, in fact, a hundred and eight.

My next thought concerned the choice of an impression, or effect, to be conveyed: and here I may as well observe that, throughout the construction, I kept steadily in view the design of rendering the work *universally* appreciable. I should be carried too far out of my immediate topic were I to demonstrate a point upon which I have repeatedly insisted, and which, with the poetical, stands not in the slightest need of demonstration — the point, I mean, that Beauty is the sole legitimate province of the poem. page 455 / A few words, however, in elucidation of my real meaning, which some of my friends have evinced a disposition to misrepresent. That pleasure which is at once the most intense, the most elevating, and the most pure, is, I believe, found in the contemplation of the beautiful. When, indeed, men speak of Beauty, they mean, precisely, not a quality, as is supposed, but an effect — they refer, in short, just to that intense and pure elevation of *soul* — *not* of intellect, or of heart — upon which I have commented, and which is experienced in consequence of contemplating "the beautiful." Now I designate Beauty as the province of the poem, merely because it is an obvious rule of Art that effects should be made to spring from direct causes — that objects should be attained through means best adapted for their attainment — no one as yet having been weak enough to deny that the peculiar elevation alluded to is *most readily* attained in the poem. Now the object, Truth, or the satisfaction of the intellect, and the object Passion, or the excitement of the heart, are, although attainable, to a certain extent, in poetry, far more readily attainable in prose. Truth, in fact, demands a precision, and Passion a *homeliness* (the truly passionate will comprehend me) which are absolutely antagonistic to that Beauty which, I maintain, is the excitement, or pleasurable elevation, of the soul. It by no means follows from any thing here said, that passion, or even truth, may not be introduced, and even profitably, into a poem — for they may serve in elucidation, or aid the general effect, as do discords in music, by contrast — but the true artist will always contrive, first, to tone them into proper subservience to the predominant aim, and, secondly, to enveil them, as far as possible, in that Beauty which is the atmosphere and the essence of the poem.

Regarding, then, Beauty as my province, my next question referred to the *tone* of its highest manifestation — and all experience has shown that this tone is one of *sadness*. Beauty of whatever kind, in its supreme development, invariably excites the sensitive soul to tears. Melancholy is thus the most legitimate of all the poetical tones.

The length, the province, and the tone, being thus determined, I betook myself to ordinary induction, with the view of obtaining some artistic piquancy which might serve me as a keynote in the construction of the poem — some pivot upon which the whole structure might turn. In carefully thinking over all the usual artistic effects — or more properly *points*, in the theatrical sense — page 456 / I did not fail to perceive immediately that no one had been so universally employed as that of the *refrain*. The universality of its employment sufficed to assure me of its intrinsic value, and spared me the necessity of submitting it to analysis. I considered it, however, with regard to its susceptibility of improvements, and soon saw it to be in a primitive condition. As commonly used, the *refrain*, or burden, not only is limited to lyric verse, but depends for its impression upon the force of monotone — both in sound and thought. The pleasure is deduced solely from the sense of identity — of repetition. I resolved to diversify, and so heighten, the effect, by adhering, in general, to the monotone of sound, while I continually varied that of thought: that is to say, I determined to produce continuously novel effects, by the variation of *the application* of the *refrain* — the *refrain* itself remaining, for the most part, unvaried.

These points being settled, I next bethought me of the *nature* of my *refrain*. Since its application was to be repeatedly varied, it was clear that the *refrain* itself must be brief, for there would have been an insurmountable difficulty in frequent variations of application in any sentence of length. In proportion to the brevity of the sentence, would, of course, be the facility of the variation. This led me at once to a single word as the best *refrain*.

The question now arose as to the *character* of the word. Having made up my mind to a *refrain*, the division of the poem into stanzas was, of course, a corollary: the *refrain* forming the close of each stanza. That such a close, to have force, must be sonorous and susceptible of protracted emphasis, admitted no doubt: and these considerations inevitably led me to the long *o* as the most sonorous vowel, in connection with *r* as the most producible consonant.

The sound of the *refrain* being thus determined, it became necessary to select a word embodying this sound, and at the same time in the fullest possible keeping with that melancholy which I had pre-determined as the tone of the poem. In such a search it would have been absolutely impossible to overlook the word "Nevermore." In fact, it was the very first which presented itself.

The next *desideratum* was a pretext for the continuous use of the one word "nevermore." In observing the difficulty which I at once found in inventing a sufficiently plausible reason for its continuous repetition, I did not fail to perceive that this difficulty page 457 / arose solely from the pre-assumption that the word was to be so continuously or monotonously spoken by a *human* being — I did not fail to perceive, in short, that the difficulty lay in the reconciliation of this monotony with the exercise of reason on the part of the creature repeating the word. Here, then, immediately arose the idea of a *non*-reasoning creature capable of speech; and, very naturally, a parrot, in the first instance, suggested itself, but was superseded forthwith by a Raven, as equally capable of speech, and infinitely more in keeping with the intended *tone*.

I had now gone so far as the conception of a Raven — the bird of ill omen — monotonously repeating the one word, "Nevermore," at the conclusion of each stanza, in a poem of melancholy tone, and in length about one hundred lines. Now, never losing sight of the object *supremeness*, or perfection, at all points, I asked myself — "Of all melancholy topics, what, according to the *universal* understanding of mankind, is the *most* melancholy?" Death — was the obvious reply. "And when," I said, "is this most melancholy of topics most poetical?" From what I have already explained at some length, the answer, here also, is obvious — "When it most closely allies itself to *Beauty:* the death, then, of a beautiful woman is, unquestionably, the most poetical topic in the world — and equally is it beyond doubt that the lips best suited for such topic are those of a bereaved lover."

I had now to combine the two ideas, of a lover lamenting his deceased mistress and a Raven continuously repeating the word "Nevermore." — I had to combine these, bearing in mind my design of varying, at every turn, the *application* of the word repeated; but the only intelligible mode of such combination is that of imagining the Raven employing the word in answer to the queries of the lover. And here it was that I saw at once the opportunity afforded for the effect on which I had been depending — that is to say, the effect of the *variation of application.* I saw that I could make the first query propounded by the lover — the first query to which the Raven should reply "Nevermore" — that I could make this first query a commonplace one — the second less so — the third still less, and so on — until at length the lover, startled from his original *nonchalance* by the melancholy character of the word itself — by its frequent repetition — and by a consideration of the ominous reputation of the fowl that uttered it — is at length excited to superstition, and wildly propounds queries of a far different character — queries whose solution he **page 458 /** has passionately at heart — propounds them half in superstition and half in that species of despair which delights in self-torture — propounds them not altogether because he believes in the prophetic or demoniac character of the bird (which, reason assures him, is merely repeating a lesson learned by rote) but because he experiences a frenzied pleasure in so modeling his questions as to receive from the *expected* "Nevermore" the most delicious because the most intolerable of sorrow. Perceiving the opportunity thus afforded me — or, more strictly, thus forced upon me in the process of construction — I first established in mind the climax, or concluding query — that query to which "Nevermore" should be in the last place an answer — that query in reply to which this word "Nevermore" should involve the uttermost conceivable amount of sorrow and despair.

Here then the poem may be said to have its beginning — at the end, where all works of art should begin — for it was here, at this point of my preconsiderations, that I first put pen to paper in the composition of the stanza:

> "Prophet," said I, "thing of evil! prophet still if bird or devil!
> By that heaven that bends above us — by that God we both adore
> Tell this soul with sorrow laden, if within the distant Aidenn,
> It shall clasp a sainted maiden whom the angels name Lenore —
> Clasp a rare and radiant maiden whom the angels name Lenore."
> Quoth the raven "Nevermore."

I composed this stanza, at this point, first that, by establishing the climax, I might better vary and graduate, as regards seriousness and importance, the preceding queries of the lover — and, secondly, that I might definitely settle the rhythm, the metre, and the length and general arrangement of the stanza — as well as graduate the stanzas which were to precede, so that none of them might surpass this in rhythmical effect. Had I been able, in the subsequent composition, to construct more vigorous stanzas, I should, without scruple, have purposely enfeebled them, so as not to interfere with the climacteric effect.

And here I may as well say a few words of the versification. My first object (as usual) was originality. The extent to which this has been neglected, in versification, is one of the most unaccountable things in the world. Admitting that there is little possibility of variety in mere *rhythm*, it is still clear that the possible varieties of metre and stanza are absolutely infinite — and yet, *for centuries, no man, in verse, has ever done, or ever seemed* page 459 / *to think of doing, an original thing*. The fact is, that originality (unless in minds of very unusual force) is by no means a matter, as some suppose, of impulse or intuition. In general, to be found, it must be elaborately sought, and although a positive merit of the highest class, demands in its attainment less of invention than negation.

Of course, I pretend to no originality in either the rhythm or metre of the "Raven." The former is trochaic — the latter is octameter acatalectic, alternating with heptameter catalectic repeated in the refrain of the fifth verse, and terminating with tetrameter catalectic. Less pendantically — the feet employed throughout (trochees) consist of a long syllable followed by a short: the first line of the stanza consists of eight of these feet — the second of seven and a half (in effect two-thirds) — the third of eight — the fourth of seven and a half — the fifth the same — the sixth three and a half. Now, each of these lines, taken individually, has been employed before, and what originality the "Raven" has, is in their *combination into stanza;* nothing even remotely approaching this combination has ever been attempted. The effect of this originality of combination is aided by other unusual, and some altogether novel effects, arising from an extension of the application of the principles of rhyme and alliteration.

The next point to be considered was the mode of bringing together the lover and the Raven — and the first branch of this consideration was the *locale.* For this the most natural suggestion might seem to be a forest, or the fields — but it has always appeared to me that a close *circumscription of space* is absolutely necessary to the effect of insulated incident: — it has the force of a frame to a picture. It has an indisputable moral power in keeping concentrated the attention, and, of course, must not be confounded with mere unity of place.

I determined, then, to place the lover in his chamber — in a chamber rendered sacred to him by memories of her who had frequented it. The room is represented as richly furnished — this in mere pursuance of the ideas I have already explained on the subject of Beauty, as the sole true poetical thesis.

The *locale* being thus determined, I had now to introduce the bird — and the thought of introducing him through the window was inevitable. The idea of making the lover suppose, in the first instance, that the flapping of the wings of the bird against the shutter, is a "tapping" at the door, originated in a wish to in- **page 460 /** crease, by prolonging, the reader's curiosity, and in a desire to admit the incidental effect arising from the lover's throwing open the door, finding all dark, and thence adopting the half-fancy that it was the spirit of his mistress that knocked.

I made the night tempestuous, first to account for the Raven's seeking admission, and secondly, for the effect of contrast with the (physical) serenity within the chamber.

I made the bird alight on the bust of Pallas, also for the effect of contrast between the marble and the plumage — it being understood that the bust was absolutely *suggested* by the bird — the bust of *Pallas* being chosen, first, as most in keeping with the scholarship of the lover, and, secondly, for the sonorousness of the word, Pallas, itself.

About the middle of the poem, also, I have availed myself of the force of contrast, with a view of deepening the ultimate impression. For example, an air of the fantastic — approaching as nearly to the ludicrous as was admissible — is given to the Raven's entrance. He comes in "with many a flirt and flutter."

> Not the *least obeisance made he* — not a moment stopped or stayed he,
> *But with mien of lord or lady*, perched above my chamber door.

In the two stanzas which follow, the design is more obviously carried out: —

> Then this ebony bird beguiling my sad fancy into smiling
> By the *grave and stern decorum of the countenance it wore*,
> "Though thy *crest be shorn and shaven* thou," I said, "art sure no craven,
> Ghastly grim and ancient Raven wandering from the nightly shore —
> Tell me what thy lordly name is on the Night's Plutonian shore?"
> Quoth the Raven "Nevermore."
>
> Much I marvelled *this ungainly fowl* to hear discourse so plainly
> Though its answer little meaning — little relevancy bore;
> For we cannot help agreeing that no living human being
> *Ever yet was blessed with seeing bird above his chamber door —*
> *Bird or beast upon the sculptured bust above his chamber door,*
> With such name as "Nevermore."

The effect of the *dénouement* being thus provided for, I immediately drop the fantastic for a tone of the most profound seri- page 461 / ousness: — this tone commencing in the stanza directly following the one last quoted, with the line,

> But the Raven, sitting lonely on that placid bust, spoke only, etc.

From this epoch the lover no longer jests — no longer sees any thing even of the fantastic in the Raven's demeanor. He speaks of him as a "grim, ungainly, ghastly, gaunt, and ominous bird of yore," and feels the "fiery eyes" burning into his "bosom's core." This revolution of thought, or fancy, on the lover's part, is intended to induce a similar one on the part of the reader — to bring the mind into a proper frame for the *dénouement* — which is now brought about as rapidly and as *directly* as possible.

With the *dénouement* proper — with the Raven's reply, "Nevermore," to the lover's final demand if he shall meet his mistress in another world — the poem, in its obvious phase, that of a simple narrative, may be said to have its completion. So far, everything is within the limits of the accountable — of the real. A raven, having learned by rote the single word "Nevermore," and having escaped from the custody of its owner, is driven at midnight, through the violence of a storm, to seek admission at a window from which a light still gleams — the chamber-window of a student, occupied half in poring over a volume, half in dreaming of a beloved mistress deceased. The casement being thrown open at the fluttering of the bird's wings, the bird itself perches on the most convenient seat out of the immediate reach of the student, who, bemused by the incident and the oddity of the visitor's demeanor, demands of it, in jest and without looking for a reply, its name. The raven addressed, answers with its customary word, "Nevermore" — a word which finds immediate echo in the melancholy heart of the student, who, giving utterance aloud to certain thoughts suggested by the occasion, is again startled by the fowl's repetition of "Nevermore." The student now guesses the state of the case, but is impelled, as I have before explained, by the human thirst for self-torture, and in part by superstition, to propound such queries to the bird as will bring him, the lover, the most of the luxury of sorrow, through the anticipated answer "Nevermore." With the indulgence, to the extreme, of this self-torture, the narration, in what I have termed its first or obvious phase, has a natural termination, and so far there has been no overstepping of the limits of the real. page 462 /

But in subjects so handled, however skilfully, or with however vivid an array of incident, there is always a certain hardness or nakedness, which repels the artistical eye. Two things are invariably required — first, some amount of complexity, or more properly, adaptation; and, secondly, some amount of suggestiveness — some under-current, however indefinite, of meaning. It is this latter, in especial, which imparts to a work of art so much of that *richness* (to borrow from colloquy a forcible term) which we are too fond of confounding with *the ideal*. It is the *excess* of the suggested meaning — it is the rendering this the upper instead of the under current of the theme — which turns into prose (and that of the very flattest kind) the so-called poetry of the so-called transcendentalists.

Holding these opinions, I added the two concluding stanzas of the poem — their suggestiveness being thus made to pervade all the narrative which has preceded them. The under-current of meaning is rendered first apparent in the lines —

> "Take thy beak from out *my heart,* and take thy form from off my door!"
>
> Quoth the Raven "Nevermore!"

It will be observed that the words, "from out my heart," involve the first metaphorical expression in the poem. They, with the answer, "Nevermore," dispose the mind to seek a moral in all that has been previously narrated. The reader begins now to regard the Raven as emblematical — but it is not until the very last line of the very last stanza, that the intention of making him emblematical of *Mournful and Never-ending Remembrance* is permitted distinctly to be seen:

> And the Raven, never flitting, still is sitting, still is sitting,
> On the pallid bust of Pallas just above my chamber door;
> And his eyes have all the seeming of a demon's that is dreaming,
> And the lamplight o'er him streaming throws his shadow on the floor;
> And my soul *from out that shadow* that lies floating on the floor
> Shall be lifted — nevermore.

page 463 /

The Principle of Composition

KENNETH BURKE

For our point of departure here, let's use Poe's essay, *The Philosophy of Composition,* where he gives his suspect account of the way in which he wrote *The Raven.* According to Poe (and few if any readers have seemed inclined to believe him) no point in the composition of the poem "is referable to accident or intuition." And his essay was designed to demonstrate "that the work proceeded, step by step, to its completion with the precision and rigid consequence of a mathematical problem."

I. A. Richards has referred to Poe's explanation as "an ostentatious parade of allegedly perfect adjustment of selected means to fully foreseen ends." (Cf. "Poetic Process and Literary Analysis," in *Style and Language*, edited by Thomas A. Sebeok.) Further: "Poe, so eager — in Harry Levin's phrase — 'to convince the world of his self-mastery,' spares no pains to make this clear." And he concludes: "However 'The Raven' may in fact have been written, we know that most poems are not composed so; the author's manuscripts, where first drafts are available, at least show us that."

It's not unlikely that Poe could at least have come close to the logically deductive procedures he retails than would ordinarily be the case. After all, he was the author of works like *The Gold-Bug.* And there's no reason to deny that such "stories of ratiocina-

---

Reprinted, by permission, from *Poetry*, October, 1961, pp. 46–53. The article substantially represents a position which the author is developing in his book, *A Symbolic of Motives*, to be published by Beacon Press.

tion" do require a kind of planning not unlike the series of logical deductions by which, according to Poe, he decided upon the length of the poem, its subject-matter, its contrasts, its tone, its refrain, etc., etc. When planning stories of this sort, "It is only with the *dénouement* constantly in view that we can give a plot its indispensable air of consequence, or causation, by making the incidents, and especially the tone at all points, tend to the development of the intention." Author and reader here reverse things. Beginning with page 46 / the solution, the author figures out the kind of situation that would require such a solution. But the reader proceeds in the other direction, by beginning with the problem and gradually progressing towards the solution. So a kind of "deductive" planning is involved in such stories, at least. And Poe himself (in a letter referring to both "the bird" and "the bug" in the same breath) spontaneously indicates that *The Raven* and *The Gold-Bug* were for him classifiable in the same bin.

There are many kinds of story, and many kinds of poem, which might conceivably be written from hand to mouth, from pillar to post, the writer himself not sure exactly where he is going until he gets there. But it's almost inconceivable that a story of ratiocination like *The Gold-Bug* could be written thus. Here the art is like that of a Houdini. Houdini didn't let the public set the conditions from which he should escape. Rather, having hit upon the device that would permit him to escape, he next figured out the exact conditions of confinement which would make such a means of escape possible. In brief, from his idea of the *dénouement* he deduced his ideas of the prior complications.

However, my concern with a possible similarity of motives between the poem of the bird and the story of the bug does not require me to believe Poe's account of how he wrote the poem. As regards our present speculations, it doesn't matter whether Poe was telling the literal truth or a bare-faced lie. In fact, to get the point I am after, let's assume that Poe's account was a fabrication from the whole cloth — and that it was done either by way of showmanship or (as Harry Levin's effective belowthebeltism seems to suggest) to supply a formal, public denial of the author's notorious personal weaknesses. For the present, we'll pass up the personal motives that may have figured in the rationalizing of his project when, having decided that the ideal topic of his poem must somehow combine death and beauty, he brought forth his crucial formula: "The death, then, of a beautiful woman is, unquestionably, the most poetical topic in the world." Whatever may be our speculations on this point with regard to Poe's poetically necrophile tendencies (as though he were proved to have been an undertaker who lost his license for morbid reasons) the question need not detain us here. Our question is: What could be said in favor of Poe's procedure in his essay on *The Raven*, even if (to make our case as clear as possible) we flatly assume that his account of how he wrote the poem is completely false? **page 47 /**

First, let's dispose of the most likely alternative: the "historical," "biographical," or temporally "genetic" account of a work's development. Here would be the hit-and-run, catch-as-catch-can record of the poem in its various stages of planning and revision. The primary evidence for such a study of poetic composition is usually taken to be various drafts of the given work, arranged as far as possible in the order of their production. Often the inspection of such material does give us new insight into the author both as a personality and as a craftsman. However, we must remember that: Even if we had a record of every such single step involved in the actual writing of a poem, of the exact order in which revisions were made, of the author's dreams and personal quandaries during the writing, of his borrowings from other authors or from situations in life itself (unrelated incidents that happened to occur at the time when the work was being produced and that the author found ways of transforming for the particular purposes of his poem) — even if we had a mountain of such data, we should have but a fraction of the information needed to chart fully the work's genesis. For obviously, if a poem is worth the trouble of a second look, the germ of its beginning had been planted long before the stage of actual writing. In this sense, the poet began "planning" his poem (consciously or unconsciously) many years before he got around to the writing of it. An inspection of successive drafts, notebooks, the author's literary habits in general, etc., helps — but in the last analysis the poem's universe of discourse dissolves into the mystery of the universe itself.

However, though studies of this sort can't possibly go deep enough, they do provide us with a high-class kind of gossip that is often worth the effort. My point is not that such pursuits should be neglected, but simply that they do not replace the "principle" involved in Poe's essay. And our problem is to see what can be said for that principle.

We come closer when we consider a second kind of derivation, the kind that has to do with the poem as a finished public product, an "art object," the formal commodity for which you pay your good money. Regardless of where the poet started, of how many revisions he made, of what he added or left out, etc., etc., here is a self-consistent symbol-system, a structure with beginning, middle, and end, a whole with internally related parts. And the critic's job is to *appreciate* this production.

The problem of derivation here primarily involves a close step-by-step analysis of the particular text, with the attempt to show how the page 48 / various elements in the work require one another in the course of shaping and guiding and exploiting the expectations of the reader.

Quite as I would not sacrifice the high-class gossip of genetic criticism so I would be all the more loath to abandon this realm of formal and appreciative criticism, ranging from mere "news" of a work (as in a book review) to such concerns with the principles of a literary species as are embodied in Aristotle's treatise on Greek tragedy.

But this reference to "the principles of a literary species" brings us to the crux of these notes, which concerns the following paradox: Once you begin asking about the principles involved in the production of a given work, you set the conditions for a surprising kind of reversal. Strictly speaking, it is not the same kind of reversal as we mentioned with regard to the way in which a Poe "story of ratiocination" might be planned by beginning at the end. But the two methods are sufficiently alike to become confused, unless there is a specific attempt to draw the distinction and maintain it. My job here is first to make the distinction clear, and then to show, on the basis of it, how significant Poe's essay becomes, as a guide for critics.

There is a third kind of "derivation," thus:

The critic, let us say, begins with the work as "art object," or "formal commodity," the finished public product. In examining it, he sees that a great many principles of judgment are implicit in it. That is, regardless of whether the author of the work explicitly asked himself why he formed the work as he did, the work embodies a series of decisions which *imply* answers to such questions. For instance, if the work is a play with a blood-and-thunder ending, implicit in its sheer nature there is, first of all, a principle that amounts to saying: "Resolved: That this kind of work should be a play with a blood-and-thunder ending." Similarly, if the author adopts certain procedures for leading to this ending, implicit in these procedures there are principles that amount to saying: "Resolved: That such-and-such kinds of characters in such-and-such kinds of situations and undergoing such-and-such transformations are the proper procedures for a work of this sort." Etc. In brief, insofar as a work is developed in accordance with the author's sense of propriety (insofar as he constructs it in ways that "feel right" to him), then no matter how spontaneous and purely "intuitive" his approach to his material may be, implied in all his choices there is a corresponding set of "principles." How- page 49 / ever, in his capacity purely as the writer of the original work, he need never state these principles.

As a matter of fact, usually authors do aim to state some of the principles by which they are guided, or think themselves guided. That is, they'll make fragmentary approaches to such "statements of policy" as are to be found grandly in Sidney's *Apologie for Poetrie,* or Wordsworth's preface to the *Lyrical Ballads,* or Shelley's *Defence of Poetry*. But usually their pronouncements along these lines are much less thorough-going than that, being confined to rules of thumb (as with notions that the kind of work they want should be statuesque rather than conversational, or conversational rather than statuesque, or should avoid rhyme, or should never be without rhyme, or should avoid inversions, etc.).

But for our present purposes, the point to be stressed is: Whether or not authors do formulate the principles of choice by which they are guided, such principles are necessarily implicit in the choices they make. Indeed, only by such an internal consistency of principles can the work itself possess the consistency needed to give it integrity and development as an artistic form.

Even if the poet does formulate such principles, however, he does so not as poet but as another self, as critic. For it is the *critic's* job to attempt systematically specifying the principles of composition that he finds (or thinks he finds) embodied in the given poem. And insofar as the poet himself makes such pronouncements, about either his own work or other people's (as for instance in the prefaces of Racine), he is here speaking as a critic. Often, on this score, he does a much better job of it than the critics themselves — but the fact remains that, at these times, he is writing not poetry but criticism. And whether or not the poet wants to concern himself with such matters, he is certainly entitled to *demand* that the critic do so. He is entitled to *demand* that the critic aim at a conceptual architectonic which will somehow contrive to translate the poet's intuitions into the terms of their corresponding critical principles.

But insofar as the critic proves himself equal to this task, the whole issue can now be turned around. For "principles" are "firsts." As such, they were "there from the very start." In the sense of purely *logical* priority, "principles of composition" implicit in a given literary species (such as a lyric like *The Raven*) "were there even *before*" they became embodied in the particular work that exemplifies them. They "were there," I say, in the sense of a purely *logical* priority — but, especially in page 50 / the history-ridden nineteenth century (and its twentieth-century vestiges), there has been a constant invitation to interpret all such purely *logical* priority in terms of *temporal* priority.

We now have the material for showing the essential rightness of Poe's concern with "the principle" of composition, however badly he got side-tracked in the effort to develop a truly "principled" theory of poetic derivation. He really did ask himself, as a *critic*, what principles he found (or thought he found) implicit in his act as *poet* (author of *The Raven*). In effect, he thus formulated the aesthetic principles (including a theory of beauty and of lyrical effects) which seemed to him the conceptual equivalents of the principles that had implicitly guided him in the writing of the poem. So far, so good.

Then he tricked himself into explaining such procedures in terms of a purely "genetic" (narrative, temporal) series, as with the first kind of critical analysis we considered in these notes. And hereby he opened himself to the distrust that his essay has aroused since the day of its publication.

As noted previously, it's possible that, because of his peculiar approach to such matters, he did come much closer to such a way of working than do most writers. But that's not the main point, for our present purposes. The main point is that he hit upon the ideal form for an "architectonic" critic to aim at.

In other words, regardless of how any work arose (as tested by the gossip available to us when narratively studying the genetic process of the poem's emergence in time), the critic should aim to formulate the principles of composition implicit in it. Then he should test the power and scope of his formulations by reversing the process. Thus, "prophesying after the event," he would proceed by showing how, if his formulations are adequate, the poem should be "logically deducible" from the principles he has formulated.

Ironically enough, the poet usually distrusts any such tendencies in critics. But the poet should reverse his attitude on this matter. He should demand that critics prove themselves worthy of poetry by performing an equally creative task of their own. For if the poet can prod the critics to performances of this sort, then criticism will help reveal the essentially *principled* nature of the judgments underlying the production of the original works. page 51 /

Thus, instead of stopping with the obvious faults in Poe's essay, let's recognize what an admirably sound critical procedure was struggling for expression there. The changes in style of presentation would be surprisingly slight (though they would amount to the kind of deflection at the center that shows up as quite a deflection at the circumference). Essentially, the shift would amount to this:

Poe need simply have said: "Implicit in my composition there are certain principles. Regardless of how I happened to write this composition, it necessarily embodies these principles. As a critic, I have sought to formulate the principles. Then (just as people check multiplication by division, or addition by subtraction) I'll check my critical formulations by reversing things; and instead of deriving the critical principles from the examination of the work, I'll try deriving the work from the principles."

Then he might have added: "Insofar as the principles I have formulated do not seem to account for as much as I would have them do, other critics should try their own hand at the same game, to see whether they can formulate the principles *they* think are needed, to account for the nature of the work."

In sum: To write the poem at all, the poet necessarily writes a certain *kind* of poem. Insofar as the poem is effective, it will necessarily produce a certain *kind* of effect. And the poem is necessarily composed of the elements by which it produced the particular kind of effect "proper" to that particular kind of poem.

Turn this situation around, and the particular methods and subject-matter of the poem can be, as it were, "deduced" or "derived" from the definition of the poem as a kind. Thus, Poe tried to persuade his readers that he deduced the topic and treatment of *The Raven* not just "in principle" but actually (genetically) from his definition of what he considered to be the ideal lyric.

However, while arguing for Poe's derivations "in principle," I still feel that his particular formulas must be considerably modified, before we shall have the best "principles" for "prophesying after the event" in Poe's case. Possibly, we need more than his definition of what he takes to be the ideal lyric, or any such definition. Possibly, for a complete job of such "derivation in principle," we should also need a formula for Poe's particular personality (at least, his particular personality as a poet, re- **page 52 /** gardless of what he may have been as citizen and taxpayer). Such considerations would also involve the belowthebeltism to which we referred in connection with Harry Levin's observation.

For instance with regard to Poe's preferences for dead women as a "beautiful" topic for a poem, we might recall that, in *La Vita Nuova,* Dante tells how he dreamed of Beatrice as dead while she was still alive. Whatever the *psychological* motives for such a fantasy, and whether or not in some cases it is "necrophile," there is the purely *logological* fact that death is a species of *perfection* (that is, "finishedness"). And however differently Dante and Poe may have conceived of poetry, both were concerned with *perfection* as a poetic motive.

Many concerns of this sort would need treatment, for a fully rounded discussion of Poe's essay. But though I have a small bbl. of notes on the subject, these would call for another, quite different presentation. **page 53 /**

CHAPTER FIVE

Disorder in the Making and Order in the Poem

ALEXANDER POPE

An Essay on Man

An Essay on Man

ALEXANDER POPE

In Four Epistles to H. St. John, Lord Bolingbroke

Epistle I

OF THE NATURE AND STATE OF MAN, WITH RESPECT TO THE UNIVERSE

ARGUMENT

Of Man in the abstract. I. That we can judge only with regard to our own system, being ignorant of the relations of systems and things, verse 17, etc. II. That Man is not to be deemed imperfect, but a being suited to his place and rank in the creation, agreeable to the general order of things, and conformable to ends and relations to him unknown, verse 35, etc. III. That it is partly upon his ignorance of future events, and partly upon the hope of a future state, that all his happiness in the present depends, verse 77, etc. IV. The pride of aiming at more knowledge, and pretending to more perfection, the cause of Man's error and misery. The impiety of putting himself in the place of God, and judging of the fitness or unfitness, perfection or imperfection, justice or injustice, of his dispensations, verse 113, etc. V. The absurdity of conceiting himself the final cause of the creation, or expecting that perfection in the moral world which is not in the natural, verse 131, etc. VI. The unreasonableness of his complaints against Providence, while, on the one hand, he demands the perfections of the angels, and, on the other, the bodily qualifications of the brutes; though to possess any of the sensitive faculties in a higher degree would render him miserable, verse 173, etc. VII. That throughout the whole visible world a universal order and gradation in the sensual and mental faculties is observed, which causes a subordination of creature to creature, and of all creatures to Man. The gradations of Sense, Instinct, Thought, Reflection, Reason: that Reason alone countervails all the other faculties, verse 207, etc. VIII. How much further this order and subordination of living creatures may extend above and below us; were any part of which broken, not that part only, but the whole connected creation must be destroyed, verse 233, etc. IX. The extravagance, madness, and pride of such a desire, verse 259, etc. X. The consequence of all, the absolute submission due to Providence, both as to our present and future state, verse 281, etc., to the end.

Awake, my ST. JOHN! leave all meaner things
To low ambition and the pride of Kings.
Let us, since life can little more supply
Than just to look about us and to die,
Expatiate free o'er all this scene of Man;
A mighty maze! but not without a plan;
A wild, where weeds and flowers promiscuous shoot,
Or garden, tempting with forbidden fruit.
Together let us beat this ample field,
Try what the open, what the covert yield; 10
The latent tracts, the giddy heights, explore
Of all who blindly creep or sightless soar;
Eye Nature's walks, shoot Folly as it flies,
And catch the manners living as they rise;
Laugh where we must, be candid where we can,
But vindicate the ways of God to Man.
I. Say first, of God above or Man below
What can we reason but from what we know?
Of Man what see we but his station here,
From which to reason, or to which refer? 20
Thro' worlds unnumber'd tho' the God be known,
'Tis ours to trace him only in our own.
He who thro' vast immensity can pierce,
See worlds on worlds compose one universe,
Observe how system into system runs,
What other planets circle other suns,
What varied being peoples every star,
May tell why Heav'n has made us as we are:
But of this frame, the bearings and the ties,
The strong connexions, nice dependencies, 30
Gradations just, has thy pervading soul
Look'd thro'; or can a part contain the whole?
Is the great chain that draws all to agree,
And drawn supports, upheld by God or thee?

II. Presumptuous Man! the reason wouldst thou find,
Why form'd so weak, so little, and so blind?
First, if thou canst, the harder reason guess,
Why form'd no weaker, blinder, and no less!
Ask of thy mother earth why oaks are made
Taller or stronger than the weeds they shade! 40
Or ask of yonder argent fields above
Why Jove's satellites are less than Jove!
Of systems possible, if 'tis confest
That wisdom infinite must form the best,
Where all must fall or not coherent be,
And all that rises rise in due degree;
Then in the scale of reas'ning life 'tis plain
There must be, somewhere, such a rank as Man:
And all the question (wrangle e'er so long)
Is only this, — if God has placed him wrong? 50
Respecting Man, whatever wrong we call,
May, must be right, as relative to all.
In human works, tho' labour'd on with pain,
A thousand movements scarce one purpose gain;
In God's, one single can its end produce,
Yet serve to second too some other use:
So Man, who here seems principal alone,
Perhaps acts second to some sphere unknown,
Touches some wheel, or verges to some goal:
'Tis but a part we see, and not a whole. 60
When the proud steed shall know why Man restrains
His fiery course, or drives him o'er the plains;
When the dull ox, why now he breaks the clod,
Is now a victim, and now Egypt's God;
Then shall Man's pride and dulness comprehend
His actions', passions', being's, use and end;
Why doing suff'ring, check'd, impell'd; and why
This hour a Slave, the next a Deity.
Then say not Man's imperfect, Heav'n in fault:
Say rather Man's as perfect as he ought; 70
His knowledge measured to his state and place,
His time a moment, and a point his space.
If to be perfect in a certain sphere,
What matter soon or late, or here or there?

The blest to-day is as completely so
As who began a thousand years ago.
  III. Heav'n from all creatures hides the book of Fate,
All but the page prescribed, their present state;
From brutes what men, from men what spirits know;
Or who could suffer Being here below? 80
The lamb thy riot dooms to bleed to-day,
Had he thy Reason would he skip and play?
Pleas'd to the last he crops the flowery food,
And licks the hand just rais'd to shed his blood.
O blindness to the future! kindly giv'n,
That each may fill the circle mark'd by Heav'n,
Who sees with equal eye, as God of all,
A hero perish or a sparrow fall,
Atoms or systems into ruin hurl'd,
And now a bubble burst, and now a world. 90
  Hope humbly then; with trembling pinions soar;
Wait the great teacher Death, and God adore.
What future bliss He gives not thee to know,
But gives that hope to be thy blessing now.
Hope springs eternal in the human breast:
Man never is, but always to be, blest.
The soul, uneasy and confin'd from home,
Rests and expatiates in a life to come.
  Lo, the poor Indian! whose untutor'd mind
Sees God in clouds, or hears him in the wind; 100
His soul proud Science never taught to stray
Far as the solar walk or milky way;
Yet simple nature to his hope has giv'n,
Behind the cloud-topt hill, an humbler Heav'n,
Some safer world in depth of woods embraced,
Some happier island in the wat'ry waste,
Where slaves once more their native land behold,
No fiends torment, no Christians thirst for gold.
To be, contents his natural desire;
He asks no Angel's wing, no Seraph's fire; 110
But thinks, admitted to that equal sky,
His faithful dog shall bear him company.
  IV. Go, wiser thou! and in thy scale of sense
Weigh thy opinion against Providence;
Call imperfection what thou fanciest such;

Say, here he gives too little, there too much;
Destroy all creatures for thy sport or gust,
Yet cry, if Man's unhappy, God's unjust;
If Man alone engross not Heav'n's high care,
Alone made perfect here, immortal there: **120**
Snatch from his hand the balance and the rod,
Rejudge his justice, be the god of God.
In pride, in reas'ning pride, our error lies;
All quit their sphere, and rush into the skies!
Pride still is aiming at the bless'd abodes,
Men would be Angels, Angels would be Gods.
Aspiring to be Gods if Angels fell,
Aspiring to be Angels men rebel:
And who but wishes to invert the laws
Of order, sins against th' Eternal Cause. **130**
  V. Ask for what end the heav'nly bodies shine,
Earth for whose use, — Pride answers, " 'Tis for mine:
For me kind Nature wakes her genial power,
Suckles each herb, and spreads out ev'ry flower;
Annual for me the grape, the rose, renew
The juice nectareous and the balmy dew;
For me the mine a thousand treasures brings;
For me health gushes from a thousand springs;
Seas roll to waft me, suns to light me rise;
My footstool earth, my canopy the skies." **140**
  But errs not Nature from this gracious end,
From burning suns when livid deaths descend,
When earthquakes swallow, or when tempests sweep
Towns to one grave, whole nations to the deep?
"No," 'tis replied, "the first Almighty Cause
Acts not by partial but by gen'ral laws;
Th' exceptions few; some change since all began
And what created perfect?" — Why then Man?
If the great end be human happiness,
Then Nature deviates; and can Man do less? **150**
As much that end a constant course requires
Of showers and sunshine, as of Man's desires;
As much eternal springs and cloudless skies,
As Men for ever temp'rate, calm, and wise.
If plagues or earthquakes break not Heav'n's design,
Why then a Borgia or a Catiline?

Who knows but He, whose hand the lightning forms,
Who heaves old ocean, and who wings the storms;
Pours fierce Ambition in a Cæsar's mind,
Or turns young Ammon loose to scourge mankind? 160
From pride, from pride, our very reas'ning springs;
Account for moral as for natural things:
Why charge we Heav'n in those, in these acquit?
In both, to reason right is to submit.
  Better for us, perhaps, it might appear,
Were there all harmony, all virtue here;
That never air or ocean felt the wind,
That never passion discomposed the mind:
But all subsists by elemental strife;
And passions are the elements of life. 170
The gen'ral order, since the whole began,
Is kept in Nature, and is kept in Man.
  VI. What would this Man? Now upward will he soar,
And little less than Angel, would be more;
Now looking downwards, just as griev'd appears
To want the strength of bulls, the fur of bears.
Made for his use all creatures if he call,
Say what their use, had he the powers of all?
Nature to these without profusion kind,
The proper organs, proper powers assign'd; 180
Each seeming want compensated of course,
Here with degrees of swiftness, there of force;
All in exact proportion to the state;
Nothing to add, and nothing to abate;
Each beast, each insect, happy in its own:
Is Heav'n unkind to Man, and Man alone?
Shall he alone, whom rational we call,
Be pleas'd with nothing if not bless'd with all?
  The bliss of Man (could pride that blessing find)
Is not to act or think beyond mankind; 190
No powers of body or of soul to share,
But what his nature and his state can bear.
Why has not Man a miscrosopic eye?
For this plain reason, Man is not a fly.
Say, what the use, were finer optics giv'n,
T' inspect a mite, not comprehend the Heav'n?
Or touch, if tremblingly alive all o'er,

To smart and agonize at every pore?
Or quick effluvia darting thro' the brain,
Die of a rose in aromatic pain? 200
If Nature thunder'd in his opening ears,
And stunn'd him with the music of the spheres,
How would he wish that Heav'n had left him still
The whisp'ring zephyr and the purling rill?
Who finds not Providence all good and wise,
Alike in what it gives and what denies?
VII. Far as creation's ample range extends,
The scale of sensual, mental powers ascends.
Mark how it mounts to Man's imperial race
From the green myriads in the peopled grass: 210
What modes of sight betwixt each wide extreme,
The mole's dim curtain and the lynx's beam:
Of smell, the headlong lioness between
And hound sagacious on the tainted green:
Of hearing, from the life that fills the flood
To that which warbles thro' the vernal wood.
The spider's touch, how exquisitely fine,
Feels at each thread, and lives along the line:
In the nice bee what sense so subtly true,
From pois'nous herbs extracts the healing dew! 220
How instinct varies in the grovelling swine,
Compared, half-reas'ning elephant, with thine!
'Twixt that and reason what a nice barrier!
For ever separate, yet for ever near!
Remembrance and reflection how allied!
What thin partitions Sense from Thought divide!
And middle natures how they long to join,
Yet never pass th' insuperable line!
Without this just gradation could they be
Subjected, these to those, or all to thee! 230
The powers of all subdued by thee alone,
Is not thy Reason all these powers in one?
VIII. See thro' this air, this ocean, and this earth
All matter quick, and bursting into birth:
Above, how high progressive life may go!
Around, how wide! how deep extend below!
Vast chain of Being! which from God began;
Natures ethereal, human, angel, man,

Beast, bird, fish, insect, who no eye can see
No glass can reach; from infinite to thee; 240
From thee to nothing. — On superior powers
Were we to press, inferior might on ours;
Or in the full creation leave a void,
Where, one step broken, the great scale's destroy'd:
From Nature's chain whatever link you like,
Tenth, or ten thousandth, breaks the chain alike.
  And if each system in gradation roll,
Alike essential to th' amazing Whole,
The least confusion but in one, not all
The system only, but the Whole must fall. 250
Let earth unbalanced from her orbit fly,
Planets and stars run lawless thro' the sky;
Let ruling angels from their spheres be hurl'd,
Being on being wreck'd, and world on world;
Heav'n's whole foundations to their centre nod,
And Nature tremble to the throne of God!
All this dread order break — for whom? for thee?
Vile worm! — O madness! pride! impiety!
  IX. What if the foot, ordain'd the dust to tread,
Or hand to toil, aspired to be the head? 260
What if the head, the eye, or ear repin'd
To serve mere engines to the ruling mind?
Just as absurd for any part to claim
To be another in this gen'ral frame;
Just as absurd to mourn the tasks or pains
The great directing Mind of All ordains.
  All are but parts of one stupendous Whole,
Whose body Nature is, and God the soul;
That, changed thro' all, and yet in all the same,
Great in the earth as in th' ethereal frame, 270
Warms in the sun, refreshes in the breeze,
Glows in the stars, and blossoms in the trees;
Lives thro' all life, extends thro' all extent,
Spreads undivided, operates unspent;
Breathes in our soul, informs our mortal part,
As full, as perfect, in a hair as heart;
As full, as perfect, in vile Man that mourns,
As the rapt Seraph that adores and burns.

To him no high, no low, no great, no small;
He fills, he bounds, connects, and equals all! 280
  X. Cease, then, nor Order imperfection name;
Our proper bliss depends on what we blame.
Know thy own point: this kind, this due degree
Of blindness, weakness, Heav'n bestows on thee.
Submit: in this or any other sphere,
Secure to be as bless'd as thou canst bear;
Safe in the hand of one disposing Power,
Or in the natal or the mortal hour.
All Nature is but Art unknown to thee;
All Chance, Direction, which thou canst not see; 290
All Discord, Harmony not understood;
All partial Evil, universal Good:
And spite of Pride, in erring Reason's spite
One truth is clear, WHATEVER IS, IS RIGHT.

Selections from Spence's Anecdotes

Spence's Anecdotes *is a collection of miscellaneous remarks made by various personages of the early eighteenth century to the Reverend Joseph Spence, during the years 1728 to 1744. The full title of the collection, which was unpublished until 1820, is as follows:* ANECDOTES, Observations, and Characters of Books and Men. Collected from the Conversation of Mr. Pope, and other eminent persons of his time, by the Rev. Joseph Spence. *We here select a few of the remarks of Pope pertaining to his poems and his methods of writing them, with special reference to "An Essay on Man."* [*Bracketed sentences are comments by Spence himself.*]

FROM SECTION I. 1728–30.

The first epistle is to be to the whole work, what a scale is to a book of maps; and in this, I reckon, lies my greatest difficulty: not only in settling and ranging the parts of it aright, but in making them agreeable enough to be read with pleasure. [This was said in May, 1730, of what he then used to call his Moral Epistles, and what he afterwards called his Essay on Man. He at that time intended to have included in one epistle what he afterwards addressed to Lord Bolingbroke in four.] — P. page 16 /

. . . . .

There are three distinct *tours* in poetry; the design, the language, and the versification. [To which he afterwards seemed to add, a fourth, the expression; or manner of painting the humours, characters, and things that fall within your design.]

After writing a poem, one should correct it all over, with one single view at a time. Thus for language; if an elegy; "these lines are **page 23 /** very good, but are they not of too heroical a strain?" and so *vice versa.* It appears very plainly, from comparing parallel passages touched both in the Iliad and Odyssey, that Homer did this; and it is yet plainer that Virgil did so, from the distinct styles he uses in his three sorts of poems. It always answers in him; and so constant an effect could not be the effect of chance.

In versification there is a sensible difference between softness and sweetness that I could distinguish from a boy. Thus on the same points, Dryden will be found to be softer, and Waller sweeter. It is the same with Ovid and Virgil; and Virgil's Eclogues, in particular, are the sweetest poems in the world. — P. **page 24 /**

. . . .

Mr. Pope's poem grows on his hands. The first four or five epistles will be on the general principles, or of "The Nature of Man;" and the rest will be on moderation, or "The Use of Things." In the latter part each class may take up three epistles. . . . These two lines contain the main design that runs through the whole:

> Laugh where we must; be candid where we can;
> But vindicate the ways of God to man. **page 48 /**

From Section IV. 1734–36.

The famous Lord Hallifax (though so much talked of) was rather a pretender to taste, than really possessed of it. — When I had finished the two or three first books of my translation of the Iliad, that lord "desired to have the pleasure of hearing them read at his house." — Addison, Congreve, and Garth were there at the reading. — In four or five places, Lord Hallifax stopped me very civilly; and with a speech, each time much of the same kind: "I beg your pardon, Mr. Pope, but there is something in that passage that does not quite please me. — Be so good as to mark the place, and consider it a little more at your leisure. — I am sure you can give it a better turn." — I returned from Lord

Hallifax's with Dr. Garth in his page 134 / chariot; and as we were going along, was saying to the doctor, that my lord had laid me under a good deal of difficulty, by such loose and general observations; that I had been thinking over the passages almost ever since, and could not guess at what it was that offended his lordship in either of them.—Garth laughed heartily at my embarrassment; said, I had not been long enough acquainted with Lord Hallifax, to know his way yet: that I need not puzzle myself in looking those places over and over when I got home. "All you need do, (said he) is to leave them just as they are; call on Lord Halifax two or three months hence, thank him for his kind observations on those passages; and then read them to him as altered. I have known him much longer than you have, and will be answerable for the event."—I followed his advice; waited on Lord Hallifax some time after: said I hoped he would find his objections to those passages removed, read them to him exactly as they were at first; page 135 / his lordship was extremely pleased with them, and cried out, "Ay, Mr. Pope, they are perfectly right! nothing can be better."—P.

. . . . .

"I have drawn in the plan for my Ethic Epistles, much narrower than it was at first."—He mentioned several of the particulars, in which he had lessened it; but as this was in the year 1734, the most exact account of his plan, (as it stood then) will best appear from page 136 / a leaf which he annexed to about a dozen copies of the poem, printed in that year, and sent as presents to some of his most particular friends. Most of these were afterwards called in again; but that which was sent to Mr. Bethel was not.*

* It run as follows.

INDEX TO THE ETHIC EPISTLES.

Book I. Of the Nature and State of Man.

Epistle 1.—With respect to the Universe.
2.—As an Individual.
3.—With respect to Society.
4.—With respect to Happiness.

Book II. Of the Use of Things

Of the Limits of Human Reason.
Of the Use of Learning.
Of the Use of Wit.
Of the Knowledge and Characters of Men.
Of the particular Characters of Women.
Of the Principles and Use of Civil and Ecclesiastical Polity.
Of the Use of Education.
A View of the Equality of Happiness in the several Conditions of Men.
Of the Use of Riches. page 137 /

. . . . .

It is a great fault in descriptive poetry, to describe every thing. The good antients, page 139 / (but when I named them, I meant Virgil) have no long descriptions: commonly not above ten lines, and scarce ever thirty. . . .

It might be a very pretty subject for any good genius that way, to write American pastorals; or rather pastorals adapted to the manners of several of the ruder nations, as well as the Americans. I once had a thought of writ- page 140 / ing such; and talked it over with Gay: but other things came in my way and took me off from it. page 141 /

. . . . .

The things that I have written fastest, have always pleased the most. — I wrote the Essay on Criticism fast; for I had digested all the matter, in prose, before I began upon it in verse. page 142 /

. . . . .

Mr. Addison would never alter any thing after a poem was once printed; and was ready to alter almost every thing that was found fault with before. — I believe he did not leave a word unchanged, that I made any scruple against in his Cato. — P. [The last line in that tragedy originally

"And oh, 'twas this that ended Cato's life."

It was Mr. Pope who suggested the alteration as it stands at present.

"And robs the guilty world of Cato's life."] — Spence.
page 151 /

. . . .

I was born in the year 1688.—My Essay on Criticism was written in 1709; and published in 1711; which is as little time as ever I let any thing of mine lay by me. page 170 /

From Section V. 1737–39.

Middling poets are no poets at all. There is always a great number of such in each age, that are almost totally forgotten in the next. A few curious inquirers may know that there were such men, and that they wrote such and such things; but to the world they are as if they had never been. page 199 /

. . . . .

I have nothing to say for rhyme, but that I doubt whether a poem can support itself without it, in our language; unless it be stiffened with such strange words, as are likely to destroy our language itself. page 200 /

From Section VII. 1742–43

When I was looking on his foul copy of the Iliad, and observing how very much it was corrected and interlined, he said, "I believe you would find, upon examination, that those parts which have been most corrected read the easiest.—P. [I read only the first page in which

> — Η *μυρι᾽ Αχαιοις αλγε᾽ εθηκε·*
> Πο*λλας δ᾽ ίφθίμας ψυχας αϊδι προϊαψεν*
> Η*ρώων* . . . .

was thus translated,

> That strow'd with warriors dead the Phrygian plain,
> And peopled the dark shades with heroes slain.

It now stands thus,

> That wrath which *hurl'd* to Pluto's gloomy reign
> The souls of mighty chiefs *untimely* slain. page 265 /

And was evidently altered to preserve the sense of the word

page 265 / προϊαψεν What a useful study it might be for a poet, to compare in those parts what was written first, with the successive alterations; to learn his turns, and arts in versification; and to consider the reasons why such and such an alteration was made. — Spence.] page 266 /

. . . . .

About fifteen, I got acquainted with Mr. Walsh. He used to encourage me much, and used to tell me, that there was one way left of excelling: for though we had several great poets, we never had any one great poet that was correct; and he desired me to make that my study and aim. — P. [This, I suppose, first led Mr. Pope to turn his lines over and over again so often, which he continued to do page 280 / till the last; and did it with surprising facility. — Spence.] page 281 /

. . . . .

From Section VIII. 1743–44.

"The great secret how to write well, is to know thoroughly what one writes about, and not to be affected." — [Or, as he expressed the same thing afterwards in other words,] "to write naturally, and from one's own knowledge." — P. page 291 /

. . . . .

I *must* make a perfect edition of my works; page 295 / and then shall have nothing to do but to die. — P. page 296 /

. . . . .

I would leave my things in merciful hands. — I am in no concern, whether people should say this is writ well or ill, but that this was writ with a good design. — "He has written in page 301 / the cause of virtue, and done something to mend people's morals:" this is the only commendation I long for. — P. page 302 /

. . . . .

I had once thoughts of completing my ethic work in four books. — The first, you know, is in the Nature of Man. — The second, would have been on Knowledge and its limits: — here would have come in an Essay on Education; part of which I have inserted in the Dunciad. — The third, was to have treated of Government; both ecclesiastical and civil — and this was what chiefly stopped my going on. I could not have said what I *would* have said, without provoking every church on the face of the earth: and I did not care for living always in boiling water. . . . **page 315 /**

. . . . .

Mr. Pope died the 30th of May (1744) in the evening; but they did not know the exact time: for his departure was so easy, that it was imperceptible even to the standers by. — MAY OUR END BE LIKE HIS! **page 322 /**

. . . . .

Pope at Work

GEORGE SHERBURN

Alexander Pope only spasmodically lived up to his philosophy of life so neatly expressed in his phrase, "One's chief business is to be really at home." In the letter to Bethel in which this symbolic remark is found, he adds, "My house is like the house of a Patriarch of old standing by the highway side, and receiving all travellers." He was much at home, and he received many guests; but he was also a traveller — in Parson Adams's style (in books) as well as in the coaches of his noble friends. If he was seldom really at home, he might have used Sir Balaam's excuse, " 'Twas such a busy life!" He fluttered from house to house in his "rambles," and he fluttered from page to page in innumerable books: between whiles he wrote, tended his mother's reposing age, rearranged his garden and his grotto, and had little time left in which to utter the cry of disillusionment and ennui, "Vive la bagatelle!"

The spring of 1730 was not perhaps his busiest, but then as always he was busy; and a page preserved in the papers of Joseph Spence makes this spring worth examining as a specimen period. The last fortnight in April Pope spent in "in a little journey" — unidentified. But at the beginning of May he was back in Twickenham entertaining visitors. For the whole first week of the month he seems to have had as guest one of his most important

---

Reprinted, by permission, from *Essays on the Eighteenth Century*, by George Sherburn (Oxford: The Clarendon Press, 1945).

and most self-effacing friends, the Rev. Joseph Spence, who came perhaps from Oxford, where he was Professor of Poetry, or perhaps from Birchanger (Essex), where he was Rector. Spence already aspired to be Pope's biographer, and during the week he listened attentively as Pope and he paced through the garden or rested in the sunny entrance to the damp grotto or (more likely!) sat by the fire in Pope's library. They talked of Machiavelli and Montaigne, of the ruling passion, and of Pope's growing works that were to advertise this passion. From the fragments already on paper or in his mind Pope read or recited, and Spence, as befitted a dutiful though inferior Boswell, retired and set down what he remembered on sheets of paper that were eventually to furnish matter for his *Anecdotes.* page 49 /

. . . .

The chief importance of Spence's record is that it shows us Pope at work on several poems at once; and from other notes page 51 / by Spence and from a study of the working manuscripts of some of the poems (several such are preserved) we can form a fairly clear idea of how Pope put his work on paper The results of our examination can concern only humble mechanics of composition and not imaginative processes. There might seem to be four stages of mental and manual labour involved in this procedure: (1) Making notes for the poem, sometimes detailed in prose; (2) the composition of verse paragraphs; (3) the arranging of these fragments in an effective structure; and (4) the polishing and perfecting of lines. This last type of activity naturally went on in all the other stages of composition.

First, then, we must recognize that for at least some of his poems he made notes in prose or a version in prose, more or less complete and organized. In another conversation, later than 1730, he told Spence, "I wrote the Essay on Criticism fast; for I had digested all the matter, in prose, before I began upon it in verse." Again, he spoke to Spence of "my *Brutus*, which is all planned already; and even some of the most material speeches written in prose." Spence's record in 1730 concerning the "very large (prose) collections on the Happiness of Contentment" (ultimately to become the fourth epistle of the *Essay on Man?*) seems to suggest that this prose stage in composition was perhaps habitual. Savage's remark on Lord Bolingbroke's "long letter" with a second under way, and incomplete, though equivalent already to many pages of print, reinforces strongly Lord Bathurst's story concerning Bolingbroke's "dissertation in prose" that helped form the *Essay on Man.* But Lord Bathurst in 1769 wrote of his dissertation: "It has never appeared since, and perhaps I am the only man now alive who has read it." Most unfortunately none of these preliminary prose collections, except the summary of *Brutus*, is known to have survived: they would be largely hypothetical if it were not for Spence's notes. One may doubt if Pope destroyed Bolingbroke's "dissertation," since the poet regarded his lordship idolatrously as "much the best writer of the age." Upon Pope's death his executor (William Murray, later the first Earl of Mansfield) returned to Pope's friends letters from them that Pope had preserved, and one suspects that Bolingbroke, also an executor, would take back his own manuscripts. It is at least conceivable that this prose dissertation written for Pope still exists.

Pope's admirers have been loath to admit the charge that in **page 52 /** the *Essay on Man* he simply versified a prose dissertation by Lord Bolingbroke. One page (the fifth) in the manuscript of the fourth epistle of the *Essay* preserved in the Pierpont Morgan Library seems to illustrate a procedure less simple than the mere turning of prose into verse. On this page Pope jotted down ideas in both verse and prose. Like so many others from Pope's workshop, it is a tantalizing confusion of fragments, with prose at the top and bottom of the page and fragments of verse in between.

. . . .

The second stage of composition was that of putting prose fragments into verse. This has just been illustrated, and here one can feel one is on surer ground, for working manuscripts of poems by Pope are surprisingly numerous, though most of those preserved are beyond the fragmentary stage. Habitually in working manuscripts from the early thirties Pope used folio half-sheets and wrote in the outer half of each page, using the inner half for possible revisions. When he had his fragments more or less cemented together, a friend (if a willing friend, such as Thomas

Dancastle — who transcribed the whole *Iliad* — or the Countess of Burlington or Jonathan Richardson, happened along) made him a fair copy, doubtless thinking the work finished. But more than once, as one can see in the fragments of the *Epistle to Dr. Arbuthnot* preserved in the Morgan Library, the insatiate reviser cut up the fair copy, rearranged the order page 54 / of the passages, inserted new sections, and rephrased lines until the manuscript page became a most confused tangle. Of this unconscionable appetite for revision we have further evidence from his publisher, Dodsley, recorded in Johnson's "Life of Pope." Of the poem that became the *Epilogue to the Satires* Johnson says:

> Dodsley told me that they were brought to him by the author, that they might be fairly copied. "Almost every line," he said, "was then written twice over; I gave him a clean transcript, which he sent some time afterwards to me for the press, with almost every line written twice over a second time."

If such a manuscript be placed in comparison with the clean fair copy of the *Essay on Criticism* preserved in Bodley, the conclusion must be that the habit of revision grew upon Pope with the years. All the working manuscripts of Pope's later poems bear out the assumption that Dodsley's experience with the *Epilogue* was quite normal. The manuscripts show, furthermore, that Pope worked by paragraphs or passages and that his great problem was arranging the paragraphs and tying them together tactfully. In December, 1730, Pope wrote to Caryll, "I have many fragments which I am beginning to put together, but nothing perfect or finished, nor in any condition to be shown, except to a friend at a fireside."

A good example of his methods of "building" a poem is found in the fragments of the *Epistle to Dr. Arbuthnot* now in the Morgan Library. In these sixteen pages or scraps of pages (not all in Pope's hand, but all contemporary with him) versions of the passage beginning "Why did I write" (11. 125–46) appear on three different leaves. In one (fol. 7) we have only the first word or words of each line. This is Pope's method of indicating that a passage has been completely composed and need not be recopied at the moment; but space is left so that, upon inspiration, revision may be entered. What he wishes to work upon are the passages preceding and following. In another page (fol. 11) we have the completed passages preceded by a transitional approach (later discarded) and followed immediately by the passage beginning with line 151 —

If meagre Gildon draw his venal quill.

In other words, here the passage as a unit has been composed, but the "approaches" that tie it to the rest of the poem remain page 55 / unsettled. The third version (fol. 4) is even more significant, and is a perfect example of Pope's growing habit of working on two or more poems at once — and of confusing them. Here the mixture involves the *Epistle to Dr. Arbuthnot* (1735) and *The First Satire of the Second Book of Horace Imitated* (1733), which he addressed to William Fortescue. page 56 /

. . . .

This example of confusion resulting from simultaneous composition of two poems is not surprising; it can be duplicated from the manuscripts of other of Pope's poems from this period, notably those of the *Essay on Man.* The very elaborateness of Pope's programme led to inevitable confusion, which persisted even after the *Essay on Man* was printed. By that time Pope's "moral" scheme, though still tentative, was more settled than when described to Spence in 1730.

This grand project for a series of poems in from two to four "books" has some importance in Pope's methods of composition, since it helps explain how poems overlapped and how passages from one were originally conceived as belonging to another. Lines in defence of satire might appear in the poems addressed to Arbuthnot and Fortescue and even in the later *Epilogue to the Satires.* The ruling passion Pope treated twice — as he did other favourite topics. He explained his grand plan more than once to Spence, who was interested enough to transcribe a suppressed page from the first collected edition of the *Essay on Man,* which gave the outline of the project in printed form. Spence's transcript, as preserved in his papers, reads as follows: page 57 /

A Page annex'd to the Quarto Edition (of 1734) of the Essay on Man.

Index to the Ethic Epistles

The First Book:

Of the Nature and State of Man.

Epistle I
With respect to the Universe.

Epistle II.
As an Individual

Epistle III.
With respect to Society.

Epistle IV.
With respect to Happiness.

The Second Book.

Of the Use of Things.

Of ye Limits of Human Reason.
Of ye Use of Learning.
Of ye Use of Wit.
Of ye Knowledge & Characters of Men.
Of ye particular Characters of Women.
Of ye Principles & Use of Civil and Ecclesiastical Polity.
— Of ye Use of Education.
A View of ye Equality of Happiness in ye several Conditions of Men.
— Of ye Use of Riches &c.

This was annext to about a dozen Books; that were sent as presents to particular friends. Most of them were call'd in again, by Mr P; but that to Mr. Bethel was not; frō wch this is copy'd.

So far Spence. This page was very probably suppressed because, almost as soon as the *Essay on Man* was completely published, some, but not all, of the poems of "Book II" were also in print in early quarto editions of the *Essay on Man* as "Ethic Epistles The Second Book. To several Persons." This publication made superfluous the description transcribed by Spence from the suppressed page.

That Pope's plan was constantly shifting may be inferred from the two holograph manuscripts of the *Essay on Man*, which are now in the possession of the Pierpont Morgan Library and the Houghton Library of Harvard University. Both include the first three epistles, and the Morgan manuscript also contains an early form of much of the fourth. In general the Morgan manuscript is the earlier. In the Harvard manuscript the poem is approaching the state of a "fair copy" almost ready for the press; but it contains many revisions and some passages not found in page 58 / the Morgan manuscript and several that had not yet found their final position in the poem. Both manuscripts of Epistle I are in almost final state, but structural confusions still exist in Pope's mind. The Morgan manuscript has, opposite line 6 of Epistle I,

> A mighty Maze! of Walks without a Plan,

the marginal note: "Inconsistencys of Character, ye Subject of Ep. 5." (This might well refer to the first Moral Essay.) Opposite line 7 ("where Weeds and Flowrs promiscuous shoot") we find the note: "Passions, Virtues &c. ye Subject of Ep. 2." — probably of the *Essay* itself. To line 8 ("Orchard, tempting with forbidden Fruit") is appended: "The Use of Pleasure, in Lib. 2" — which may possibly be a reference to Epistle IV of the *Essay on Man* or to some never written part of "Book II." Opposite line 10 ("Try what the *open*, what the *covert* yield") we find "Of the Knowledge of Mankind Epistle 1st of Book 2"; and opposite 11 ("Of all who *blindly creep*, the tracks explore"), "Learning & Ignorance, Subject of Epist 3. of Book 2." Opposite line 88 ("a sparrow fall") is "Vid Epist. 3. of animals." Evidently the plans were still in process of formation; for in the Harvard manuscript Epistle II had opened with an abbreviated form of the passage beginning —

> Come then my *Friend*, my Genius come along!
> Oh Master of the Poet and the Song!

and a fairly complete form of the apostrophe to Bolingbroke is appended at the end of Epistle II (but not as a part of it). This last is labelled marginally "Peroratio Lib. I," and at the foot of the page "Finis Lib. Prim." The Morgan manuscript unfortunately lacks the last leaf of Epistle III, and the Harvard manuscript includes in the ending of Epistle III passages that eventually were to be placed in Epistle IV (e.g. iv. 361–72).

After Epistle III in the Harvard manuscript occur seven blank pages, on which Pope probably intended to insert Epistle IV when done; and after these blank leaves comes an inserted leaf (never a proper part of the manuscript) on which appears the following surprise:

Incipit Liber Secundus
Epist. I. of ye Limits of Reason
And now, transported o'er so vast a Plain,
While the free Courser flies with all the Rein; page 59 /
While heav'nward, now, his mounting Wings he feels,
Now stoops where Fools fly trembling from his heels;
Wilt thou, my Laelius! keep ye Course in sight,
Confine ye Fury, or assist ye Flight?
Laelius, whose Love excus'd my labours past,
Matures my present, & shall bound my last.

This fragment, representing Pegasus as somewhat like a dive-bomber with Bolingbroke as pilot and Pope as gunner, presents a contamination of the "Peroratio Lib. I" with the opening couplet of the imitation of *The First Epistle of the First Book of Horace*, which Pope addressed to Bolingbroke in 1738, more than four years after the *Essay on Man* was completely in print. The last couplet here quoted occurs also in the discarded apostrophe to Memmius-Laelius that opened Epistle II in both the Morgan and the Harvard manuscripts.

A similar curious contamination is seen in a passage reserved for better service but originally designed to follow the famous lines of the *Essay on Man* concerning vice as a monster of such frightful mien (ii. 217–20). Both manuscripts of the *Essay* have the following lines in slightly varying forms:

A *Cheat!* a *Whore!* who starts not at the Name
In all the Inns of Court, or Drury Lane?
B—t but does business, Huggins brings matters on*
Sid *has the Secret,* Charters *knows the Town.*

(*Marginal variant: Y —but *serves the Crown*)

Along with practically all details of personal satire these lines disappeared when the *Essay* was printed; but they show up brilliantly near the beginning of the *Epilogue to the Satires* (1738):

But *Horace*, Sir, was delicate, was nice;
Bubo observes, he lash'd no sort of *Vice:*
Horace would say, Sir Billy *serv'd the Crown,*
Blunt *could do Bus'ness*, H-ggins *knew the Town*, . . .

And possibly the first of these manuscript couplets (omitted from the *Essay* after the first edition) is bitterly inverted later in the *Epilogue*:

> The wit of Cheats, the Courage of a Whore,
> Are what ten thousand envy and adore.

Obviously Pope could not prosecute his elaborate plan for many related poems and compose with several in mind at once without confusing them. page 60 /

When Pope told Spence in 1730 that there was "no judging of a piece from the scattered parts," he was being modest and was recognizing the confused state of his fragmentary manuscripts. Spence properly interpreted the remark: one should "survey the whole" —

> 'Tis not a lip, or eye, we beauty call,
> But the joint force and full result of all.

Pendantry may be permitted to remark, however, after examining Pope's manuscripts, that he composed by fragmentary paragraphs fully as often as by individual couplets, and far more often than he did from any sort of structural "outline" of the whole poem. As he told Spence, the greatest trouble was in "settling and ranging" these parts aright. The poet's habit of working in verse paragraphs can be seen anywhere. In the Harvard manuscript of the *Essay on Man,* Epistle I, for example, lines 29–34 of the standard editions are placed after line 22; lines 61–8 come after line 28, and are followed by lines 35–42; after line 186 come 207–32, &c. A comparison of early printed texts of the fourth "Moral Essay" ("Of Taste") with later texts will show that the habit of rearranging paragraphs continued even after the poem was published. Both in the Harvard manuscript of the *Essay on Man,* Epistle I (which was obviously regarded as a final fair copy when begun), and in the fourth "Moral Essay," the parts shuffled involve nearly always more than a single couplet. There has been too much stress on Pope's artistry in couplets; he is, as a matter of fact, quite as notably an artist in verse paragraphs. His art in varying the mood and tone and pace of succeeding paragraphs gives a diversity that indemnifies for any supposed monotony resultant from the closed couplet.

One may well suspect that in later days the *Essay on Man* would have been more favourably regarded by critics if the poet had printed his verse paragraphs frankly as such — if, in the manner of Traherne's *Centuries of Meditations* or of Tennyson's *In Memoriam,* he had been content to leave his verse units as fragmentary reflections on philosophic ideas that are bound to have recurrent interest. Pope did, of course, indicate units by marginal Roman numerals; yet he wished finally to think of his work as "a short, yet not imperfect, system of ethics."

Of this "system" he fell short, and of all the stages of poetic page 61 / composition that of "settling the parts" into a coherent and effective order worried him most. The difficulty is especially acute in the early thirties, when he is at work on different poems simultaneously; but perhaps the difficulty is inherent in the attempt to write fairly long poems that are discursively reflective.

Coming to the last stage of composition to be considered, we can have no doubt that the poet did make his fragmentary reflections "agreeable enough to be read with pleasure." Of his *limae labor et mora* already much has been said, and perhaps it is all summed up in the general opinion that Pope seldom altered without improvement. Examples may be superfluous, but the manuscripts of the *Essay on Man* are so full of them that one cannot forbear quoting. The opening lines of Epistle II —

> Know then thyself; presume not God to scan;
> The proper study of mankind is man —

are so natural an example of the firm, lapidary style that one can hardly imagine the couplet is the result of much reshaping. But in the Morgan Library manuscript the Epistle begins with the comparatively feeble

> we ourselves
> Learn ~~then Thyself,~~ not God presume to scan
>
> But
> ~~And~~ know, the Study of Mankind is *Man.*

And the Harvard manuscript has as lines 13–14 of the Epistle (after 12 lines of apostrophe to Bolingbroke):

> Know
> ~~Learn~~ we ourselves, not God presume to scan,
>
> The only Science Convincd
> ~~But know~~, the Study of Mankind is *Man.*

Obviously the real inspiration here came after some floundering. The couplet is a superb example of Pope's process of perfecting his utterance. One may note that there is nothing inherently "decorative" about the process. Another type of perfecting is seen in the famous passage in Epistle I concerning the Indian concept of Heaven. In part the Morgan manuscript reads:

> Yet Nature's flattery this Hope has given;
> Behind his cloud-topt Hills he builds a Heaven,
> Some happier World, wch woods on woods infold,
> Where never christian pierced for thirst of Gold. **page 62 /**
> Some safer World, in depth of Woods embrac'd
> Some happier Island in the watry waste,
> Where slaves once more their native land behold,
> No Fiends torment, nor Christians thirst for Gold.
> Where Gold n'er grows, & never Spaniards come,
> Where Trees bear maize, & Rivers flow wth Rum,
> Exil'd, or chain'd, he lets you understand
> Death but returns him to his native Land;
> Or firm as Martyrs, smiling yields the ghost,
> Rich of a Life, that is not to be lost.

In the Harvard manuscript Pope had improved the first of these lines into its standard printed form, doubtless because of the unsatisfactory implications of *flattery*, which later Mr. Elwin was at pains to point out. Other verses, of some merit, were omitted to secure a firmer line of thought or at least greater brevity. The problem *proprie communia dicere* was encountered by Pope at every point in his revisions.

Of the fourteen lines just quoted Pope has crossed through for deletion lines 3 and 4 and the last six: the printed texts give variants of the remaining six. The case may serve as occasion to remark that Pope's method of composition by accreting paragraphs is in part balanced by this art of blotting. The Morgan manuscript of the four epistles of the *Essay on Man* contains almost 250 lines that did not appear in versions printed by Pope. Dr. Johnson concluded from the Homer manuscripts of Pope that the poet's method "was to write his first thoughts in his first words, and gradually to amplify, decorate, rectify, and refine them." This statement is largely, but not completely, true. There exists, for example, an early manuscript form of what was to become the *Epistle to Dr. Arbuthnot;* and the manuscript runs only to about a hundred lines — less than one-fourth the final length of the poem. But Pope practised condensation as well, and omitted much that he set down on paper in his working manuscripts. Concerning the decorative quality of his later composition there may be argument. If added illustrative details be regarded in the manner of gargoyles, these accretions are decorative. But if one considers Pope's imaginative phrasing after the *Dunciad* of 1729 — and apart from Book IV of that poem (1743) — the effect is not decorative but functional. His labour to produce

Know then thyself, presume not God to scan **page 63 /**

is a fair example. The diction is chiselled and "rectified," but not ornate. Through all the stages of composition — the turning of prose hints into verse paragraphs, the ranging of these paragraphs, and the final *limae labor* — Pope's object is the rectification of expression. For him poetry is perfected utterance, and his working manuscripts, especially those from the early thirties, testify to his unwearied attempts to polish his paragraphs and make them "agreeable enough to be read with pleasure." **page 64 /**

The Scale of Wonder

R. A. BROWER

In the bravura address to Bolingbroke at the close of the *Essay on Man,* Pope declares

> That urg'd by thee, I turn'd the tuneful art
> From sounds to things, from fancy to the heart;
> For Wit's false mirror held up Nature's light . . .

In the language of the *Essay on Criticism,* Pope is saying that he has put behind him the "wit" of fancy that distorts and decorates, and that he has now written a piece of "true Wit." In other words, he has seen and expressed the true nature page 206 / of things, especially the truth of human nature ("the Heart"). But true wit does not exclude "sprightliness," and so the *Essay on Man* like the *Essay on Criticism* is a poem of "nature" *and* "wit," of "Nature to advantage dressed." If it is easy in reading the earlier essay to forget that "the heart" is there, it is still easier for readers of the *Essay on Man* to become very solemn indeed and treat the poem as a Lucretian *De Rerum Natura* rather than as an Horatian essay. At times Pope may have fancied that he was actually writing in Lucretius' manner. In a letter to Swift written a few months after the publication of the fourth epistle (1734), he raises the question, though not too seriously, as shown by the context. He is speaking of his amusement at not being

---

Reprinted, by permission, from *Alexander Pope: The Poetry of Allusion,* by R. A. Brower (Oxford: The Clarendon Press, 1959).

recognized as the author when the epistles were published earlier without his name:

> The design of concealing myself was good, and had its full effect; I was thought a divine, a philosopher, and what not? and my doctrine had a sanction I could not have given to it. Whether I can proceed in the same grave march like Lucretius, or must descend to the gayeties of Horace, I know not, or whether I can do either?

Although he had earlier written to Swift of the *Essay on Man* and Bolingbroke's parallel prose work as "aspiring to philosophy," he had followed this remark with a quotation from Horace that again indicates a certain lightness of tone. He says in effect, "Let us forget about politics and like Horace 'spend our Time in the Search and Enquiry after Truth and Decency'."

Whether Horace or Lucretius won the day in the completed poem can be best answered not by a philosopher or a literary critic, but by the "common reader." He will know, for example how seriously to take the last couplet of Pope's opening address to Bolingbroke:

> Laugh where we must, be candid where we can;
> But vindicate the ways of God to Man.
> (I. 15–16)

The mere reader of poetry will note the chummy, clubby "we's," the comfortable and worldly invitation to "laugh" or view with generosity (eighteenth-century "candour") "this page 207 / scene of man." He will observe too the shift from Milton's "justifie" to "vindicate." Milton's grammatical form is purposive or optative, a clause of purpose used in a prayer: "that . . . I may assert Eternal Providence,/And (may) justifie . . ." To "justifie" in Milton's context is to demonstrate largely the divine order and justice; but such meanings taken with Milton's prayerful tone have a very different effect from Pope's "vindicate." Though "vindicate" refers to similar kinds of justification, the word reeks with the atmosphere of debate and points scored. As qualified by Pope's tone the meaning becomes positively hearty and jaunty, an assertion of divine justice in the voice of a man ready to take on all comers. Justification seems to come in almost as an afterthought to other concerns: "Laugh where we must, be candid . . ./*But* vindicate. . . ." The study of nature is all but subdued to the purpose of wit, the happy hunting of the poet and friend in their rural retirement:

> Together let us beat this ample field,
> Try what the open, what the covert yield;
> The latent tracts, the giddy heights explore
> Of all who blindly creep, or sightless soar;
> Eye Nature's walks, shoot Folly as it flies;
> And catch the Manners living as they rise . . .
> (9–14)

More often than not in the liveliest passages of the *Essay* the grand exploration of nature's plan is closely linked with "shooting folly" and "catching the manners," with critical observation and witty dramatization of human nature as we generally know it. For the student of Pope's development, the *Essay on Man* marks his arrival at maturity as a poet who combined moral seriousness with satiric wit. In the *Essay on Man,* as in occasional passages of the *Dunciad* of 1728 and 1729, we see how brilliantly Pope can exploit various literary traditions and earlier "imitations" in the pursuit of his critical and satirical aims.

But we can hardly say what kind of a poem the *Essay on Man* is, or where and when it is poetry, or whether it has imaginative unity, unless we attend to what Pope says, to his "argument." He certainly does not have an argument in the Miltonic and heroic sense of a myth that dramatizes impor- **page 208 /** tant values and beliefs. But it is clear enough that he has an argument in the persuasive sense of the word, and it is equally apparent that he claims to have an argument in the sense of a discourse with an ordered series of inferences that follow from certain first principles or assumption. Few readers who have looked for this kind of logic in the poem, from Dr. Johnson to recent students of philosophy in literature, have been very happy with what they have found. Pope's language has the look of argument, his "then's" and "hences" indicate logical sequence, and some logical connexion can usually be discovered between the stages of his discourse. But as in most defective arguments, we are troubled less by what is present than by what is absent. If, for example, we look for full proof of Pope's most important principles either by example or by deduction, we shall not find it. Pope constantly *refers* to historic arguments about man and the universe without ever presenting them adequately in the poem. One illustration —

from a passage that troubled Dr. Johnson — is worth looking at, since it summarizes some of the main principles that Pope assumes:

> Of Systems possible, if 'tis confest
> That Wisdom infinite must form the best,
> Where all must full or not coherent be,
> And all that rises, rise in due degree;
> Then, in the scale of reas'ning life, 'tis plain
> There must be, somewhere, such a rank as Man;
> And all the question (wrangle e'er so long)
> Is only this, if God has plac'd him wrong?
>
> (I. 43–50)

Most readers will recognize the "system" of nature, the great scale or Chain of Being, to which we referred in discussing the *Essay on Criticism.* Thanks to Lovejoy's study and to the writings of numerous followers, this view of the universe has become almost as much of a commonplace for us as for Pope's contemporaries. One happy result of its return to the realm of the familiar is that like eighteenth-century readers we can attend to the poetry without being surprised or confused by the doctrine. page 209 /

The main features of this traditional view appear in Pope's summary. "Wisdom infinite," the Platonic "Good" that later became identified with God, must create "the best" of universes. The "best" is a "full" universe, one in which all possible forms of being are created, and it is also a "coherent" universe, one in which there is an unbroken continuity of created beings arranged hierarchically from the lowest to the highest forms. "Then," says Pope, if we grant these principles, "there must be, somewhere," in the scale of beings who have reason, the "rank" of man. In the immediate context "then" is logically exact, but if we reconsider the principles to which we are assenting we may feel decidedly uncomfortable. Pope does not present here or elsewhere the reasoning by which the Neoplatonists explained why God must create "the best" universe and why the "full" one is the best. He flatly states the principle, just as he lightly assumes the necessity of coherence and hierarchical order. Coherence is a most troublesome principle, as anyone can see who considered whether every conceivable form of being between fish and birds or monkeys and man has in fact been created. Or if we ask with Johnson what "somewhere" means, doubts arise as to what exactly Pope is concluding from his principles. The local exactness of "then" diminishes in importance when we discover how little support Pope offers for his dogmas. It is then too much to be told that "all the question" is only whether God has placed man in the wrong place, since — as Johnson saw — there could be no question of a wrong place in a universe created by "Supreme Wisdom." The thought occurs that Pope had not attended very closely to his own argument. The aside, "wrangle e'er so long," which is surprisingly low in tone, is probably a sign of his impatience with the refinements of logical discourse. We are reminded of Dryden's brusque way of squelching arguments in the *Religio Laici:*

> For points obscure are of small use to learn;
> But common quiet is mankind's concern
>
> (449–50)

But though not closely built as an argument, the poem page 210 / illustrates in a large way Pope's first principles and a number of related philosophical doctrines and ideas fashionable in the eighteenth century. For example, much of the poem centres on the typical optimist proposition that "Whatever is, is Right," a statement, it must be emphasized, not expressive of naïve cheerfulness. When Pope and his contemporaries speak of this as the best of possible worlds, their emphasis is on *possible.* Of worlds possible, given the nature of God and the necessity of impartial and unchanging laws of nature, ours is the best that can be conceived. The creation is not designed for the individual, but for the whole, and of the whole man is not an adequate judge. Evil, though real and inevitable, is explained in terms of the ancient and Renaissance doctrines of the harmony of opposites:

> All Discord, Harmony, not understood;
> All partial Evil, universal Good:
>
> (I. 291–2)

After setting forth these general views of Nature's order in the first epistle, Pope goes on to illustrate them, first with respect to man as an individual (Epistle II), and next with respect to man as a member of society (Epistle III). He defends the rightness of the overall plan by showing how reason and self-love (in the various "modes" of the passions) are harmonized within the individual. Reason, the guiding, restraining power, is given a fairly negative role in this process as compared with the "ruling Passion," which in some inexplicable way strengthens our "best principle" and provides the motive power of virtue. In society "self-love," the drive to self-fulfilment in man, happily works for the good of the whole. Pope thus finds support for another favourite eighteenth-century conviction that "Self-love and Social are the same." It might seem that "Happiness" (the theme of Epistle IV), in the sense of "Good, Pleasure, Ease Content!" could hardly be "our being's end and aim" under a plan that necessarily involves evil and suffering and even complete disaster for many individual persons. Pope avoids the inconsistency by redefining happiness as virtue, a Stoic-Christian virtue which is not dependent on externals but an achievement of the inner life. The conclusion to the four page 211 / epistles, that "all our Knowledge is OURSELVES TO KNOW," is not unexpected since a dominant theme of the earlier epistles is the ancient Greek and Socratic doctrine that the "proper study of Mankind is Man." This humanist conviction, adjusted to the Christian doctrine that the greatest of the virtues is love, is probably not quite consistent with the emphasis put on the study of nature's plan in the physical universe.

But with all its minor and major inconsistencies the *Essay on Man* has a structure of ideas that are historically important and that were regarded by many of Pope's readers as valuable and true. It need hardly be said here that a structure of ideas, however consistently worked out, does not of itself make a poem. One could almost certainly dig out a set of propositions of considerable if not equal importance and involving no more contradictions, in Prior's *Solomon*, Akenside's *Pleasures of Imagination*, or the *Night Thoughts* of Young. While granting that all three are better poems for having included some important ideas in some sort of order, we shall hardly be tempted to regard any of these awesome "philosophic" pieces as poetry of a high quality. It is a happy thought that we should not think of putting the *Essay on Man* among these monuments of vanished minds. The dulling effects of the eighteenth-century grand subject on the brightest of minds have never been more perfectly illustrated than in Prior's colossal bore. A poet of urbane wit, who wrote at least one poem of finely serious reflection, the lines *Written in the Beginning of Mezeray's History of France*, he became a plodding, relentlessly elevated teacher when he addressed himself to *Solomon on the Vanity of the World.* Pope was not untouched by the same blight, but he comes off remarkably well when compared with his contemporaries. Unlike any other long "philosophic" poem of the century, the *Essay on Man* is continuously readable, and at its best it is poetry of a high order. To put it baldly, Pope succeeded because he did not write the poem he seems to have thought he was writing, at least in moments when he was discussing his grandiose project with Bolingbroke or Spence. It is worth page 212 / noting that he did not take an august tone in writing of the poem to Swift, who had a way of bringing out Pope's most human, least polite, or pretentious qualities. It is also quite certain that Pope did not write the kind of philosophic essay Bolingbroke would have written in prose, as it is equally clear that he did not systematically versify Bolingbroke's philosophy.

To see how Pope escaped into poetry, how he made his own kind of poetry out of ideas that he had gathered from many sources besides his talks with Bolingbroke, we must consider the texture of his verse and the modes of expression that give the *Essay on Man* its special character. We may then be able to describe its poetic structure or design and see what emphases appear and where — if unconsciously — Pope was putting his weight and revealing his concerns. For Pope, almost invariably, a mode of expression includes a mode of imitation or allusion, a remark true even of the *Essay on Man*, probably the least obviously allusive of Pope's longer works. Although imagery plays a fairly important part in the *Essay*, allusion, as so often in Pope and Dryden, works as an equivalent for metaphor.

To anyone who examines the poem without presuppositions, the most characteristic uses of language are almost always modes of address, ways of indicating tone and shifts of tone. The essence of Pope's "drama" in the *Essay*, as in later satirical epistles, lies in the play of tone, the tone he takes to the fictive characters he is addressing, whether they are a set of readers, a friend, or a victim, any one of the many dramatic impersonations of the poet's other selves. The common reader who is surprised by the jauntiness and social heartiness with which Pope announces his "high argument" is noticing something important if obvious, that the *Essay on Man* is written within the dramatic framework of an eighteenth-century Horatian epistle. But as Pope is speaking page 213 / to a noble lord on a pompous theme, he has brought his tone nearer to the grand address of Dryden than to the casualness of Horace. The *Essay on Man* is on the whole closer to the more vigorous and less intimate passages of the *Essay on Criticism* than to the *Epistle to Dr. Arbuthnot.* Or to take examples from Horace — it is closer to the aloof nobility of *Nil admirari* than the inwardness and friendliness of *Hoc erat in votis.* As in the *Essay on Criticism* "good breeding" is much — at times a little too much — in evidence:

> Awake, my St. John! leave all meaner things
> To low ambition, and the pride of Kings.

Throughout the four epistles Pope keeps up the illusion of well-bred good talk, injecting the conversational note by devices of many kinds: parenthetic asides to the reader, sensible observations often marked by an introductory "'tis," persuasive "know's" and "think's," more casual "say's" (to introduce another point of view or a stronger argument), and rather too insistent questions as if to keep the reader's attention from wandering.

The two most frequent modes of address that give this conversation-lesson its peculiar quality go well beyond the usual conventions of intimacy and politeness. In the midst of his exhortation to Bolingbroke Pope steps aside for a moment to marvel at the universe,

> A mighty maze! but not without a plan . . .
> (I. 6)

Some thirty lines later he interrupts his argument to marvel in another way to another auditor,

> Presumptuous Man! the reason wouldst thou find
> Why form'd so weak, so little, and so blind!
> (I. 35–36)

In the course of the *Essay* Pope keeps running up and down this scale of marvelling, from the grandly solemn to the rudely ironic. A rhetorical fever chart of such exclamations would reveal the interesting fact that as they increase in intensity and number, the poetic life of the verse increases in vigour and variety and also in fun or in profundity, whether "the Muse now stoops, or now ascends." The "marvelling" page 214 / expressions take almost every conceivable form, although a number of types keep recurring. In context of both the higher and lower attitudes, we find many lines or passages beginning with "Lo!" "Behold!" "Mark!" "Look!" "See!" and "Go!," salutes to abstractions ("Oh Happiness!" "Vast chain of being!") and wondering questions (often hard to distinguish from exclamations in Pope's punctuation). In purely ironic contexts, such expressions (especially "Go!" and "See!") appear in even greater numbers as the whole repertory of marvelling devices is turned on the unwilling pupil, that "Vile worm!," man. Though an occasional "my lord" or "friend," or "you," or a polite exhortation to "know" or "learn" remind us that the well-bred auditor is not forgotten, Pope's most striking addresses are in the vein of scornful wonder. "Thou fool!" and "fool!" or equivalent compliments are showered down on the "wond'rous creature!" (Some samples: "Go, wiser thou!" "Oh blind to truth!" "Oh sons of earth!" "foolish man!"). Another type of expresssion also equating man and fool — though with an accent of wonder — is the aloof imperative, "let fools," "let graceless zealots," "let subtle schoolmen." But the two types of marvelling are always merging, and the nature of Pope's art and his central attitudes are clearest in addresses poised neatly between the extremes like "great standing miracle!" or "painful preheminence!"

To see the kind of glissade Pope executes in passing from one attitude to its opposite, and the poetry of ideas he is creating, consider what happens between "A mighty maze!" and "Presumptuous Man!" the two examples with which we began. After urging St. John to join him in "vindicating the ways of God to Man," the poet continues with another Miltonic echo,

> Say first, of God above, or Man below,
> What can we reason, but from what we know?
> Of Man what see we, but his station here,
> From which to reason, or to which refer?
> Thro' worlds unnumber'd tho' the God be known,
> 'Tis ours to trace him only in our own.
> He, who thro' vast immensity can pierce,
> See worlds on worlds compose one universe,
> Observe how system into system runs,
> What other planets circle other suns,
> What vary'd being peoples ev'ry star,
> May tell why Heav'n has made us as we are.
> But of this frame the bearings, and the ties,
> The strong connections, nice dependencies,

> Gradations just, has thy pervading soul
> Look'd thro'? or can a part contain the whole?
>   Is the great chain, that draws all to agree,
> And drawn supports, upheld by God, or thee?
>   Presumptuous Man, the reason wouldst thou find,
> Why form'd so weak, so little, and so blind!
> (I. 17–36)

The rich adjustment of ideas and style through learned reference and literary allusion is astonishing. The epic command of the first line becomes in the next the question of men who argue by analogy from the known order to the unknown, the change in style making way for the contrasting picture of a mind that embraces the whole universe and its plan. This wondrous mind is described in language recalling Lucretius' high praise of Epicurus and also Virgil's lines on the Lucretian philosopher, the passage of the *Georgics* echoed in *Windsor Forest*. The philosopher's comprehensive view is artfully presented in terms appropriate partly to a contemporary astronomer and partly to poets and theologians in the Platonic-Christian tradition of the Great Chain of Being. The final question, which calls for assent to the argument that we can reason only from "what we know," alludes to the golden chain of Milton and Homer. Thus the reader is prepared for the thrust of the next line, "Presumptuous Man!" which sounds on the surface like an heroic epithet and is of course cuttingly sarcastic.

The modulation of tone to this level from the awe of "mighty maze" is truly marvellous and shows how Pope felt his way through his philosophic "materials" to an attitude and a kind of poetry peculiarly his own. As we noted above, the "Say first" that he starts with does not remain Miltonic for long. Milton was addressing the Holy Spirit (half-merged with the "Heavenly Muse"), but Pope, it soon appears, is much nearer earth. **page 216 /**

> Say first, of God above, or Man below,
> What can we reason, but from what we know?

The heroic "say" is inclined toward the later argumentative "say's," and "we" is very much "men like you and me," or "man" addressed as "thee" at the end of the passage. The high Lucretian praise of the all-seeing philosopher seems close in effect to wondering at the "mighty maze," but unlike the ancient poets and the

Pope of *Windsor Forest,* the poet of the *Essay* is ironic. He speaks in the voice of a man finely withdrawn from pretensions to "Wisdom infinite." The naïve listener who has been taken in by the encomium is gently knifed as the moral is brought home,

> . . . has thy pervading soul
> Look'd thro'? or can a part contain the whole?

"Thee" in the next couplet is cruelly *ad hominem:* "Is the great chain . . . upheld by God, or *thee?*" "Presumptuous Man!" is the final blow to aspiring "wit" and the battery of unanswerable questions that follows reduces man to his finite "foolish" status.

What has happened to the "argument" and the "structure of ideas" in Pope's poetic transformation? Certainly very little has been proved, either by deduction, or by citing evidence, and yet a great deal of "doctrine" has been implied and, in spite of the irony, it has been made impressive and dramatically convincing. We get a sense of the great order of nature according to both the Newtonian and Platonic views, we have also a vivid impression of the fine ordering of parts within the whole, and we are left with a grand Homeric image of the lively dependency of the whole order on God. Here is wonder with some substance to it, wonder that is more than a rhetorical gesture. But the poetic drift is always towards irony, a tendency that has a marked effect on the philosophic "content' and that gives us a clear indication of Pope's deepest concerns. What moves him, the feeling that shapes his style and governs the way in which he combines allusions and the tone with which he expresses them, is his strong antipathy to man's presumption, to pride, especially of mind or "wit" (in the older sense of intelligence):

> In Pride, in reas'ning Pride, our error lies . . . **page 217 /**
> (I. 123)

Absurd trust in human reason is as usual for Pope inseparable from fullness:

> When the proud steed shall know why Man restrains
> His fiery course, or drives him o'er the plains;
> When the dull Ox, why now he breaks the clod,
> Is now a victim, and now Egypt's God:
> Then shall Man's pride and dulness comprehend
> His actions', passions', being's, use and end . . .
> (I. 61–66)

Behind Pope's attitude is the enlightened distrust of scholastic logic that can be traced in Bacon, Hobbes, and Locke:

> Let subtle schoolmen teach these friends [Reason, Self-love]
> to fight,
> More studious to divide than to unite,
> And Grace and Virtue, Sense and Reason split,
> With all the rash dexterity of Wit:
> Wits, just like fools, at war about a Name,
> Have full as oft no meaning, or the same.
> (II. 81–86)

Such "Wits" in philosophy, like merely clever "wits" in literature are little better than fools. In Pope this attitude toward over-confidence in reason is identified with Socratic confession of "ignorance," which is accompanied as always by the belief that the most valuable knowledge is to "know thyself."

In the movement from wonder at the mighty maze to scorn of presumptuous man and in the way Pope presses traditional views and styles in the service of his irony lies the essence of his poetry in the *Essay on Man.* To feel the link between these modes of "marvelling" is to grasp the key to its imaginative design, to see how it is composed as a poem and what it mainly expresses. We may now ask whether the design is continuous and where and why the *Essay* succeeds or fails as poetry. Our answers will also give us further insight into the relation between Pope's achievement as a moral and satirical poet and his earlier successes in quite different poetic modes.

The First Epistle of the *Essay on Man,* on "Man, with respect to the universe," is commonly regarded as the best page 218 / of the four. It includes more of the passages that are generally known and remembered, nearly all of the famous purple patches, except for the lines on man's "middle state" in the Second Epistle. There are also relatively fewer moments in reading it when we are disturbed by doubts as to whether we are surely reading a *poem* (even of the conversational variety). The poetic design is clearest and most continuous in this first epistle since the polarity of man and the universe almost inevitably issues in a polarity of attitudes and rhetorical modes. As soon as Pope begins to expatiate on the blessings that accompany man's state — his ignorance of the future, his eternal hopefulness — irony intrudes:

> Oh blindness to the future! kindly giv'n,
> That each may fill the circle mark'd by Heav'n . . .
> (85–86)

Like the lamb that "licks that hand just rais'd to shed his blood," man fortunately does not know the time and the manner of his end. The Advice to "Hope humbly then" is brought home in the first passage of serious marvelling, the picture of the "poor Indian" content with a simple hope, his soul uncorrupted by "proud Science." Pope's noble savage is a reincarnation of the shepherd-hero of the *Pastorals* and the *Iliad,* a dweller in the visionary American of *Windsor Forest,* where

> . . . the freed Indians in their native groves
> Reap their own fruits, and woo their sable loves . . .
> (409–10)

page 219 /

The diction has touches of the heroic-descriptive manner of *Windsor Forest* and the *Iliad:* "the solar walk" (originally from Dryden's *Annus Mirabilis*), the "cloud-topt hill," and "the watry waste." There is some civilized amusement in this picture of the Indian's simple desires, but in the first line that follows, the irony is turned on proud "enlightened" man:

> Go, wiser thou! and in thy scale of sense
> Weigh thy Opinion against Providence . . .
> (113–14)

a couplet in the idiom and tone of Horace's advice in *Nil admirari,*

> i nunc, argentum et marmor vetus aeraque et artes suspice . . .
> (*Epp.* I. vi. 17–18)

(A similar contrast between low and high stations is made by Horace in the satirical diatribe of slave to master, *Satires* II. 7. 95–101.) Pope clinches the lesson in a piece of antithetical wit recalling a well-known couplet in the *Essay on Criticism:*

> In Pride, in reas'ning Pride, our error lies;
> All quit their sphere, and rush into the skies.
> (123–4)

But Pope could hardly fail to observe that primitive man can also be a victim of pride, and in the "Keatsian" lines on the happy child of nature ("For me kind Nature . . ."), he writes an ironic pastoral rhapsody. The pastoral dream-world of "eternal springs and cloudless skies," referred to here in mocking accents, is contrasted with the true course of Nature, which works through unchanging laws that produce "plagues" and "earthquakes" as a part of "Heav'n's design."

Mock admiration for "Man . . . whom rational we call" gives way to the most effective deflation of our desire to "act or think beyond mankind":

> Why has not Man a microscopic eye?
> For this plain reason, Man is not a Fly.
> Say what the use, were finer optics giv'n,
> T' inspect a mite, not comprehend the heav'n?
> Or touch, if tremblingly alive all o'er,
> To smart and agonize at ev'ry pore?
> Or quick effluvia darting thro' the brain,
> Die of a rose in aromatic pain?
> (193–200)

The final couplet is one of the few in the poem where we are tempted to compare Pope's poetry of ideas with Donne's. In its exquisite accuracy and wit the image is inseparable from the subject of the metaphor, the disturbance that must follow if man were given powers not belonging to his place page 220 / in the order of being. Though the bond of feeling and thought is less close and the economy of style is less metaphysical in the lines that continue the argument, they are almost the best passage of serious marvelling in the whole poem:

> Far as Creation's ample range extends,
> The scale of sensual, mental pow'rs ascends:
> Mark how it mounts, to Man's imperial race,
> From the green myriads in the peopled grass:
> What modes of sight betwixt each wide extreme,
> The mole's dim curtain, and the lynx's beam:
> Of smell, the headlong lioness between,
> And hound sagacious on the tainted green:
> Of hearing, from the life that fills the flood,
> To that which warbles thro' the vernal wood:
> The spider's touch, how exquisitely fine!
> Feels at each thread, and lives along the line:
> In the nice bee, what sense so subtly true
> From pois'nous herbs extracts the healing dew:
> How Instinct varies in the grov'ling swine,

Compar'd, half-reas'ning elephant, with thine:
'Twixt that, and Reason, what a nice barrier;
For ever sep'rate, yet for ever near!
Remembrance and Reflection how ally'd;
What thin partitions Sense from Thought divide:
And middle natures, how they long to join,
Yet never pass th' insuperable line!
(207–23)

The language brings sharply to our senses what the scale means in extensiveness and variety, in the distance between the extremes, and in the thin partitions dividing successive classes of being. The attitude of wonder and the "ideas" of order are expressed through minute particulars of visual and tactile imagery: "the green myriads in the peopled grass," "the mole's dim curtain," and (a couplet that Tennyson especially admired)

The spider's touch, how exquisitely fine!
Feels at each thread, and lives along the line . . .

The art of the lines is (like Tennyson's) Virgilian in delicacy and exactness of epithet, a quality pointed out by Joseph Warton. The diction has touches of Pope's georgic-pastoral **page 221 /** style, and the description of animals, especially of smaller creatures, is very close to the semi-human and playfully heroic descriptions of the *Georgics*. But Pope's eye is so much on the detail and the image that relevance to the idea is not always kept clearly in mind: the "spider's touch" and the bee's "sense so subtly true" ought according to the argument to be matched by balancing extremes, but they are not. We are reminded of a similar fuzziness in the more philosophic lyrics of *In Memoriam*.

But in spite of some blurring of this sort, the large sequence of thought and feeling is clear and dynamic from here to the end of the epistle. We move naturally from wonder at fine details to the grand view of

See, thro' this air, this ocean, and this earth,
All matter quick, and bursting into birth.
Above, how high progressive life may go!
Around, how wide! how deep extend below!
(233–6)

But Pope's generalized *O altitudo*'s are a little vacuous, and we are relieved when he returns to the more concrete "beast, bird, fish," and "insect." The chaos that would follow any break in the chain of being leads to a fine passage of marvelling in the style of an Homeric oath:

> Let Earth unbalanc'd from her orbit fly,
> Planets and Suns run lawless thro' the sky,
> Let ruling Angels from their spheres be hurl'd,
> Being on being wreck'd, and world on world,
> Heav'ns whole foundations to their centre nod,
> And Nature tremble to the throne of God . . .

This Newtonian-Biblical (and Miltonic) apocalypse has a destination we have been anticipating since the fairly complimentary question addressed to man,

> The pow'rs of all subdu'd by thee alone,
> Is not thy Reason all these pow'rs in one?
> (231–2)

The scene of chaos ends rudely with

> All this dread ORDER break — for whom? for thee?
> Vile worm! — oh Madness, Pride, Impiety!

page 222 /

The awe has been too extreme, the rhetorical exclaiming too obvious to hold, and the heroic oath has a quality of mocking magnificence that easily turns to sarcasm. We know from the *Rape of the Lock* how easy it is to pass from imprecation to bathos:

> Sooner let Earth, Air, Sea, to *Chaos* fall,
> Men, Monkies, Lap-dogs, Parrots, perish all!
> (IV. 119–20)

But ridicule of man's "ruling Mind" bounces us back to its opposite (the swing is almost inevitable in Pope), "the great directing Mind of All," and prepares us for the lines that express best the sense of wonder at the great life glowing within each part. By combining images from astronomy, gardening, and organic form in art, Pope alludes deftly to other expressions of harmony and order at other points in the epistle and the poem:

> All are but parts of one stupendous whole,
> Whose body Nature is, and God the soul;
> That, chang'd thro' all, and yet in all the same,
> Great in the earth, as in th' aethereal frame,

> Warms in the sun, refreshes in the breeze,
> Glows in the stars, and blossoms in the trees.
> Lives thro' all life, extends thro' all extent,
> Spreads undivided, operates unspent,
> Breathes in our soul, informs our mortal part,
> As full, as perfect, in a hair as heart;
> As full, as perfect, in vile Man that mourns,
> As the rapt Seraph that adores and burns;
> To him no high, no low, no great, no small;
> He fills, he bonds, connects, and equals all.
> (267–80)

The oscillation from the great to the small prepares us for the final sharp injunction to proud man's "erring reason,"

> Cease then, nor ORDER Imperfection name . . .
> (231)

Though Pope may not have written the parts of this epistle in their present sequence, he has composed them into poetry with an order of linked attitudes and modes of expression that grow easily out of the "structure of ideas." **page 223 /**

. . . .

CHAPTER SIX

Poetic Process and Literary Analysis

I. A. RICHARDS

Poetic Process and Literary Analysis

I. A. RICHARDS

My title, I notice, can seem to break my subject up into two halves. I would therefore like to begin by suggesting that it would be unfortunate if we let any clear-cut division, much less any opposition or contrast, form *too early* in our thought. ?Poetic Process? . . . ?Literary Analysis?.[1] Each phrase can be highly elastic, each serves to name many very different things. And their boundaries can shift very suddenly. What I would wish on this occasion to be concerned with chiefly is the fruitful interactions of the energies so describable (Poetic Process — the activities through which a poem comes into being; Literary Analysis — the attempt to anatomize a poem) with side glances only at the possibilities of mutual frustration. A good deal of Poetic Process consists in, and advances by, Literary Analysis and, on the other hand, Literary Analysis is often Poetic Process attempting to examine and appraise itself.

One other preliminary: there are sayings that truly deserve to be called "ever memorable" in the sense that the more constantly we bear them in mind the more error we shall be spared. Among these, should we not give a high place to Coleridge's "Do not let us introduce an Act of Uniformity against Poets"?[2] There are many ways of passing Acts of Uniformity: one is by

[1] The marks ?________? mean 'query'.
[2] Coleridge, letter to Thelwall, December 17, 1796.

From *Style in Language*, edited by Thomas A. Sebeok (1960). Reprinted by permission of the publishers, John Wiley & Sons Inc. and M.I.T. Press.

framing definitions. Here are four lines in which Wordsworth reminds Coleridge that they are no friends of

> that false secondary power, by which
> In weakness, we create distinctions, then
> Deem that our puny boundaries are things
> Which we perceive, and not which we have made.[3]

It will be only to some Poetic Processes, occurring in some poets only, and on some occasions only, that what I may contrive to say will apply. page 9 / Similarly with Literary Analysis: there are more ways than one of exploring our enjoyments.

Among our more obvious sources of information upon Poetic Process, where shall we place the poet's own account of the matter? It is customary at present to play it down—although any scrap of paper carrying any reference, however oblique, to circumstances of composition or any gossip about occasions is hoarded for the record as never before. Poets of standing—whatever their friends and relatives may be doing—remain as sparing of explanations as ever: to be mysterious and unforthcoming about his own work seems a part of the poet's role. Those who have departed from it have often seemed to feel the need of a cloak. Stephen Spender, in his *The Making of a Poem*, is one of the few exceptions. Edgar Allan Poe uses both cloak and mask: in explaining how "The Raven" came into being he begins by dressing the revelation up as a mere "magazine paper." Coming from such a "magaziner" as Poe, this is surely an ambivalent phrase.

> I have often thought how interesting a magazine paper might be written by an author who would—that is to say who could—detail, step by step, the processes by which one of his compositions attained its ultimate point of completion. Why such a paper has never been given to the world, I am much at a loss to say—but perhaps the authorial vanity has had more to do with the omission than any other cause.

We may perhaps linger on this phrase "authorial vanity." We are on ticklish ground here as Poe very well knows. He goes on:

> Most authors—poets in especial—prefer having it understood that they compose by a species of fine frenzy—an ecstatic intuition—and would positively shudder at letting the public take a

[3] Wordsworth, *The Prelude*, (1805–1806) Book II, 221–224.

> peep behind the scenes, at the elaborate and vacillating crudities of thought — at the true purposes seized only at the last moment — at the innumerable glimpses of idea that arrived not at the maturity of full view — at the fully matured fancies discarded in despair as unmanageable — at the cautious selections and rejections — at the painful erasures and interpolations — in a word at the wheels and pinions.

Alas, we find nothing of all this in what follows. Instead we are given an ostentatious parade of allegedly perfect adjustment of selected means to fully foreseen ends. Poe, so eager — in Harry Levin's phrase — "to convince the world of his self-mastery," spares no pains to make this clear.

> It is my design to render it manifest that no one point in its composition is referable to accident or intuition; that the work proceeded, step by step, to its completion with the precision and rigid consequence of a mathematical problem.

What species of "the authorial vanity" is this? Who shall say? But, however "The Raven" may in fact have been written, we know that most poems are not composed so; the authors' manuscripts, where first drafts are available, at least show us that.

page 10 /

Now to the group of questions with which I am most concerned. It is time to state them, and in somewhat provocative form, so that — whether or not I can do anything toward answering them — the questions themselves may be strikingly posed for your consideration. "What, if anything, have its occasion, origin, motivation, its psychological and compositional history to do with the being of the completed poem?" I am trying to pose this group of questions in such a way that — for readers with the scatter of prepossessions which you, I conjecture, enjoy — a sizable section will reply at once with (*a*) "Why, *everything*, of course!" and another sizable section with (*b*) "Why, *nothing*, of course!" and yet another with (*c*) "Well, it depends, of course!" And I will be happy if those in the last section outnumber those in the first two.

I will try now to bring the problem into better focus in two very different ways: *first*, by sketching some of the reasons that may prompt a thinker to reply with *a* or *b* or *c; secondly*, by taking a short poem for which I have special information — since I wrote it myself — and detailing some of "the elaborate and vacillating crudities of thought . . . the true purposes seized only at the last moment . . . the painful erasures and interpolations," in a word the sort of thing Poe left out of his account of the composition of "The Raven." I am doing this in the hope of making the problem as concrete as possible, so that we may possibly be able to put our fingers on questions about the Poetic Process which concern the Being or Nature of the poem and separate them from questions where "the answer little meaning — little relevancy bore." That is the program.

First, why should anyone answer "Why, *everything* . . .!"? Chiefly — don't you think? — because he takes the questions historically, or psychologically or biologically, as asking "By what steps, through what causal sequences, has the poem come to consist of these words in this order?" If so, the occasion, the motivation, the psychological and compositional history do have *everything* to do with the poem.

Then, why should anyone answer "Why, *nothing* . . .!"? Chiefly — don't you think? — because he takes the question linguistically, or stylistically, as asking: "Given these words in this order, what gives them the powers they have?" Asked so, we can see, I think, that the poet's biography need have nothing to do with the powers of the poem.

Finally, the deliberations and discriminations of those who might answer "It depends . . . !" are more complex to describe. Here come in questions about the kind of poetry it may be and its relations to the rest of the known poetry of the author, to his other utterances, to the literature and colloquial of the period, to possible sources, to echoes, and so forth. page 11 / Perhaps I can best summarize these considerations by remarking that the author in his Poetic Process, in his actual work on the poem, is an imaginary construct — a handsome creation of the imagination — based on our understanding of the poem. Such is the normal case, the type situation. We then use this imaginary construct — the poet at work — to help us in further interpretation, and we often forget meanwhile that he is our theoretical invention.

Let me turn now to the unusual, the abnormal case, the non-typical situation when we *have* access through the author's testimony — made from the best of his knowledge and belief — about what went on in the Poetic Process. After looking at this poem and at the privileged commentary or explanation, we may, I hope, be in a better position to ask certain questions about what Literary Analysis can tell us of *what is* and *is not* in the poem.

A poem may be regarded as a suitcase (I regret that my metaphor is so old-fashioned) which the poet may think he packs and the reader may think he unpacks. If they think so,

> They know not well the subtle ways
> I keep, and pass, and turn again.

So, at least, the poem, I think, is entitled to retort.

Here is the poem:

HARVARD YARD IN APRIL
APRIL IN HARVARD YARD

Or, rather, here is not the poem but only its title — otherwise I should not tax your patience long. It was, I believe, said of the library at Yale "This is not the library; the library is inside!" In a moment I will be putting on the page what? . . . not the poem itself but its lines. A poem "itself" is a most elusive thing, I suggest, that can never be put on any screen or page. Can we even put the words of a poem on a page? I wonder. We can put a notation for them there. But there are many linguists and the like about these parts these days, and I know better than to use the word lightly.

When I put a notation for the words of my poem on the screen, I shall avail myself of another of my authorial privileges *and read them.* That is, I shall give you, through the auditory channel, another notation: an acoustic notation ?parallel? (but we must question this word) to the optical notation. This reading, of course, acts as a most powerful persuader as to how the words are to be taken — much more subtle, penetrating, and comprehensive than the glosses and comments which follow. But, I need hardly point out — or need I? — that an author's reading (like any other reader's) has no authority which does not derive from the poem itself. These page 12 / readings, these renderings, these vocal interpretations are ways of packing, or finding, in the poem what may or may not be there. The author no more than his reader, I submit, can wish things into his poem — or wish them out. Consider the title. It is supposed to have a great deal to do with the poem. But I (as author) cannot settle that. No more can you (as reader). It is something to be settled between the poem and its title. They settle it; we do not. With its duplications and the time-space shift of "in," and the quasi-personification of April and the seesaw of emphasis, the title was added after the poem was finished. It was added partly to summarize, partly to give warning of, certain balancings within the poem.

Words in titles operate in a peculiar suspension and here we have a name within the title. "Harvard Yard," in particular, and "yard" in more general uses, will be charged very differently for different readers: for alumni of different universities and for American and British usage. For the British a yard is a rather humbly useful, limited, outdoor working space, unlike a garden and with no suggestion — with almost an anti-suggestion — of groves academic or sacred. Echoes of "prison yard" I would expect to be weak, although certain lines in the poem might invite them.

HARVARD YARD IN APRIL
APRIL IN HARVARD YARD

To and fro
Across the fretted snow
Figures, footprints, shadows go.

Their python boughs a-sway
The fountain elms cascade
In swinging lattices of shade
Where this or that or the other thought
Might perch and rest.
And rest they ought
For poise or reach.
Not all is timely. See, the beech,
In frosty elephantine skin
Still winter-sealed, will not begin
Though silt the alleys hour on hour.
Débris of the fallen flower,
And other flowery allure
Lounge sunlit on the Steps and there
Degrees of loneliness confer.

Lest, lest . . . away!
You may
Be lost by May page 13 /

The poem began, I recall, as a not-at-all wish-fulfilling dream of spring flight from Harvard — in lines in part contained in the *coda*: something like

Happiest they
Who would away
Who may be gone
By May.

These and similar tentatives were nursed awhile in traverse through the Yard to and from my office — the Yard's character as a pre-eminent locus of "to-and-fro-ing" (physical and spiritual) not coming into clear consciousness until the poem was almost finished. Only then, argument and counterargument (often not meeting) come to mind as a ground justifying some comparing of the fretted snow with tracked and retracked sheets of paper, together with a feeling that "figures" (line 3) could be numerals. There was earlier an echo from a lecture remark I had made: "The printed words of a poem are only its footprints on paper."

To and fro
Across the fretted snow
Figures, footprints, shadows go.

"Shadows," on the other hand, in actual composition looked forward from the first to "shade" (line 6). Afterward, as confirmation and support, I thought of de la Mare's

When less than even a shadow came
And stood within the room . . . ,

also of

Coming events cast their shadows before them . . . ,

and of T. S. Eliot's

The lengthened shadow of a man
Is history, said Emerson.

and, beyond all, of F. H. Bradley's "The shades nowhere speak without blood and the ghosts of Metaphysic accept no substitute. They reveal themselves only to that victim whose life they have drained and to converse with shadows he himself must become a shade."

How soon the day-by-day doings of the trees with the coming of spring began to belong to the poem I cannot clearly recall: "fountain" from my very first sight of American elms had seemed the obvious descriptive word; but only after 21 years and through the poem did I learn it is just that, the obvious descriptive word.

Python boughs: in and for the poem the peculiar writhe of boughs, at once sinous and angular, emphasized itself. Early drafts plrayed with "snakey," but with "a-sway," "cascade," and "shade" present, another page 14 / vowel seemed desirable, and since "lithe" and "writhe" were highly active in attempts to describe what was striking me, "python" felt final.

A-sway: the slighter motions of bare boughs are more visible before leafage comes, and in spring, when the eye is watching for every advance, there is more occasion than in winter to observe them. Winter gales agitate them, but with spring breezes they seem to stir of their own will as an outcome of the mounting sap.

Cascade: the thickening fringes and tassels of budding leaf and flower on outermost pendent sprays were green or golden drops defining the outline of the fountain's fall; their "shade," although thin, softening and cooling the glare of sunlight on the snow.

Perch: comparison of thoughts with birds seems inevitable. Trumbull Stickney's grand lines, for example:

> Sir, say no more. Within me 'tis as if
> The green and climbing eyesight of a cat
> Crawled near my mind's poor birds.

Timely: when thoughts turn to trees, in academic groves at least, Mother Eve and her Tree of Knowledge are not far off. I would like to think that the poem contained originally a suggestion that the Tree (python boughs) was itself the Tempter, but that was an afterthought.

Silt the alleys: "silt" proposed itself as suggesting sand — product of breakup, unlubricative, arid, unfruitful; "alleys," channels for to-and-froing, worn into grooves, out of true, and clogged by the grit of work.

Debris: hourly wastage of new, ungerminated, uncared for ideas, which may choke the channels; the wreckage and waste of "essential omission" — to use Whitehead's phrase — the saving neglect, which strains (and trains) the academic.

Allure: a lure is an apparatus used to recall hawks, a bunch of feathers within which, during its training, the hawk finds its food. Catachrestically, it can be both a snare and a mark to be shot at. The young scholar might be glad to borrow Cupid's bow to use on selected members of Radcliffe who at this season begin to decorate the chapel steps in their spring fabrics.

Degrees of loneliness: very different from the degrees that are conferred on those very steps at commencement. The line consciously echoed Donne's "The Extasie" (1. 44): "Defects of loneliness controls" — "Degress of loneliness confer."

Lost: in terms not only of the allure but of examination results and the perplexities of study. The coda uses, as I have mentioned, what was the temporal germ of the poem.

Now from such detail, what, if anything, of general import can be extracted? How far can knowledge of what went on in the process of page 15 / composition, however faithfully or tediously reported, serve as evidence of what is or is not *in the poem?*

You will recognize, I believe, that all this is chiefly a device — somewhat elaborate, I grant — for directing our attention to this tricky phrase "in the poem." If you can bear it, let us look through this little collection of samples of things I must aver *were* in the process of composition and ask of some of them whether and how they may not also be IN THE POEM.

First, this impulse — spring fever, nostalgia for the beyond, itchy-footedness — what I describe as a "not-at-all wish-fulfilling dream of spring flight" out of which the poem started and with which, in the coda, it ends: if any of this feeling has got in, it will not be — will it? — simply because it is talked about, mentioned, or even, in any obvious sense, implied — as by

away!
You may
Be lost by May.

We plainly have to, and do, make a distinction between the overt or manifest content — the inventory of terms that should not be omitted in a paraphrase — and what is truly operative in a poem. We would all agree that things may be mentioned and even insisted upon in a poem and yet remain perfectly inert, helpless, and noncontributive. (We should not, however — should we? — conclude that because they are inert [mere dead matter] they are therefore *always* unnecessary and better away. They may serve as catalysts or supporting tissue.)

This distinction between what is overt or manifest and what is operative — whether overt or not — is dangerous, of course. It lets us allege things about poems and deny things about them too easily. It opens the doors, typically, to allegations about the Unconscious.

For example, a friend to whom I had shown this poem and who had liked it — which pleased me because he is an admirable and well-recognized poet — was disappointed by and most suspicious, I believe, of the annotations I have been offering you. They did not, for him, contain the right sort of revelations of hidden passions in me. Alas! Is it any good my saying that *although there may be that sort of thing in the poem* there was nothing of the sort anywhere in the process of composing it. There may be murder in a poem without the author himself being either murdered or a murderer. But, no, once certain dealings with the Unconscious are on the tapis, the best-informed denial turns into addtional evidence.

To talk of evidence, what sorts of evidence are really available for the presence or absence of X (whatever it may be) in the poem? This, to me, is the central question, as important as it is difficult to answer. And it is my hope that I may find support for the view that the best, if not the only, page 16 / sorts of evidence are fundamentally linguistic — have to do with relations of words and phrases to one another — and furthermore (to retort with suspicion to suspicion) that evidence from a poet's alleged biography or psychology is seldom competent in any honest court.

To return to my example, if there *is* spring fever in this poem, it is there as outcome of a very complex set of mutual influences among its lines: in their movement as far as that is a derivative from their meaning, and in their meaning, in and through such things as the optative "might" in

When this or that or the other thought
Might perch and rest

in and through the fatigued flaccidity of "this or that or the other thought," in and through the alliterative pattern of

perch and rest.
And rest they ought
For poise or reach.

in and through the subjunctives following "though"

silt lounge confer.

Mind you, I am painfully aware that it is easy enough to allege such things: to pick this or that out of the inconceivably complex fabric of an utterance and say that here are more particularly the conveyors of this or that impulse and part of the poem. It is quite another matter to *prove* anything of the sort. We do not, I imagine, even know what the criteria of good proof in such matters would be. We can, of course, consent — agree to find them there — but that falls far short of proof.

On the other hand, the sorts of agreement which I am pointing to with this word "consent" are indispensable. Proof in these matters, if we ever attain it, will be by consent rather than by compulsion. Moreover, it is through such agreement about how words work together — the minute particulars of their cooperations — that discussion, analysis, and criticism must proceed. When two readers *differ*, they can discover and locate and describe their differences of interpretation only thanks to their consent together on other points.

Here let me touch on a misconception which, nowadays, I think — in my experience as a teacher — frustrates more potentially good readers of poetry than any other. To the word "shadow" (and "shade") a few minutes ago I appended a little string of quotations from de la Mare, a proverb, T. S. Eliot, and F. H. Bradley. These were uses of "shadow" that the Poetic Process considered in fixing — although not in forming — its third line "Footprints, figures, shadows go." But, of course, of course — I mean it *should* be of course — no sort of identification of these particular quotes and references page 17 / is required for the understanding of the line. They belong to the Poetic Process, not to the Literary Analysis. None the less, Literary Analysis, in trying to bring out the force of a word such as "shadow" in such a setting, very often finds it necessary to adduce a number of such other uses. Poetry cannot and does not use such words as though they had never been used before or as though they had only been used in one way. And the teaching of the reading of poetry to students who (somehow or other) have read little poetry anyhow, and very little of it reflectively, does have to play the part of a leisurely dictionary and acquaint students with "this and that and the other" relevant use.

This is a characteristic part nowadays of the technique of Literary Analysis. It is parallel to much that is done for the other arts, a necessary way of helping words to mean more nearly all they should. But, — and here is where the frustrating misconception I spoke of comes in — far too many students somehow suppose that *they*, as readers, ought somehow to have known and thought of just those instances of the use of the word that the analyst has found convenient and illuminating to adduce for his purpose. So Literary Analysis gives rise, by accident as it were, to a set of unreal difficulties and imaginary obstacles quite parallel to those we would have if we supposed that to read aright we must somehow divine all the uses of a word that may have beguiled and guided a poet in the manifold choices of Poetic Process.

This sort of avoidable frustration comes up especially when a Literary Analysis — to bring out the force of a line — sets, say, a passage of Plato beside it. He does not mean necessarily that the poet in the Poetic Process was thinking of the passage, or that the poet need know the passage or even have heard of Plato. All he means is that in the line, in the cooperations among its words, there is active something which can also be exemplified (and often can best be exemplified) in the Plato passage. In brief, he is using a historical reference technique to make what is a linguistic and not a historical point. The "Platoism" he is concerned with is something which is *in the language*.

You remember Emerson's farmer to whom he lent a *Republic*. The farmer returned it saying "That man has of lot of my ideas!" It was true — if we will allow that the farmer's ideas are the ideas offered him, in some way, through the semantic structure of his language. My ideas are, in a deep sense, *in* my language — in the relations between words which guide me in their use. I have to admit, though, that these phrases, "*in* the poem" and "in the language," persuade me that I very imperfectly understood this innocent-seeming little word "in."

Let us look now at another example of relevant relations among words, equally active this time in Poetic Process and Literary Analysis. Among page 18 / the factors operative in choosing "python boughs a-sway" — in place of, say, "snakey boughs a-sway" — in line 4 were the marginal presence, as I mentioned, of the words "lithe" and "writhe." I may well have thought of "withe" and "scythe," too; and there would also be the less perfect rhyme "alive." For "snakey," on the other hand, there was no such morphemic support; on the contrary; "shakey" — no good at all; "break" — no, no; "fake" — oh, horrors! So "python boughs" it had to be.

I take this as my type specimen of mutual influences among words of the order that is most conspicuously exemplified in rhyme: similarities in sound introducing and reinforcing relevancies of meaning. "Python" was not a rhyme word here, but where rhyme is in use other words than rhyme words do often have their susceptibility to influence from their rhyme field increased.

Now all this, with many other mutual influences among words which need never come into clear consciousness, belongs alike to Poetic Process and to Literary Analysis. In choosing his words, the poet is allowing himself to be guided in ways in which (he hopes) his reader may also be guided. The reader, in turn, may be following — in his awareness of the meaning, in his analysis, and in his appraisal — very closely in the footsteps of the Poetic Process. But the important thing, as I see it, is that both are under the control of the language, both are subject to their understanding of it.

Contrast, now, this happy and healthy condition with the sad state of a reader who is trying to guess — he knows not how — about what some poet at some precise, but unidentified, minute of his mortal journey may have been undergoing.

Of course, we all know that much in criticism and commentary which seems to be discussing the poet and reads as if it were about what he was doing as he wrote, *is not* really about that sort of thing at all. No, it is about what the poem has done and is doing to the critic — the critic who is inventing and projecting a poet's mental processes as a convenient way of talking about something else.

Mr. T. S. Eliot remarked — in his BBC talk, "Virgil and the Christian World" — that for a poet "his lines may be only a way of talking about himself without giving himself away." Well, a great deal of criticism which looks like microscopic biography — a minute by minute, line by line, blow by blow account of the poet's battle with his poem — is no more than the *critic's* way of talking about *himself* without giving the critic away either. Thus a reviewer will quote a line: "One wondered whether the loaded earth . . ." and go on to wonder: "Did one (i.e., the poet, who should be *I*, not *one*) really wonder that, or did one think one ought to wonder something?" This looks like an almost insane attempt to nose into another page 19 / person's private reflections, but it is not. It is merely the reviewer's way of trying to indicate that the line does not seem very good to him.

Sometimes, however, the biographic assumption hardens: "Even when the pioneer work was completed anybody attempting a fresh critical appraisal of Wordsworth's poetry was faced with some dispiriting machete work if he was to establish the biographical detail to which the criticism would have to be referred."

A *fresh critical appraisal* of poetry *having to be referred* to *biographical detail:* doesn't that make you feel a little uncomfortable? Suppose some barrelful of papers were to roll out of some attic in Stratford-on-Avon. Could it really force us to revise our critical approach of *King Lear* or could another batch of Dead Sea Rolls or Scrolls demote the poetry in *The Book of Job?* Personally, I would be extremely sorry to learn one more fact about either author. And I confess that, if I were to be granted such opportunities in the next world, I would as lief *not* meet Homer as any man.

To be more serious, if possible: what I am hoping to suggest is that some of the criticism of Literary Analysis which seems so often nowadays to be pegged to the poet's personality would be more profitable if it discussed the linguistic grounds — the powers in the words and the movement of the poem — which make the reader invent and project spiritual characteristics and spiritual adventures for the poet. In short, I have a hope that in time this amalgam of the gossip column and the whodunit will become a less dominant ingredient in criticism. Poetry is so much more than a source for lowdown on the lives of poets. To let a thing of the seeming scale of *Ulysses* become chiefly a ground for speculations about Joyce's sexual history — is that not rather a sad comedown from more important sorts of concern with literature? I know, of course, that to an individual nothing can seem more important than his own sexual history. But are we not in some danger of forgetting that general communications should be about matters of general interest?

To take as a minute, a tiny, innocuous, example the second line of "Harvard Yard in April":

To and fro
Across the *fretted snow*

fret: eat; eat away; consume; torture by gnawing; gnaw at; wear away by friction; chafe; roughen; cause to ripple, as a breeze frets the surface of water; tease; vex; worry . . . (OED).

Over this "fretted snow" a reader could, if he cared, *either invent* a particularly disgruntled, impatient, spring-fever-beset author who projects his own discomfort even on the very snow, and so on, *or* let the word "fretted" itself — as a highly charged meeting point of various meanings — come to page 20 / livelier life. The dictionary spreads the meaning out for us. But I am thinking of how the word can strike us before we separate such things — if, indeed, apart from dictionaries, we ever do. The dictionary adds a comment apropos of "gnaw at" which pleased me when I saw it. It says "Now only of small animals." A mouse, I suppose, can fret a bit of cheese (as a fret saw does plywood); but when a grizzly bear chaws up a man, that is not fretting. I liked that; it seems to offer my line "Across the fretted snow" a sort of bonus of meaning I had not been clearly aware of. It turned the people who had been leaving all those tracks on the snow into only small animals after all and gave a diminishing-glass sharpness to the scene.

But by point is that "fretted," if it has this power, gets it from its relations to other words — as a node of possibilities of meaning — not from the fact that an author (me in this case) had been pumping petulance into it. No matter how fevered, or how cool, the author may be, he cannot do anything with the word unless the language lets him, unless it is willing to work for him so: "For words it is not poets make up poems."

Perhaps I have overlabored this plea for the emancipation of Literary Analysis from biographic explorations or conjectures. I realize that it will not be welcome everywhere: it looks like an attempt to put a great many people out of their jobs. I would like before I close, to turn to another aspect of contemporary literary analysis — an increasing tendency to read meanings into poems at random, regardless of linguistic limits. I have a small but choice exhibit of awful warnings to show you — all written by people who were at the time of their writing doomed of their own choice to hard labor for the rest of their natural lives — no, I mean for the rest of their employable lives — teaching helpless children in classrooms how to be discerning readers.

The first two lines of Mr. Eliot's "A Cooking Egg" read:

> Pipit sate upright in her chair
> Some distance from where I was sitting.

There has been, as you know, some discussion among critics

about what sort of a person Pipit may best be supposed to be *in the interests of the poem as a whole.* Views have ranged from taking her as a retired nurse or governess to taking her as a Bloomsbury *demi-vierge.* The discussion came to a climax in an appeal from Dr. E. M. W. Tillyard, Master of Jesus, to the poet to explain the poem and set our minds at rest, an appeal to which Mr. Eliot, very wisely I think, has not responded.

However, one of my students, being faced with the problem, bethought her of the dictionary. There she found grounds for this:

> Pipit sate upright in her chair . . . **page 21 /**
>
> According to Webster's New Collegiate Dictionary, "sate" may mean "to satisfy or gratify to the full a desire" or "gratify to the point of weariness or loathing, satiate." Pipit has obviously satisfied the "I" for she sits upright, at a distance; a state of satiation has occurred.

It is an interesting point in *linguistics* to consider why we are sure that words in such an instance do not work like that.

Or consider this. The last verse of Donne's "The Extasie" reads

> And if some lover, such as wee,
> Have heard this dialogue of one,
> Let him still marke us, he shall see
> Small change, when we'are to bodies gone.

> *To bodies gone:* there is an ambiguity in the phrase; is it "gone away from our ecstasy to our bodies" or "gone (in respect) to bodies" — gone entirely away from them? I think this ambiguity is operative.

Another comment on these same last three words of the poem:

> *To bodies gone:* "to" may be a play on words: if read aloud and thought of as "two," it signifies the sacrifice of spiritual union necessary for two people to indulge in physical love.

Observe that both these teachers-to-be feel free to ignore the rest of the line:

> he shall see
> Small change, when we'are . . .

Their prepossessions enable them to find a meaning accurately opposite to "I must not say 'that which Donne put there' — (I don't know anything about that) but 'that which the rest of the poem expressly requires.' "

Compare another commentator who, perhaps, moves toward the point — but by what strange means!

> *Let him still marke us:* the word "still" can mean "without moving" and the sense of the line is changed to "let him notice that we are quiet and motionless."

Are you completely worn out? Or may I show you another double right-angle swivel?

An important movement in Coleridge's "Dejection: An Ode" begins

> Hence, viper thoughts, that coil around my mind
> Reality's dark dream!
> I turn from you, and listen to the wind
> Which long has rav'd unnotic'd.

> The poet retunes himself by *turning* inward to his soul. . . . He is coming through a storm which has made him hear the tune. His horror upon noticing makes him *turn* from the world of the senses and the outside. page 22 /

Lastly, the last verse of Marvell's "The Garden" opens with the lines:

> How well the skilful Gardner drew
> Of flow'rs and herbes this Dial new

> First, the word "well" draws its meaning from a pun. It seems to mean how carefully constructed the world is. It would seem to me that "well" has the connotation of a source of water, a deep hole in the ground. That is, nature is a well which has great depth and from which deep and eternal meanings and values can be drawn.

All very true, no doubt, but not anything that the semantic texture of the language will allow the two lines to mean or that the rest of the poem will invite us to understand here. Surely a teacher-to-be should have a better sense than this of what is and is not admissible in an interpretation.

What can have been happening to cause this alarming condition, this reckless disregard of all the means by which language defends itself? I have not been exaggerating; such things are far too frequent in the English studies of those who are likely to become teachers. My instances could be duplicated by every teacher of teachers. Some essential control over interpretation seems to have been relaxed.

At an occasion on which so many authorities in linguistics, criticism, and related studies are gathered together, it seemed appropriate to offer evidence that their work may have more immediate, practical relevance to education than is sometimes supposed. **page 23 /**